The Politics of
International Law

The Politics of International Law

U.S. Foreign Policy Reconsidered

David P. Forsythe

Lynne Rienner Publishers ▪ Boulder and London

Published in the United States of America in 1990 by
Lynne Rienner Publishers, Inc.
1800 30th Street, Boulder, Colorado 80301

and in the United Kingdom by
Lynne Rienner Publishers, Inc.
3 Henrietta Street, Covent Garden, London WC2E 8LU

Library of Congress Cataloging-in-Publication Data
Forsythe, David P., 1941–
    The politics of international law : U.S. foreign policy
  reconsidered / David P. Forsythe
        p. cm.
    Includes bibliographical references
    ISBN 1-55587-207-7 (alk. paper)
    ISBN 1-55587-208-5 (pbk. : alk. paper)
    1. United States—Foreign relations—1981–1989. 2. International
law—United States. I. Title.
JX1417.F675 1990
341'.04'0973—dc20   90-32486
                                                                CIP

British Cataloguing in Publication Data
A Cataloguing in Publication record for this book
is available from the British Library.

Printed and bound in the United States of America

The paper used in this publication meets the requirements
of the American National Standard for Permanence of
Paper for Printed Library Materials Z39.48-1984.

The current disorientation in American foreign policy derives from our having abandoned, for all practical purposes, the concept that international relations (and also to a degree the internal conduct of governments) can and should be governed by a regime of public international law.
— Senator Daniel Patrick Moynihan

Contents

Preface

This book is intended for introductory students of international relations, U.S. foreign policy, international law, and policy-making in Washington. I am not one to nitpick over academic boundaries.

Its origin lay in my difficulty in finding suitably political material to use in my international law classes, and suitably legal material for my classes in international relations and U.S. foreign policy. Most of the published material on international law was written by law professors and lacks a realistic sense of the political struggle involved in applying international law to public policy. This legalistic material lacks especially a sense of the conflict between the Executive and Congress that so pervaded Washington politics in the 1980s (and even before, say from the early 1970s).

The present book tries to capture and represent international law, warts and all, as it really functions in the policy-making process in Washington. Rather than presenting that law as interpreted by the International Court of Justice or by a distinguished legal scholar, I present it as interpreted by policy-making institutions, then compare that interpretation—and especially the political factors behind it—with a more cosmopolitan view of international law oriented to a stable and equitable world order.

The question may be raised as to why I limit myself in this book to the Reagan era. First, to students, going back more than a decade seems like ancient history. While there is much to be learned from a longer historical perspective, there are sufficient lessons to be learned just by concentrating on the more recent past. I believe that one should not attempt too much in a short book designed for teaching purposes.

Second, that more recent past feeds directly into the present. For example, decisions in the Reagan era about U.S. financial assessments to the United Nations affect the Bush administration. President Bush inherited the controversy over U.S. assessments; and when Bush continued to threaten unilateral withholding of those U.S. payments, in order to block U.N. de facto recognition of Palestine as a state, he resurrected all the old arguments that had been brought into play both for and against such U.S. action. By understanding unilateral withholding of assessed U.S. payments to the U.N. by Congress and the Reagan administration, one understands the context within which the Bush policy-making team considered its options.

The same type of linkage between the recent past and the present can be demonstrated with regard to other issues covered in this book, such as strategic defense and arms control treaties, refugee policy, and intervention in Nicaragua. The Reagan past contributed directly to U.S. foreign policy under Bush. When President Bush decided to use military force in Panama in the fall of 1989, his decision was facilitated by Reagan's intervention in Grenada. George Bush even used many of the same arguments employed by his predecessor in trying to justify the forcible change of government in Panama—i.e., an asserted right of intervention in the name of democracy and human rights. The two situations were not identical, but in large part they played themselves out in similar fashion. Both uses of unilateral force proved politically popular at home, while they were clearly criticized at the United Nations and the Organization of American States as a violation of international law. There were other similarities as well. The more novel and sweeping arguments by the president were downplayed by professional diplomats and lawyers, who stressed traditional international legal arguments concerning self-defense and humanitarian intervention. Understanding Reagan and Grenada provides an appropriate frame of reference, not identical but still highly useful, for understanding Bush and Panama.

In addition President Bush retained Abraham D. Sofaer as the legal adviser in the State Department, and that ensured some continuity between the Reagan and Bush administrations on international legal questions.

Finally, at the time of writing, many policy positions of the Bush administration were not entirely clear, thus precluding detailed and definitive treatment of that era.

* * *

The central value judgment permeating this work is that the United States cannot make a lasting contribution to world order by seeking short-term national advantage, but rather will promote its most fundamental national interests by adjusting its foreign policy to the transnational and cosmopolitan values found in contemporary international law. I am highly skeptical of the long-term benefits, even to ourselves and most certainly to others, of a moralistic and crusading American manifest destiny, which tends to confuse American nationalism and advantage with stable and equitable global order.

Realistically, attempts to build world order on disproportionate U.S. advantage are likely to prove unsuccessful in the late twentieth and early twenty-first centuries, given the relative decline of U.S. power, especially economic power. Stable and lasting order must entail a reasonably equitable sharing of values, advantages, and benefits. One of the geniuses of the American political experience, with the major exception of the Civil War era, has been the ability to compromise, to share values, between federalists and advocates of states' rights, between northerners and southerners, between liberals and conservatives, between developers and environmentalists. This point seems largely to have escaped those who manage U.S. foreign policy, and who have confused a temporary U.S. predominance in the world after World War II with the requisites of stable equilibrium in a basically polycentric world in which power, as well as other values such as wealth, must be shared. Greater U.S. attention to the legal rules of the game of international politics, since those rules encompass a sharing of benefits over time, is in fact in the real, if long-term, U.S. national interest.

* * *

The intellectual roots of this central value judgment, as well as of my approach in general to understanding law and politics, can be traced to Richard Falk's seminar on international law at Princeton University some decades ago. There were more recent and direct contributions to this book from a variety of persons who at least refined my biases, if they did not succeed in totally eliminating them. The manuscript was read in whole or part by Margaret Galey, consultant to the House Foreign Affairs Committee; Frank A. Sieverts, an aide to Senator Claiborne Pell, chair of the Senate Foreign Relations Committee; Larry D. Johnson, a principal legal officer in the United Nations Office of Legal Counsel; Patricia Fagan from the Washington office of the United Nations High Commission for Refugees; Margaret Crahan, Luce Professor at Occidental College in Los Angeles; Burns Weston, Murray Professor of Law at the University of Iowa; and of course Richard Falk and Francis Boyle. Lynne Rienner and her chosen readers were also more than helpful, as well as gracious, in producing the final version—the contents of which are, as usual, the final responsibility of only the author.

The University of Nebraska, through its "Congress Fund" as administered by the Political Science Department, greatly facilitated this study with a grant that made possible some concentrated research and uninterrupted writing during the summer of 1989. My graduate assistant for much of the preparation of the book, Kelly Pease, was diligent in locating material and checking sources, particularly with regard to Chapter 5. My daughter, Lindsey, then a political science major at Davidson College, read parts of the manuscript and told me what undergraduates might like or dislike, might find confusing or need elaboration. Finally, my wife, Annette, helped me recover from a brief hospitalization, which allowed a more rapid completion of this book.

DPF

Foreword

Richard Falk

For too long, the importance of international law for the study of international relations and foreign policy has been undervalued, especially here in the United States. It is fairly obvious why this has happened. It was, first of all, a reaction to the widely shared view that an unwarranted emphasis on international law by the United States had led diplomats astray in the period prior to World War II. Legalism in foreign affairs was held responsible for two equally unhealthy attitudes by government officials—either an unwarranted confidence that a legally correct diplomacy could overcome the impulse of aggressive states to wage war, or a misleading belief that a legalistic isolationism from the geopolitical stage would keep the country out of foreign wars. The failure of appeasement to hold Hitler in check produced the lesson of Munich, whereas the surprise attack on Pearl Harbor overcame the U.S. isolationist impulse. The combination of these pre-1945 learning experiences was interpreted by the U.S. foreign policy establishment as reason enough to be wary about international law and international lawyers.

Getting rid of illusions stemming from a legalistic view of international political life has been interpreted during the Cold War years since 1945 to mean emphasizing the unavoidably central role of military capabilities for purposes of both deterrence and defense. Foreign policy has been built around the doctrine of containment in the setting of an East-West rivalry of such a deep ideological character that the opposing sides perceived each other as committed more or less unconditionally to a world of conflict in which, to be sure, rules of the game existed, but not an operative legal framework based on shared values, including a respect of legality.

And then there was a related factor at work. The United States emerged after World War II as the main guardian of the established international order. With the collapse of colonialism and the partial transfer of East-West tensions to Third World arenas, U.S. leaders were reluctant to acknowledge any legal limitations on government discretion—not just in the East-West rivalry but in Third World politics as well. This insistence on freedom of maneuver in "the periphery" helped generate a national controversy during the Vietnam War, and then reached its climax during the Reagan years, when U.S. representatives seemed to take pride in flaunting their defiance of international law, perhaps most flagrantly in repudiating the World Court in the aftermath of its decision condemning U.S. support for contra efforts to disrupt Sandinista rule in Nicaragua.

Political scientists tended to follow the policy-makers' lead during this period. A realist consensus emerged among academics in which states were treated as the dominant actors in a world shaped by patterns of military and economic power. The subdiscipline of international relations gradually clustered around two nodes of concern: security studies on matters of war and peace, and international political economy on issues of money, trade, and investment. International law had little role to play in such a worldview, providing at most technical instruments for formalizing regimes set up to enable rational types of cooperation among states in various areas of international life.

This realist image of the world was always an exaggeration, although its ideological utility was evident during a period of protracted ideological struggle on an international level. It corresponded with the view that international security is mainly a matter of military balances and that the United States needed its freedom of action to combat its ideological enemies, who were being unscrupulously orchestrated from Moscow. The depreciation of international law followed naturally from the zero-sum logic of the Cold War. But realism as an explanatory perspective even in Cold War settings left too much of reality out of the picture. Realist diplomats all through this period were busy negotiating legal instruments for various areas of international life. Great care was devoted to the shaping of obligations in a manner that corresponded with the perceived priorities of the national interest. During the four decades after World War II, international law experienced unprecedented growth in several critical issue-areas: arms control, human rights, international economic arrangements, regulation of the oceans, and technical cooperation. Of course, realists could point to weak enforcement prospects in the event of noncompliance, but the record suggests high degrees of compliance and an increasing dependence on law to sustain stable expectations about behavior in international life.

Now, with the moderating of East-West tensions, the prospects for international law seem brighter than ever before. This optimistic assessment is reinforced by Mikhail Gorbachev's stress on strengthening international law and organization as a key ingredient of Soviet "new thinking" in foreign policy. Further encouragement for giving greater attention to the role of law in world affairs comes from the Third World, whose government representatives are now campaigning to have the United Nations formally dedicate the 1990s as the decade of international law.

These political developments occur at a time when the complexity and fragility of the ecological and economic dimensions of international life are becoming more apparent to all of us, providing the occasion—some would say the necessity—for the emergence of a global-scale legal order.

Against such a background, David Forsythe's book is beautifully adapted for teachers and students of international relations and foreign policy who want to move beyond *realism* so as to get a better grasp of *reality*. His approach to the relevance of international law has several attractive features: It grounds an affirmation of international law on a careful calculus of national interests, and thereby avoids certain preachy, legalistic tendencies to advocate adherence to law for its own sake; it explores the relevance of international law within the sinews of U.S. governmental decision-making (especially by the Executive and Congress) in circumstances of policy choice that range across several illustrative issue-areas, thereby introducing a modified "case" approach to the study of international law; it places law within the wider setting of an evolving political order and premises its advocacy on the desirability of conceiving of national interests in longer time cycles than has been habitual for policy-makers, who have tended in the past to be overly preoccupied with opinion polls and national elections; it puts the stress on the U.S. policy setting, but in a manner that casts light on the workings of the international system as a whole.

Forsythe's pedagogy is attractive. The role of law is presented as the outcome of carefully constructed narrative accounts of international events, such as a particular intervention, enabling an appreciation of the interplay of law and politics without the need to master a complex technical apparatus requiring years of law school study. Also, Forsythe understands clearly that most public international law is the work of the "political" branches, not courts. In the past, international law has often been artificially presented as a series of judicial decisions, an approach designed to make the subject matter seem more similar to the traditional subjects of legal study such as torts, contracts, and constitutional law. Forsythe realizes that this gain in respectability for international law as an object of academic inquiry is a turn-off to students of politics who are aware that the Judiciary is only marginally and inconsistently connected to the foreign policy process, which usually involves executive predominance reinforced or challenged by Congress.

It should be remembered that international relations as a serious subject of study has emerged rather recently, earlier in this century. And further, that it emerged by separating the study of politics and diplomacy from the study of law. Before the twentieth century, aside from the insights of historians like Thucydides and philosophers like Machiavelli, international law completely dominated the study of international life. In a sense, international law has served as the parent of international relations, and the latter, as it has come into its own, has acted out the role of rebellious adolescent, a necessary and desirable stage in achieving independence and a separate identity. However, once the work of differentiation has been completed, as is certainly the case for international relations, maturity has been achieved and the occasion for reconciliation is at hand; one way to perceive David Forsythe's fine book is as a reconciling initiative undertaken, significantly, by a political scientist rather than by a lawyer.

My hope would be that Forsythe's book will help make political scientists, generally, more inclined to reintegrate international law into the study of international relations as a central element. It is difficult to imagine a positive future for our own country and for the peoples of the world that does not include a much enhanced role for international law. It is not merely an aspiration on the part of idealists; it seems more like the necessary prudence that we should expect from practical diplomats entrusted with foreign policies built around the real security of the citizenry. In a constitutional democracy, one cannot always wait for enlightened bureaucrats to guide official policies. There is a responsibility to educate the citizenry, especially the young, in such a way as to ensure that democratic pressures will induce more enlightened patterns of governance. Here, too, we can be grateful to David Forsythe for putting into our hands a tool to educate a citizenry better prepared to face the challenges of the twenty-first century.

I

Introduction: A Framework for Analysis

Too often public international law has been taught as if it were just another black-letter law course whose subject matter was about as straight-forward as the federal income tax code. . . . Unless we reestablish the integral connection between the study of international law and the practice of international relations, public international law professors will probably become as extinct as the dinosaurs. —Francis A. Boyle

International law exerts considerable influence on the political life of the United States, although this fact is not widely appreciated. While international law's influence is known to specialists of the subject, most observers of U.S. foreign policy do not perceive that influence so readily. Most textbooks and other academic works covering U.S. foreign policy do not usually treat international law. It is thus no wonder that beginning students of both international law and politics approach this central thesis about international law's influence with a good deal of initial skepticism. It is not uncommon to find students who believe that international law is not really law, but some kind of political morality. Skepticism is healthy, but the ultimate conclusion is inescapable. As a generalization, it is not politically realistic to dismiss international law as if it were an intellectual sandcastle built by moral philosophers, destined to be overwhelmed by the first wave of unmitigated national interest. There are exceptions to this generalization. But one can safely say that, although international law may not be always decisive and controlling, it usually exerts an influence nevertheless on the making of foreign policy in Washington. Refining our knowledge of how much, and when, international law is brought to bear on U.S. foreign policy is the major objective of this essay.

The conscious antecedent of this work is Louis Henkin's classic *How Nations Behave: Law and Foreign Policy.*[1] Like that work, a first theme of this essay finds international law to be a pervasive influence on foreign policy, as suggested above, since the law usually reflects a prior judgment that the rules enhance national interest. Seen thusly, it is no wonder that states abide by most of the law most of the time, for by doing so they advance their long-term national interests in orderly international relations. As Werner Levi has made clear, international law is a subset of international politics.[2] In order to have international law in the first place, in either of its two basic forms of treaty law and customary law, states explicitly or implicitly have had to consent to the emergence of the rules.

This consent is based on a perception that the rule is consistent with national interests as understood at the time the rule is created. Thus, it is wrong to think of international law as a set of technical rules divorced from politics. International law results from a political process. The central problem is that national perceptions of interests change. Particular circumstances arise that generate a tension between current perceptions of national interest and the perceptions dominant at the time a particular international law was created. This situation results in a further political process in which the old rule of law is applied to the new situation.

But a second major theme of the present work differs from Henkin's excellent study. Henkin treated the United States as if it were a single, unitary, rational actor. Such an approach is normal in many legal studies, and it is certainly a well-established approach to the study of U.S. foreign policy in political science.[3] Many studies, both legal and political, speak of *the* United States, and *the* national interest. This book, however, stresses the separation of powers in Washington—or more accurately, the separation of institutions that share authority and power. In Washington in the 1970s and 1980s, as at other times in U.S. history, the Executive's conduct of foreign policy, mandated by the Constitution, had to compete principally with decisions made by Congress. Sometimes even the courts limited the Executive's freedom of decision, although there was a fairly strong tradition in the United States of judicial deference to the Executive concerning foreign affairs.[4]

Hence, a second theme supplements the first: Congress as well as the Executive, and indeed even the Judiciary, may interject international law into U.S. foreign policy. Particularly during those eras when Congress is assertive, or on issues where the Congress or the Judiciary refuses to be deferential, the careful observer who seeks a full understanding of U.S. foreign policy must look beyond the Executive alone to understand law's role in affecting policy. This point was fully appreciated in some of Professor Henkin's other splendid works,[5] but he did not incorporate it fully into *How Nations Behave*.

A third major theme springs from the second. It will become clear that I believe that the Executive's conduct of foreign policy during 1981–1988 frequently revealed a complete lack of serious respect for international law, and was therefore inherently dysfunctional to world order over time. Robert Pastor, a former staffer of the National Security Council, was persuasive when he argued, "The [Reagan] administration showed a blatant disregard for international law."[6] Herbert W. Briggs, an honorary editor of the *American Journal of International Law,* wrote in early 1987, "It remains for the United States to acquire once again a decent respect for the opinions of mankind—and rules of law."[7] Thomas M. Franck, current editor of the same prestigious journal, when looking at the Reagan administration's treatment of international law, recalled Manley Hudson's erudite but witty analysis of an earlier American era: the United States "seldom loses an opportunity to profess its loyalty to international arbitration in the abstract. . . . the expression of this sentiment has become so conventional that a popular impression prevails that it accords with the actual policy of the United States."[8] So during the Reagan era, the profession of interest in international law may have wrongly created the impression that U.S. policy was law-abiding.

This is an important point in and of itself, especially for young students of international law and politics inclined—naturally enough—to associate their government inherently with order, legality, justice, motherhood, and apple pie. Because most American families are nonpolitical, and because most public schools exist to inculcate patriotism, among their other duties, it is to be expected that many if not most younger students are blissfully ignorant of many historical facts in their nation's public life. They find it surprising to learn that the Federal Bureau of Investigation (FBI) has consistently violated the civil rights of many Americans, especially of dissenters and minorities.[9] And they find it surprising to learn that abroad the United States has participated in assassinations, massacres, suppression, and repression.[10] I seek no personal vendetta against Reagan the man or Reagan the president. But I do wish to emphasize the yawning chasm between Reagan's personal popularity within the United States and the reality of the policies he endorsed. One goal of this book is to give readers ample reason to scrutinize the actions and rationalizations of any U.S. president.

It will become clear enough in the following pages that the two administrations of Ronald Reagan treated international law mostly as a self-serving afterthought to policy decisions. More will be said in the conclusion about how this orientation was based on a self-righteousness commonly referred to as American exceptionalism, or the "city-on-a-hill syndrome."[11] In this view, Americans constitute an especially good people with a manifest destiny to remake the world in its own image, so when the United States acts, it inherently acts for the good of all. It has no need of international legal rules as determined by others, for that would impede U.S. freedom of action. Any reinterpretation by the United States of traditional rules is for the good, by definition, and therefore both desirable and permissible.

To the extent that this pronounced tendency has been corrected in U.S. foreign policy, it has come from either Congress or the courts. It is part of the purpose of this work to explore when and why the legislative and judicial branches will challenge the Executive's use (and misuse) of international law. Richard Falk wrote, after the Reagan administration disregarded the World Court's judgment in the mid-1980s case involving Nicaragua and the United States: "We must rethink the question of judicial effectiveness in the broader setting of public opinion and political democracy, and not confine our evaluation to conventional concerns about governmental [viz., executive] nonresponsiveness."[12] In other words, if one is interested in U.S. compliance with international law as adjudicated by the International Court of Justice, one has to look to Congress and public opinion, and on occasion to the courts, not just to the Executive.

There is a fourth theme as well. It is commonplace to observe a shrinking world in the sense that communication and transportation have made nation-states at least more interconnected, if not more interdependent. Without doubt states interact more (whether this interaction leads to real dependence or interdependence is debatable as a generalization applying universally). And as a result, at least partially, of this increased interaction among states (and also non-state parties), there is a great deal of international law on the books. Interaction may or may not breed conflict (it probably does)—but it certainly breeds regulation. Moreover, the growth in the number of public and private international organizations has been well documented.[13]

U.S. foreign policy is thus subject to increased review, some sort of increased reaction, from other states and also from international organizations—frequently in reference to international law. But however much one might read of resolutions passed by the United Nations Security Council or General Assembly, or read of protests by foreign friends or adversaries, this book argues that most such international influences do not have the impact on the Executive that Congress and the courts do. We may live in a shrinking world, but when decisions are made in Washington, congressional or judicial opposition to the Executive is usually far weightier in terms of actual influence than the response of the so-called international community. That this point may be distressing to those concerned with a cosmopolitan world order does not lessen its veracity.

This is not to suggest that Washington is the world. The assumption that the world centers on Washington, or follows Washington, or that the world outside the Washington beltway does not matter, is certainly one of the short-term problems in the making of U.S. foreign policy. Along with Michael Reisman in his useful book, *International Incidents: The Law That Counts in World Politics*,[14] it is important to chronicle the response of the international community—viz., the other states and international organizations—to U.S. foreign policy decisions. Whether that legal community supports, aquiesces in, or opposes U.S. policy affects both international law and world order in the long term. Indeed, international law is not simply the law on the books—the static law written down in treaties and found in court decisions interpreting customary international law. The living international law is also composed of how important states and the larger legal community understand and apply that law in concrete situations. Part of that process entails how the international community reacts to legal claims made by a state, the United States included.

But in the short term, what matters most to the Executive, which remains the primary institution for the conduct of U.S. foreign policy even in times of congressional assertiveness and judicial activism, is the position taken by those other U.S. branches of government. International influences, to the extent that they are not already incorporated in U.S. decisions in some form, usually occupy a tertiary position in impact on the Executive. As will be shown, the subject becomes highly complex when international influences seep into congressional or judicial deliberations. In many ways the boundary between what is national and what is international is highly permeable. Nevertheless, to the extent that national and international influences are distinguishable, the former usually count for more than the latter in Washington politics.

* * *

I chose the cases of decision-making for study in this book to elucidate these four basic themes. No short list of case studies could capture all the complex dimensions of international law and politics worth noting. Different cases could be utilized to drive home different emphases. All these cases show, however, that international law should be viewed in political context and that international law is usually an important part of the Washington debate on policy choice—although the importance varies. All the cases show that the legal arguments, claims, and justifications offered by Reagan officials raised major questions about their seriousness and credibility. All of the cases show that if the Executive's policy were altered to increase conformity to international law, that change transpired primarily because of congressional or judicial counter-decisions. Distinctly foreign influences were usually inconsequential, at least in terms of direct influence.

The first case, the Strategic Defense Initiative (SDI, or Star Wars Defense), shows that Congress, through the Senate, successfully forced a change in the administration's position concerning how to interpret the Anti-Ballistic Missile (ABM) treaty. Here is a case showing the clear influence of international law on U.S. policy; the law works, and it works because of the Senate. It will also be shown that the Senate's institutional self-interest had more than a little to do with a willingness to fight the Executive determinedly on the somewhat arcane subject of how to interpret an arms control treaty—with the mass public being indifferent to the outcome.

The second case, concerning the U.S. policy of forceful intervention in Nicaragua via a proxy army, shows a more mixed congressional response. While Congress opposed the president's policy in several respects, it made explicit reference only occasionally and inconsistently to international law. Thus the law worked partially, again through congressional action since the courts refused to treat legal issues arising out of the situation. American public opinion also seemed to be a factor of some importance.

The third case, dealing with the U.S. invasion of Grenada, shows that Congress did not check a highly questionable executive policy. This direct use of U.S. force was condemned even by our closest European allies. But because of political advantages inherent in the Executive, and because of American public opinion, congressional critics of the operation were few and powerless. The law did not work at all—at least not on the big issues.

The fourth case, involving U.S. handling of refugees from Central America and the Caribbean, highlights the role of the Judiciary. Whereas Congress was an important player in setting the stage for this issue, later it was the Judiciary that offered some opposition to repeated misinterpretations by the executive branch of both international and U.S. law. To the extent that the law worked, it did so because of judicial activism.

Finally, the case study on financing the United Nations shows how complex it can become to determine just what contemporary international law requires in some areas, and also to determine which branch, the executive or legislative, is more disrespectful of traditional international obligations. This case is appropriately the last, for it raises the troubling question of whether decisions in Washington stand much chance of contributing to a more orderly world. If international rules are repeatedly violated by both political branches in Washington in pursuit of particular U.S. advantage, and if this occurs at a historical juncture when overall U.S. influence is declining relative to its past and relative to others, what contribution can the United States make to a stable world order based on a mix of various national interests?

* * *

The themes of this book lead to a certain structure for the case studies. Each case study will be organized according to seven questions.

I. What are the central facts of the issue to be examined that give us an introduction to the subject? We cannot write a definitive history of any issue in a short treatment. Hence the text speaks of "some" relevant facts. But one cannot evaluate whether the use of legal rules is appropriate and/or influential unless one has an accurate understanding of at least the central facts. No law is self-executing as a practical matter. All law must be applied to factual situations not completely foreseen by the law's drafters. Whether or not there is a reasonable application of the law requires a contextual analysis entailing attention to facts.

II. What was the main thrust of the Executive's policy objectives? In other words, what did the Executive, as the predominant branch for the conduct of foreign policy, want to achieve in political terms? What were the primary policy goals? This approach assumes that politics is primary and that law is secondary. As John Stoessinger has shown clearly with regard to the evolution of the United Nations, the driving force behind nation-states' foreign policies is consideration of immediate policy and power; law is a factor derived from those political considerations.[15] This essay, for example, assumes that President John Kennedy during the Cuban missile crisis was a typical decision-maker in the following sense. He said that the Soviet missiles in Cuba had to go; he then tried to get them out in a way that least violated accepted international legal standards. He did not first ask himself: What does international law allow me to do?[16] Legal arguments made by states do not spring, politically untarnished, from the minds of legal advisers; they arise, at least in public form, as part of the overall political calculations.

III. What was the role of international law for the Executive? What legal claims, arguments, justifications were offered by the Executive as part of its policy? How easy was it for the Executive to fit its policy objectives into established legal rules? To the extent that a conflict between the two arose, what was the resulting mix of emphases in executive statements and action? Do we have evidence that international legal advisers played an important role in policy-making, and what was the nature of that role and advice? To what extent did the need of the Executive to justify its policies in international legal terms affect the policy, or to what extent did the policy and its accompanying legal claims exist in uneasy or contradictory form?

IV. What was the domestic response to executive initiatives? Did Congress or the Judiciary challenge the Executive's use of international law? If so, to what extent and with what results? What other factors affected this domestic response, such as institutional commitment, party alignment, public opinion, lobbying by interest groups? Can we establish any generalization about when and how strongly the other branches will offer an alternative to the Executive's interpretation of international law?

V. What was the response of foreign parties to executive action and claims? Did powerful states or international organizations challenge the president's policy cum legal claims? What was the relationship between international response and congressional or judicial action? To the extent that international response existed as a separate factor, what influence did it generate on the Executive?

VI. What was the outcome of policy in its dominant form for the United States? That is, given the final and controlling version of U.S. policy on the issue under study, did the policy achieve important U.S. objectives, such as improved security for the United States, better protection of human rights for U.S. nationals, increased wealth for Americans, improved protection of the American ecology?[17] Were there any negative features to the policy for the United States specifically in the short term as the policy evolved and was applied?

VII. What was the outcome of U.S. policy for world order? Did U.S. policy enhance orderly international relations? Did U.S. policy enhance other values in addition to order, such as security broadly defined, human dignity in general, increased distribution of wealth, improved environmental protection? Beyond attempts to secure particular and short-term advantage for the United States, did U.S. policy make the world a more orderly and more just place?

*   *   *

Finally, I am not much concerned whether authors or students find themselves in faculties of political science or law—or any other academic discipline, for that matter. Academic boundaries are what people talk about when they don't have any good ideas. But I am concerned, like Francis Boyle of the University of Illinois, that we seem to have so many formal studies of international law, full of attention to the effect of a semicolon, or developing a technical approach to a problem that has not the slightest chance of impacting political reality.[18] This work, above all, seeks to capture and communicate the political reality of how international legal rules intersect the process of policy-making in Washington.

NOTES

The epigraph that opens Chapter 1 is quoted from Francis A. Boyle, *American Journal of International Law*, 83, 2 (April 1989), 403.

1. New York: Praeger, 1968.

2. *Law and Politics in the International Society*, Beverly Hills, CA: Sage, 1976.

3. See Graham T. Allison, *Essence of Decision: Explaining the Cuban Missile Crisis*, Boston: Little, Brown, 1971, for a clear distinction between the state-as-rational-actor and other foci for the study of international relations. Classical studies of international law assume the nation-state is one unitary actor, whether or not rational.

4. For a brief treatment of cycles of congressional assertiveness see I. M. Destler, "Congress as Boss?" *Foreign Policy*, 42 (Spring 1981), 167–181. On judicial

deference to the Executive in foreign affairs see John Spanier and Eric M. Us-laner, *American Foreign Policy Making and the Democratic Dilemmas*, Pacific Grove, CA: Brooks/Cole, 1989.

5. *Foreign Affairs and the Constitution*, Mineola, NY: Foundation Press, 1972.

6. *Condemned to Repetition: The United States and Nicaragua*, Princeton: Princeton University Press, 1987, 70.

7. *American Journal of International Law*, 81, 1 (January 1987), 86.

8. *Judging the World Court*, New York: Priority Press, 1986, 22–23.

9. See, e.g., Herbert Mitgang, *Dangerous Dossiers: Exposing the Secret War Against America's Greatest Authors*, New York: Fine, 1988; and William Walton Keller, *The Liberals and J. Edgar Hoover: Rise and Fall of Domestic Intelligence State*, Princeton: Princeton University Press, 1989.

10. One excellent treatment of misdeeds abroad is by Thomas Powers, *The Man Who Kept the Secrets: Richard Helms and the CIA*, New York: Washington Square Press for Pocket Books, 1979.

11. Tammi R. Davis and Sean M. Lynn-Jones, " 'City Upon a Hill,' " *Foreign Policy*, 66 (Spring 1987), 20–39.

12. *American Journal*, note 7, at 112.

13. H. K. Jacobson, *Networks of Interdependence*, New York: Knopf, 1979, chps. 1, 3.

14. Princeton: Princeton University Press, 1988.

15. *The United Nations and the Superpowers*, New York: Random House, 1966.

16. See further Abram Chayes, *The Cuban Missile Crisis: International Crises and the Role of Law*, New York: Oxford, 1974.

17. I accept the usefulness of the World Order Models Project and its emphasis on four issue-areas: security, economics, human rights, ecology. See further, e.g., Samuel S. Kim, *The Quest for a Just World Order*, Boulder, CO: Westview, 1984.

18. In a book review in the *American Journal of International Law* (April 1989), Boyle noted only nine books that are, in his judgment, politically relevant.

II

Interpreting the ABM Treaty

The Reagan Revision of the ABM Treaty is a flagrant act of Treaty distortion which totally undermines the very object and purpose of the Treaty and which, accordingly, has raised deep concern even among America's staunchest allies. The consequences for international law are dismal when the world's erstwhile champion of international law chooses to disregard its obligations so blatantly. —1987 U.S. Senate Report

I SOME RELEVANT FACTS

On May 26, 1972, President Richard Nixon for the United States and Leonid Brezhnev for the Soviet Union signed an arms control agreement that came to be known as the ABM treaty. The Senate gave its advice and consent to ratification by an overwhelming vote of 88 to 2, far more than the two-thirds majority required by the Constitution, and it did not attach any reservations or understandings to the treaty. Not surprisingly, the Soviet side followed through with its procedures, and both states ratified the treaty quickly. By early October 1972, the treaty entered into legal force.[1] According to the Constitution, Article 6, paragraph 2, treaties are part of the highest law of the land, on a par with the Constitution itself.

The treaty pertained to defensive weapons systems designed to intercept or block an attack on a nation by ballistic missiles. Therefore, such defensive systems were referred to as anti-ballistic missile systems, or ABMs. In the 1970s, these systems were not regarded by most people on either side as very effective, certainly not against an intentional, large-scale attack. The assumption remained widespread that there was no defense against that type of attack; one could only hope to deter it by the promise of unacceptable damage to the potential attacker through assured retaliation. Security against a nuclear strategic attack was sought through mutual assured destruction, or MAD. If there were any credible argument in support of deploying an ABM system, then, it was as a defense against a small, perhaps accidental, attack.

Given the relative unimportance of ABMs in military terms, the treaty limited each side to two noncomprehensive systems: one per capital city, and one other. This was later reduced to one. The United States never constructed the ABM it was allowed; the Soviet Union constructed one around Moscow. The real value of the treaty was political rather than military. It was a confidence-building measure between the two nuclear superpowers, useful—as long as it was observed—for increasing trust and thereby promoting further arms control and perhaps even disarmament measures.

For more than a dozen years, all knowledgeable people in both the United States and the U.S.S.R. held the same view as to the meaning of the treaty on the main points. Particularly on the central issues of the purpose and intention of the treaty—on what it regulated in general—there was no major difference of opinion between Washington and Moscow, and certainly none within official Washington. Some differences did arise between the two parties over whether a particular radar site was or was not prohibited, or whether alteration of a radar site constituted modernization with the same technology (permitted) or replacement with new technology (impermissible). These more minor disputes did not jeopardize the existence of the treaty, but were raised and debated in the Standing Consultative Commission (SCC)—a forum created under the treaty in which the two parties sought to ensure compliance through on-going bilateral diplomacy.[2]

According to everyone involved, the main points of the treaty meant the following. Article 1, paragraph 2, said: "Each party undertakes not to deploy ABM systems for defense of the territory of its country and not to provide a base for such a defense, and not to deploy ABM systems for defense of an individual region except as provided for in Article III of this treaty." On its face this language meant that deployment of a comprehensive ABM system of any type was flatly prohibited, and any limited or noncomprehensive system of any type could only be deployed as provided for in the treaty.

⌈Article 2 said in part: "An ABM system is a system to counter strategic ballistic missiles or their elements in flight trajectory, currently consisting of . . . ." (There followed a description of a land-based ABM system [omitted here], the only type then extant.) The evident meaning was that all ABM systems were covered by the treaty, including space-based systems.⌋

Article 3 limited each party to one land-based deployment around its capital city, and one other deployment. A detailed description of what was allowable as part of each deployment was included. All details pertained to a land-based ABM, since that was the only type extant.

Article 4 drew the distinction between deployment (permitted only in two sites as specified) and "ABM systems or their components used for development or testing" (not allowed except as pertaining to replacement of existing, permitted components).

[Article 5, paragraph 1, said: "Each Party undertakes not to develop, test, or deploy ABM systems or components which are sea-based, air-based, space-based, or mobile land-based." The plain meaning was that, although research on such advanced-technology ABMs was permitted, testing, development, and deployment of them were prohibited.]

Other articles provided that the treaty was of unlimited duration, that it could be amended through bilateral diplomacy and constitutional procedures, and that either party could withdraw upon six months' notice.

Finally, the parties attached seven "agreed statements" to the treaty that had the same legal status as treaty articles. Agreed Statement D read:

> In order to ensure fulfillment of the obligation not to deploy ABM systems and their components except as provided in Article III of the Treaty, the Parties agree that in the event ABM systems based on other physical principles and including components capable of substituting for interceptor missiles, ABM launchers, or ABM radars are created in the future, specific limitations on such systems and their components would be subject to discussion in accordance with Article XIII [the SCC] and agreement in accordance with Article XIV of the Treaty [amendment and review procedure].

This meant that ABMs based on advanced or exotic technologies (rather than the land-based mode then currently extant) were prohibited, but could be subject to negotiation and amendment through the forum established.

The Reagan administration did not initially challenge this traditional—also called restrictive—interpretation of the ABM treaty. Despite some pressure from circles of opinion that wanted the administration to withdraw from the treaty altogether, Reagan adhered to it and to the same interpretation as Presidents Nixon, Ford, and Carter. Then on March 23, 1983, President Reagan gave his "Star Wars" speech. In it he launched his "Strategic Defense Initiative," or SDI, designed to move the United States away from MAD and toward a national security policy based on a high-technology, space-based intercept system. He envisaged a world free of nuclear weapons altogether, along with a comprehensive defensive system encompassing the entire nation, and he promised to give the relevant technology—when perfected—to the U.S.S.R. so as to lessen its fears about U.S. superiority.[3] This speech, radical in its implications for the past forty years of thinking about how best to ensure the physical security of the United States from military attack, gave rise to protracted national debate.

Nothing in the ABM treaty prohibited laboratory research on any type of ABM system. This was not only the traditional understanding, but also the practice of the two parties.[4] Therefore, scientific research under the president's SDI plan could go forward, and it did; even with the controversies noted later in this chapter, Congress authorized and appropriated $3.9 billion for Star Wars research during fiscal year 1988. But at some point it became clear that the president's quest for a comprehensive, or even limited but space-based, defensive system would violate the ABM treaty as then interpreted. It was widely understood that there was a legal prohibition on the deployment of any type of comprehensive defensive system, as well as a prohibition on the testing and development of "exotic" systems or their components beyond the two land-based systems allowed since 1972. One might argue over the difference between research and testing, or testing and development, but the intent of the treaty had been recognized all around. For "exotic" and comprehensive components, field testing as opposed to laboratory testing was prohibited; so was development in the sense of production; so was deployment beyond the two land-based sites—later one—that the treaty authorized.

This evident conflict between later stages of SDI and the ABM treaty went unresolved for about two years after the much-heralded Star Wars speech. Then, in the context of a continuing national debate about U.S. security policy, a Reagan official announced on October 6, 1985, that the administration was following a new interpretation of the ABM treaty, which permitted field testing and development of components for a space-based ABM.[5]

II EXECUTIVE POLICY

That the Reagan administration would announce a policy of giving high priority to SDI without dealing with how such a defensive system would contradict the ABM treaty as traditionally understood suggests a good deal about that administration's tendency to act first and think about international law second. Be that as it may, by the mid-1980s it was evident that the Executive was chafing under the traditional interpretation of that treaty.

Debate continues as to the real motivations of policy-makers in pushing SDI. One view is that Reagan, who was generally uninformed and inattentive about the specifics of nuclear and other high-tech weaponry,[6] genuinely believed that a comprehensive ABM could be effective and could substitute for the morally questionable and functionally dissatisfying doctrine of mutual assured destruction. Another view saw the president's romanticism and naivete being used by certain persons in his administration who wanted to deploy an advanced ABM in pursuit of military superiority over the Soviet Union. After all, if the United States had a reasonably effective ABM, it could launch a devastating first strike against the U.S.S.R., then avoid unacceptable damage in return via the ABM. "Defensive" systems had offensive potential. At a minimum such a situation would lead to increased U.S. political leverage on the U.S.S.R., while increasing the burdens on a suffering Soviet economy. There was also a third view that held that a marginally effective ABM might be possible in the future, and if developed and deployed even in limited form it might enhance deterrence by improving the unlikelihood of a successful first strike.

Whichever one or more of these views—or other views—really drove key policy-makers in the Reagan administration, by autumn 1985 it was clear that key parts of the Executive wanted out from under the ABM treaty. This was a matter of no small importance. It involved the standing of the United States in the world at large, based in part on its reputation for attention to international law and in particular the observance of treaties in good faith. U.S. relations with the Soviet Union were obviously at stake, and many were worried about the prospects for a renewed and unlimited arms race. In the early 1980s the Cold War had been resumed with vigor, military budgets were expanding, and the Reagan team, especially, had projected a bellicose image. The situation also affected U.S. relations with its NATO allies, many of whom were already worried about an unnecessarily belligerent alliance leader.

Executive dealings with an assertive Congress were also at stake. Since 1973, Congress had been projecting itself more and more into foreign policy, and the early years of the first Reagan administration had seen numerous battles over U.S. foreign policy in Central America and elsewhere. And finally, the Reagan policy team had to contend with that amorphous and elusive but periodically important element called the voting public. Administration statements and policies about foreign and security policy had already produced many street demonstrations and other forms of public unrest. The unilateral reinterpretation of an effective arms control treaty, in this context, was hardly insignificant. Treaty interpretation certainly involved legal analysis, but it involved even more so policy choice on major issues affecting both the power of the Executive at home and the power of the United States abroad.

For those who wanted to move ahead rapidly on phases of SDI that went beyond laboratory research, there were five procedural strategies.[7] The United States could withdraw from the treaty, as provided by the treaty itself. This seemed unattractive to Reagan officials, although it was advocated by several outside the Executive, since abandoning a successful arms control agreement would not enhance the overall status and reputation of the administration either at home or abroad. The United States could seek a revision of the treaty through amendments, but these would have to be negotiated with the Soviet Union, and there was no likelihood that the Soviets would agree to what the administration wanted. The United States could present a new interpretation to the International Court of Justice (the World Court) at the Hague, ask the U.S.S.R. to consent to adjudication, and hope that the court ruled in its favor.[8] But even if the Soviets gave their consent, there was no guarantee that the court of 15 independent judges would rule as desired. The United States could ask its own courts for a ruling in behalf of a new interpretation, but there was no guarantee that the courts would accept the case or rule as desired. Or the United States could put forth unilaterally a new executive interpretation and hope to prevail through political means over both the Soviet Union and the Congress (Senate). This latter option was the one reflected in the announcement of October 6, 1985, although some further information about that statement is highly relevant.

There were some who did not like the limitations on U.S. freedom of decision reflected in the ABM treaty, and who had tried to discredit that agreement through reinterpretation almost as soon as the ink was dry on the treaty.[9] In both 1975 and 1977, commentators in conservative think tanks offered an interpretation that would negate the traditional one held in official circles; their argument was essentially that the ABM treaty covered only land-based systems. These revisionist views were apparently laid to rest by the published responses of some of those who had negotiated the treaty. But in 1985 the ultraconservative Heritage Foundation in Washington revived this reinterpretation, and it was picked up and pushed in bureaucratic maneuvering by people in the Department of Defense—primarily Richard N. Perle and Fred C. Ikle—who held important positions and were supported by Secretary of Defense Caspar Weinberger. On October 6 National Security Adviser Robert McFarlane stated in a televised interview that the administration had adopted a new interpretation of the ABM treaty. This was a modification of the same position that had been discredited almost a decade earlier by treaty negotiators.

At the time this announcement was made in an informal and off-handed and perhaps inadvertent way, it was not clear that the president had made a formal decision on the matter.[10] It seemed that Secretary of State George Shultz had not approved the reinterpretation as U.S. policy and was not prepared for a public statement. While the leading State Department lawyer, Abraham D. Sofaer, had advised the secretary that field testing and development of ABM components based on new physical properties could be justified, other lawyers in the State Department, the Justice Department, the Department of Defense, and the Arms Control and Disarmament Agency disagreed. It was certainly true that the Soviets had been neither consulted nor informed, nor had NATO allies, nor had any member of Congress.

As even Sofaer was to say later, "This is a perfect example of how law and policy should not go forward in the political world. . . . This is not the way one should handle a legal question."[11] Nevertheless, once the public statement had been made, whether intentionally or not, it was difficult for the administration to completely reverse policy. Apparently, Secretary of State Shultz engineered a compromise statement in October 1985 indicating that, while the new interpretation was justified, the administration's policy would remain consistent with the traditional understanding—that is, no field tests would be conducted that violated the restrictive interpretation. But in legal terms, the Reagan administration had committed itself to the view that for thirteen years all other knowledgeable persons had held an erroneous view of the terms of the 1972 ABM treaty.

III EXECUTIVE LEGAL CLAIMS

It is not easy to pinpoint the administration's exact legal brief in support of the reinterpretation.[12] The State Department's legal adviser, Sofaer, made one argument in 1985, but he abandoned it when criticized in detail by Senator Sam Nunn (D, GA). Sofaer made another study in 1986, but he then said it was inadequate. He published an argument in a law review, but refused to back its contents completely. If one pieces together different administration statements, however, it appears that the Executive's arguments entailed three types of issues: (1) an interpretation of the treaty; (2) a judgment about the role of the legal adviser in the State Department; and (3) an argument about the role of the Senate in treaty interpretation. Each type of issue had its legal dimension, either international or constitutional, but each also was political since public policy and power were involved.

Interpretation of the treaty. The administration's reinterpretation of the ABM treaty, which was in reality a fundamental change in substance without participation by any other interested party, foreign or domestic, involved ignoring parts of it, reconstructing parts, and suppressing contradictory evidence.[13]

The Executive ignored the parts of Articles 1–5 that stated that all ABM systems were included; that testing and development were limited to replacement components for existing, land-based, limited systems; and that there could be no testing, development, or deployment of other than land-based systems.

The Executive reconstructed major parts of the treaty. Sofaer asserted that the restrictive interpretation was "plausible," but that other interpretations were possible because the treaty's terms were ambiguous. These other interpretations were supposedly supported by executive documents never presented to the Senate in 1972. He suggested that the Soviet Union had never agreed to any ban on the testing and development of space-based components in particular, and he tried to argue that Agreed Statement D permitted the unilateral testing and development of high-tech components. According to Sofaer, Agreed Statement D, contrary to its own language, pertained not to Article 3 (permitting only two land-based systems), but to Article 5 (dealing with exotic systems of the future). Thus, the Executive's reading of the treaty was that, although it might or might not cover only land-based systems, testing and development of components for other systems were permitted. The Reagan team argued that this was the true intent of both the United States and the U.S.S.R., but somehow treaty negotiators and higher Nixon officials never realized it and never communicated it to the Senate.

Reagan's assistant secretary of defense for international affairs, Richard Perle, told the Senate: "We undertook a systematic, deliberate, and thorough review of the treaty. . . . This review was conducted in good faith and with the integrity and conscientiousness that we, who have taken solemn oaths of office, have pledged to uphold." His substantive argument, however, and that of some of his supporters, essentially was that the Soviets would cheat if they got the chance, so the United States should cheat first. Perle said:

> If the Soviets were to have tested an ABM system or a component based on other physical principles in space . . . how would they have responded if challenged under the treaty . . . ? There is no doubt in my mind that they would have invoked Agreed Statement D. . . . What is really at issue is whether we will restrict ourselves in a manner that the Soviets would refuse to be restricted [by] if they were in our position and we were in theirs.[14]

Finally, the Executive suppressed evidence that did not support its view. One of the junior lawyers working under Sofaer in the State Department concluded that the reinterpretation was not justified; his conclusions were not reported, and he was denied further access to information. Lawyers in the Department of Defense and the Arms Control and Disarmament Agency also disagreed with the reinterpretation; their opinions were not reported to Congress or the public by the State Department, and they were prohibited from testifying before the Senate. Sofaer and the State Department did not report that all treaty negotiators save one opposed the reinterpretation. That one, Paul Nitze, was an official of the Reagan administration, had publicly supported the traditional interpretation through the spring of 1985, and had changed his mind apparently after McFarlane's announcement in October of that year.[15]

One does not have to be a lawyer or to be trained in international law to conclude that Reagan's reinterpretation was implausible on its face; one has only to read the treaty. One can also look to, as supplementary information for legal interpretation, state practice since 1972. This latter evidence also contradicts the reinterpretation, because both parties behaved according to the restricted, not permissive, interpretation. Finally, one can look at the legislative history, or negotiation record (the preparatory works or *travaux préparatoires*), of the treaty. This historical record likewise contradicts the Reagan reinterpretation, especially with the additional weight of the commentary of the negotiators.

All of the standard techniques for interpreting a treaty (looking at language, practice, and legislative history) so contradict the reinterpretation that one is led to question how the State Department's legal adviser could have let the reinterpretation become the administration's official legal position. Sofaer, after all, had been a judge, not a politician; a Democrat, not a Republican; and had taken no policy positions on SDI or ABM matters, having entered the State Department's legal office only in early 1985.

The role of the State Department's legal adviser. In retrospect, it is clear that Sofaer saw himself as analogous to the private lawyer who is paid to do what his client wants him to do. A Senate report was to castigate him for not being the primary international lawyer for the United States as a whole, and thus for not upholding the state's commitment to international law properly understood. According to Senator Joseph Biden (D, DE): "We cannot change the rules in the middle of the game simply by ordering lawyers of the State Department to find some loophole, as if they were high-paid counsel to some tycoon who wants to welsh on a bad deal. Besides, the ABM Treaty was not a bad deal."[16]

An independent role for the legal adviser would entail telling a particular government when it was transgressing the law. Other inquiries in the past had also argued for an independent legal adviser in State,[17] but it was difficult to find clear historical examples of any legal adviser's having carried out that role. One of the legal scholars called to testify in the Senate against the reinterpretation was Abram Chayes of Harvard University, who had been the State Department's legal adviser at the time of the Cuban missile crisis in 1962. But at that time he had projected dubious legal arguments trying to justify President Kennedy's policies, for which he was persuasively critiqued by Louis Henkin of Columbia University (who also testified against the reinterpretation.)[18]

The legal adviser's situation was well summarized by another lawyer with governmental experience: "People who don't like Sofaer say that the legal adviser should be a sort of chief justice, telling the Administration what it can't do. What has made him a controversial character is that instead he has used his creativity and legal skills in order, where possible, to advise his client on how to do what he wants to do."[19]

According to Sofaer himself: "I am just a legal adviser. People have got to understand that as a legal adviser you can't throw your weight around. You can't tell a national security adviser or a Cabinet member what he or she cannot do, particularly if you are not asked."[20]

This prevailing conception of the legal adviser's role was and is troubling. In U.S. law, the claims of lawyers doing what their clients want are frequently subjected to authoritative review by a judge and/or jury. In international law, legal claims often are not enforced by adjudication; they are implemented in a political process centering on power. Frequently, there is no authoritative third party utilized to evaluate legal counsel's claims. Such parties exist, in the form of the World Court or the United Nations Security Council, but they are prevented from acting through denial of state consent. Where, therefore, the government lawyer represents only his or her client to the exclusion of the integrity of the law itself, the law suffers. Where there is not a good-faith effort to implement treaties freely entered, both the law and the treaty party suffer. In the case of the ABM treaty, the Reagan reinterpretation was so incredible that the law, the Executive, and the legal adviser were all discredited. In the view of more than one person, the Reagan reinterpretation was a "charade."[21]

The role of the Senate. The administration's new version of the ABM treaty also entailed an argument about U.S. constitutional law. Essentially, the Reagan team argued that even though the Senate had given its advice and consent to a treaty based on certain representations by the Executive as to what the treaty meant, the Executive could change that interpretation without any further Senate role. The legal adviser testified that he was still finding memoranda hidden away in executive offices concerning the meaning of the ABM treaty, and that such "discoveries" could lead to unilateral reinterpretation. This point of view the Senate respectfully—and sometimes not so respectfully—declined to accept, as the following excerpt from Senate hearings shows:

> Judge Sofaer: The Senate, of course, is entitled to full and fair presentations by executive officials on the meaning of every aspect of treaties under Senate consideration. But the Senate's interest in full and fair consideration and presentations is to inform itself of the treaty that was actually made. When it gives its advice and consent to a treaty, it is to the treaty that was made, irrespective of the explanations it is provided.
>
> Chairman Biden: Would you say that again? It is to the treaty that is made, irrespective of the explanations of what the treaty means, given by the Executive to the Senate?
>
> Judge Sofaer: That is your main interest. Yes, Mr. Chairman, I would say that.
>
> Chairman Biden: That is incredible. That is absolutely staggering.
>
> Judge Sofaer: Well, let me finish.

> Chairman Biden: I'd like to hear the rest of this.
> Judge Sofaer: And I'd love to talk to you about it.
> Chairman Biden: Oh, we will. [Laughter.][22]

There was no doubt that the Senate in 1972 had consented to ratification of the ABM treaty according to the traditional—that is, restrictive—interpretation. Nixon administration officials had clearly presented that interpretation as the correct one. In fact, one of the two dissenting votes, by Senator James Buckley (R, NY), was on the basis that the treaty prevented future deployment of, and testing and production for, a space-based ABM system.[23]

The Judiciary was on the sidelines in this dispute over how to interpret law. It had never pronounced on the Executive's claim to unilateral reinterpretation because no such real dispute had ever arisen of exactly this nature. During the Carter presidency the Supreme Court had ruled that the Executive had the right to unilateral abrogation of a treaty; there was no constitutional role for the Senate in that type of action.[24] (And therefore, ironically, the Reagan administration could have avoided at least some conflict with Congress by withdrawing from the treaty as provided in the treaty.)

The Congress continued to insist throughout the Reagan presidency that the reinterpretation of the ABM treaty by the Executive was both an incorrect understanding of the substance of international law and procedurally a violation of constitutional law. As we shall see, this was as much a political battle as a legal one.

IV THE DOMESTIC RESPONSE

Immediately after McFarlane announced the reinterpretation in early October 1985, House Democrats exercised their majority position (which gave them control of committee and subcommittee chairs) to direct hearings toward the new administration position.[25] But this effort was unfocused and ineffectual. The House could claim to be involved through its role in providing funds for SDI, but the Senate had an even stronger claim to review because of its special role in giving advice and consent to treaties. However, the Republicans were the majority party in the Senate, and Republican committee chairs were not anxious to challenge the policies of a president of their own party. Party loyalty, not to mention support for SDI, overrode concern about the integrity of treaty interpretation. From the start of congressional review of this issue, party politics was to be—and remained—an important factor. With Republican inactivity in the Senate undercutting Democratic criticism in the

House, the administration seemed to be coasting along with its reinterpretation; it secured sizable funding from the Congress for SDI research for fiscal year 1986. But surface appearances were deceiving.

Two key factors changed the situation.[26] The first was that the Democrats regained control of the Senate in the 1986 elections. With Claiborne Pell (D, RI) as chair of the Foreign Relations Committee and Joseph Biden (D, DE) as chair of the Judiciary Committee, two liberal Democrats were poised to challenge the disliked policies of a Republican president. The second key factor pertained to personality. Two Democratic senators not members of the above committees went public with careful critiques of the administration's arguments. Carl Levin (D, MI) first challenged the Executive in December 1986; Sam Nunn (D, GA), the new chair of the Armed Services Committee and one of the most respected senators on security policy, followed. These factors converged into a concerted Democratic effort in the Senate to force the administration to abide by the restrictive interpretation of the ABM treaty during 1987. There were continuing parallel efforts in the House spearheaded by Les Aspin (D, WI). The key move was by Biden, who introduced a resolution attacking the reinterpretation and got Pell to agree to a joint hearing by their two committees.

Many like Nunn tried to focus on the constitutional issue of the proper role of the Senate in treaty interpretation, but this was impossible to separate from the international legal issue of how to properly interpret a treaty. The intertwining of international and constitutional law was nicely captured as Senator Nunn replied to Senator Jesse Helms:

> Senator Helms: Why are we so concerned with the technicalities and the dispute about what is the right on the one side and the right on the other of a 17-year-old negotiating record when the Soviets have violated the fundamental provisions of the ABM Treaty?
>
> Senator Nunn: But what we have here is the law of the land which is being reinterpreted. I think that is a fundamentally different thing.
>
> I think the Senate, as I indicated, has a much larger stake than just this treaty. So, my contention is that the two ought to be separated and we ought to adhere to the law of the land or we ought to get out of those treaties based on the accepted international practice.[27]

The Democratic majority in the Senate Foreign Relations Committee approved a report saying that the "Reagan Administration's 'reinterpretation' of the ABM Treaty constitutes the most flagrant abuse of the Constitution's treaty power in 200 years of American history."[28] But scholars of international law had been called to testify about the proper techniques for interpreting treaties, and lead-off witnesses in the joint Senate hearing focused on the terms of the treaty, not constitutional law. There is no denying that attention was also given to party politics, as well as to the issue of whether to move ahead as quickly as possible with an expanded defensive weapons system.

It should be stressed that the integrity of international law was only one, and at times not the most important, of the issues raised about SDI and the ABM treaty. In the view of some respected observers, the key question was whether SDI could be supported as a reasonable and workable scheme.[29] Clearly the traditional interpretation of the treaty interfered with the implementation of SDI. Not a few members of Congress argued, like Senator Helms, that the national security of the United States was at issue; given that "fact," and because the United States was dealing with the U.S.S.R., one should not pay so much attention to either international or constitutional niceties.[30] Others argued in favor of scrapping the treaty altogether, or deferring to the Executive's conduct of foreign affairs, or conversely upholding the role of the Senate. International law and its interpretation, however, were interwoven with all of these positions.

It was not clear which of these considerations, or of others, were uppermost in the minds of Reagan's critics, but it became obvious during 1987 that those critics took the complex of issues seriously. Nunn had said publicly in February 1987 that if the administration persisted in its views it would provoke a constitutional crisis. The administration did persist, despite the weakness of its case on purely international legal grounds. As the year progressed, therefore, Democratic majorities in both houses began to attach language to the bill that authorized money for the Department of Defense, requiring the strict interpretation of the treaty. In the House there was a 100-vote margin in support of this language, with 34 Republicans joining most of the majority Democrats. In the Senate there was a comfortable 58–38 vote for similar language, with 8 Republicans voting with the Democrats. The inability of the Reagan administration to keep all Republicans in its camp had been foreshadowed in the Senate Foreign Relations Committee when Nancy Kassebaum (R, KS) voted to uphold the traditional interpretation. Among Senate Democrats, only Senator Ernest Hollings (D, SC) defected to support Reagan's position. Thus, Congress manifested its view through the power of the purse. If Reagan got a defense bill, he would also get language requiring the traditional interpretation of the treaty.

Given the strength of congressional opposition to Reagan's reinterpretation, whether based on international law, constitutional law, security policy, or some other reason, Congress was stalled by filibusters in the Senate during the summer of 1987. The president's supporters, lacking the votes, resorted to dilatory maneuvers to block reaffirmation of the traditional understanding. Then the Reagan team accepted a short-term defeat in order to avoid a permanent one. A deal was finally struck between Congress and the Executive covering FY 1988: In exhange for dropping, in conference committee, the language requiring that the administration accept the restrictive interpretation as the law, the administration agreed not to conduct any tests violating that interpretation and not to purchase any equipment that could be used for violative tests during FY 1988. This was a congressional victory in substance, although the Executive saved some face in not having its reinterpretation formally rejected.

In retrospect, it is clear that the administration wanted to move ahead with SDI testing and development and that the ABM treaty was going to be sacrificed to this cause—but without formal abrogation. This did not happen because of Congress, which paid considerable attention to the integrity of treaties. The Judiciary was not directly involved; nor was mass public opinion, since the issues were technical if not arcane and did not seem to impinge on daily lives. Congress acted through the personal convictions and party loyalties of its members, not because it was pressured by public opinion, however conceived.

V FOREIGN RESPONSES

Foreign responses to Reagan's reinterpretation of the ABM treaty seemed to have little direct and clear impact on the administration and only slight impact on congressional proceedings. The Soviet Union predictably disagreed with the reinterpretation, shortly after McFarlane's announcement, through a statement in *Pravda*.[31] This was but a restatement of Soviet commitments to the restrictive interpretation that they had made even before October 6, 1985.[32] It is not generally known what representations the U.S.S.R. made through quiet diplomatic channels, but one might assume it protested the reinterpretation to the State Department.

The United Kingdom and the Federal Republic of Germany both contacted the U.S. government immediately after the reinterpretation was announced,[33] raising questions that indicated their concern about administration policy. They and other states in NATO feared an expanded arms race in offensive weapons if the 1972 limits on ABMs were effectively discarded. This was because the easiest way to defeat a defensive system is to overwhelm it with sheer numbers of attack weapons and decoys, which are cheaper to build than defensive or intercept systems. The administration tried to buy off this criticism, offering allies some of the military contracts under the SDI program.

One can only speculate about how important officials in the Executive evaluated this foreign response. It was clear that key policy-makers in the Defense Department were committed to rapid advance on SDI regardless of foreign backlash. It does seem likely that they thought outright abrogation would antagonize NATO allies, and world opinion, more than the reinterpretation route. It also seems likely that Secretary of State Shultz was the most sensitive of the high-level administration officials with regard to foreign complications. Fear of Soviet and NATO negative reactions may have helped Shultz push the compromise policy of no violative field tests, even while Secretary of Defense Weinberger was referring to the reinterpretation as TLC: the legally correct interpretation. These same considerations about disruptive foreign reactions may have played a role in the administration's acceptance of the 1988 compromise over the defense bill, although that agreement would never have been reached had the administration not lost roll call votes over reinterpretation in the Congress.

Both Soviet and West European positions were noted in passing in congressional debates, but they were not emphasized. Much more important were domestic factors such as party politics and the Senate's interest in preserving its institutional role in giving advice and consent to treaties. As already shown, there was also persistent but not exclusive interest in upholding treaties as originally understood. This was both a domestic and an international influence, but abstracted from any particular foreign party.

In general, it can be said that those pushing the reinterpretation were only minimally affected by foreign responses and would have continued in that direction absent congressional opposition.

VI OUTCOME FOR THE UNITED STATES

There were two major outcomes for the United States from the battle over how to interpret the ABM treaty. First, it did maintain its reputation as a state that tried to implement treaties in good faith. This was achieved only through congressional action on the basis of mixed motives; the bright side, though, was that there were sizable majorities in both houses, including a number of moderate Republicans, who voted for the traditional, restrictive, interpretation of the 1972 treaty despite considerable pressure from a popular president to uphold his reinterpretation attempt.

The second outcome was not so sanguine. Because the Reagan administration never rescinded officially its reinterpretation attempt, but only accepted tactical compromises, there remained a residue of mistrust between the Senate and the Executive. In 1987 when the Reagan administration negotiated a treaty with the Soviet Union for the removal of intermediate-range nuclear forces (INF) from Europe, and then submitted it to the Senate for advice and consent, the Senate, after some senators threatened to hold the new treaty hostage to the old debate, attached the following understanding (among others):

The Senate's advice and consent to ratification of the INF treaty is subject to the condition, based on the Treaty Clauses of the Constitution, that—

(A) the United States shall interpret the Treaty in accordance with the common understanding of the Treaty shared by the President and the Senate at the time the Senate gave its advice and consent to ratification;

(B) such common understanding is based on:

(i) first, the text of the Treaty and the provisions of this resolution of ratification; and

(ii) second, the authoritative representations which were provided by the President and his representatives to the Senate and its Committees . . . ; and

(C) the United States shall not agree to or adopt an interpretation different from that common understanding except pursuant to Senate advice and consent to subsequent treaty or protocol, or the enactment of a statute; and

(D) if . . . a question arises as to the interpretation of a provision of the Treaty on which no common understanding was reached . . . that provision shall be interpreted in accordance with applicable United States law.[34]

President Reagan indicated concern about this understanding and later sent a letter to the Senate taking issue with it. He argued that the understanding elevated executive statements unduly above treaty intent, negotiating record, and subsequent practice. His letter said in part that treaties "must be interpreted in accordance with accepted principles of international law and United States Supreme Court jurisprudence." He went on to say that "Executive statements should be given binding weight only when they were authoritatively communicated to the Senate by the Executive and were part of the basis on which the Senate granted its advice and consent. . . . This Administration does not take the position that the Executive branch can disregard authoritative Executive statements to the Senate."[35]

This letter seemed to be consistent with international law and usual state practice, and it could be read as abandoning the president's position during the debate on how to interpret the ABM treaty. On the other hand, if the Executive's argument in the past had been that the United States and the U.S.S.R. had agreed to the 1972 treaty with the intent to exempt exotic testing and development, and that this intent had not been properly communicated to the Senate, the 1987 letter might not change the fundamental dispute. Such a reading of the historical record, however, implies an inordinate amount of incompetence to both treaty negotiators and Nixon officials.

Thus, the second major outcome of the reinterpretation debate was a continuing battle between the Senate and the Executive concerning the meaning of a treaty to which the Senate consented. Until that battle was resolved, every treaty submitted to the Senate was likely to produce some language intended to protect the Senate's role and the integrity of the advise and consent process. Leading senators such as Sam Nunn had predicted this course of events during the reinterpretation battle, warning that treaties might sink under the weight of these additional provisions. As of the time of writing (during the Bush administration), the Senate was determined to avoid another unilateral executive reinterpretation of a treaty's fundamental meaning.

ⅦⅡ OUTCOME FOR WORLD ORDER

The Reagan reinterpretation would have wreaked havoc with U.S.-U.S.S.R. and U.S.-NATO relations had Congress not resisted this blatant attempt to violate the traditional understanding of the meaning of the ABM treaty. The Soviets would have had ample reason to doubt U.S. good faith in implementing what had been agreed, and it is highly doubtful that Mikhail Gorbachev could have moved forward with other arms control and disarmament treaties, such as the INF accord of 1987, had the ultra-hardliners in Washington been successful in what they attempted. There is also no doubt that the NATO alliance, already strained by various issues, would have been troubled further by the violation of the basic international legal principle *pacta sunt servanda*—pacts must be observed. As the Senate Report put it, "The full picture is of a policy process not merely unusual, but so substandard as to breach the requirement of international law that a treaty be interpreted in good faith."[36] Had the Congress not opposed the Reagan team, the overall reputation of the United States for responsible and lawful behavior in the world arena would have been damaged further.

As we shall see, the Reagan reinterpretation was but one of several Reagan policies that treated international law in a most cavalier manner. Yet, in most of these other situations, as in the debate over the meaning of the ABM treaty, international law was an important part of the political debate in Washington, even if it was not the sole factor.

NOTES

The epigraph that opens Chapter 2 is quoted from the *1987 U.S. Senate Report*, 54.

1. For background and overview, see the publication by the respected Stockholm International Peace Research Institute, Walter Stutzle, et al., eds., *The ABM Treaty: To Defend or Not to Defend?* Oxford: Oxford University Press, 1987.

2. The United States had long complained in the SCC that one of the new Soviet radar sites violated the ABM treaty because it was not on the periphery of the U.S.S.R. and could look outward for missile defense as well as inward for

tracking of test missiles. Some U.S. experts agreed this site was a violation, but thought it was militarily insignificant. In October 1989, the U.S.S.R. admitted that the radar site in question was a treaty violation and began dismantling it (*New York Times*, October 24, 1989, 1). The U.S.S.R. had long complained in the SCC that what the United States called modernization of some NATO radar sites was in fact replacement with new technology. Some senators seemed to agree when they suggested that U.S. action could be viewed as a proportional response to Soviet violation. Given these disputes, particularly ultraconservative circles argued that the ABM treaty should be abrogated because of Soviet violations (these were never specified beyond the one radar site; possible U.S. violations were not addressed). The early position of the Reagan administration was that the treaty remained in the overall national interest, despite these controversies.

3. *New York Times*, March 24, 1983, 1.

4. The U.S.S.R. first argued that even research on ABMs that were exotic, used advanced physical principles, or were space-based, was prohibited under treaty language referring to "testing," but later accepted as correct the U.S. view that laboratory research was permitted.

5. "Mr. McFarlane's Interview on 'Meet the Press,'" *Department of State Bulletin*, 85 (December 1985), 33.

6. Strobe Talbott, *Deadly Gambits*, New York: Knopf, 1984.

7. For a slightly different view, see Kevin C. Kennedy, "Treaty Interpretation by the Executive Branch: The ABM Treaty and 'Star Wars' Testing and Development," *American Journal of International Law*, 80, 4 (October 1986), 854–877.

8. For an analysis of how a case gets to the World Court, see Chapter 3.

9. Raymond L. Garthoff, *Policy Versus the Law: The Reinterpretation of the ABM Treaty*, Washington: Brookings, 1987, 2–9. Garthoff was a negotiator of the 1972 treaty as a foreign service officer; he is a recognized scholar of Soviet-U.S. relations.

10. Ibid.

11. *New York Times*, March 1, 1988, 22.

12. See the collection of Sofaer's statements and writings in "The ABM Treaty and the Constitution," *Joint Hearings*, Senate Committees on Foreign Relations and the Judiciary, 100th Congress, 1st session, Washington: GPO, 1987, appendix starting at 227.

13. Garthoff, note 9.

14. *Joint Hearings*, note 12, at 121.

15. Garthoff, note 9. See also "The ABM Treaty Interpretation Resolution," *Report*, Senate Committee on Foreign Relations, 100th Congress, 1st session, Report 100-164, Washington: GPO, 1987, 25; and Paul Nitze, "Treaty Interpretation," *Department of State Bulletin* (January 1987).

16. For an extended analysis of the legal adviser's role, see *Report*, note 15, at 62–65. Biden's comment is recorded in *Joint Hearings*, note 12, at 3.

17. Richard A. Falk, *The Status of Law in International Society*, Princeton: Princeton University Press, 1970, chp. 10; and Richard Bilder, "The Office of the Legal Adviser: The State Department Lawyer and Foreign Affairs," *American Journal of International Law*, 56, 3 (July 1962), 633–684.

18. Chayes summarizes his arguments in *The Cuban Missile Crisis: International Crises and the Role of Law*, New York: Oxford University Press, 1974. In the same work, see the comment by Louis Henkin at 149–155.

19. *New York Times*, March 1, 1988, 22.

20. Ibid.

21. Senator Patrick J. Leahy (D, VT), in *Joint Hearings*, note 12, at 146. Of the various independent legal scholars who subjected the reinterpretation to legal analysis, none sided with the administration.

22. *Joint Hearings*, note 12, at 130.

23. Ibid., and *Report*, note 15.

24. *Goldwater v. Carter*, 48 USLW 3402 (Supreme Court December 13, 1979); analyzed in *American Journal of Law*, 74, 2 (April 1980), 441–447.

25. "The ABM Treaty Dispute," *Hearing*, House Subcommittee on Arms Control, 99th Congress, 1st session, Washington: GPO, 1986. See also "Strategic Defense Initiative," *Hearing*, Senate Armed Services Committee, 99th Congress, lst session, Washington: GPO, 1986.

26. The well-informed account in Garthoff, note 9, stresses personalities, but does not cover party alignments and voting.

27. *Joint Hearings*, note 12, at 66.

28. *Report*, note 15, at 66.

29. *Congressional Quarterly Almanac 1987*, Washington: Congressional Quarterly Press, 1988, 203.

30. See Helms, *Joint Hearings*, note 12, at 66.

31. Statement by Marshall Akhromeyev, October 19, 1985. See further Garthoff, note 9, chp. 5; and Vladimir Semenov, "The Treaty's Basic Provisions," and Vladlen S. Vereshchetin, "Issues Related to Current U.S. and Soviet Views of the Treaty," both in *The ABM Treaty*, note 1, at 62–74 and 105–120.

32. Garthoff, note 9.

33. Ibid.

34. *American Journal of International Law*, 82, 4 (October 1988), 810–815.

35. Ibid.

36. *Report*, note 15, at 62.

III

"Covert" Intervention in Nicaragua

Our purpose, in conformity with American and International Law, is to prevent the flow of arms to El Salvador, Honduras, Guatemala, and Costa Rica.   —President Ronald Reagan

I hold no brief for the Sandinista regime, but whatever one thinks about it, it is the internationally recognized government of a sovereign nation. It should not be the function of the United States to overthrow regimes because it does not like their ideological character.
      —Senator Patrick J. Leahy

I will say to my friend that the real issue is being obscured, that issue being whether we are going to fail to do whatever we can to prevent a Marxist takeover of Central America. That is the issue.
      —Senator Jesse Helms

I often feel in Washington that I am in Alice in Wonderland where black is white, and up is down, and in is out, and war is peace.
      —Representative Gerry Studds

1   SOME RELEVANT FACTS

In July 1979, Anastasio Somoza Debayle—the corrupt and brutal dictator of Nicaragua who was long supported by the United States—having unsuccessfully tried to suppress a revolution through mass murder and other unsavory policies—accepted Jimmy Carter's offer of safe passage to Miami and relinquished power.[1] Despite the diplomatic efforts of the Carter administration, which first sought Somoza's orderly removal through the Organization of American States (OAS) and then sought a caretaker military government from Somoza's National Guard, the new Government of National Reconstruction, distinct from the Nicaraguan communist party but using the language of Marxism, consolidated power. This new Sandinista government, named for a former Nicaraguan rebel, alienated some of those Nicaraguans who had helped make the revolution against Somoza, and these alienated Nicaraguans went into opposition or exile.

The Carter administration, in order to learn the "lessons" of Cuba in 1959–1960, tried to co-opt the Sandinista government with a sizable foreign aid program and the promise of normal relations. Thus, Carter hoped to avoid driving the new government into the arms of the Russian bear through implacable hostility, as some believed the Eisenhower administration had done when dealing with Fidel Castro immediately after his Cuban revolution. The primary quid pro quo was that Managua was expected to stay out of the Cuban–Soviet orbit. Carter may nevertheless have continued a covert aid program to opposition political parties, newspapers, and individuals.[2]

Daniel Ortega and the other core Sandinistas, however, contradicted U.S. hopes. Flushed with unexpected victory, young in years, and perhaps guided by the belief that their revolution could only be secured from imperial counterrevolution through international solidarity, the new leaders entered into diplomatic and military arrangements with Cuba, the Soviet Union and its East European allies, and other governments then adversaries of the United States. The Sandinistas also struck shadowy deals with the Palestine Liberation Organization and other nonstate parties that at the time were also adversaries of Washington. There is no doubt that in the period 1979–1981, Managua facilitated leftist revolutions in neighboring countries—especially in El Salvador—by providing military assistance, safe haven, radio contact, and other support for rebel forces.[3]

The Carter administration responded, in one of its last acts of governance, by suspending the foreign aid program to Nicaragua. This set the stage for the incoming Reagan administration. While many other facts could be brought to bear on this situation, such as the long history of U.S. military intervention in the region mostly in support of repressive regimes, several legal facts deserve special mention. They remained constant despite the change of governments in Washington.

Both the United States and Nicaragua were (and are) members of the United Nations and thus a legal party to the U.N. Charter. According to that treaty, Article 2, paragraph 4: "All members shall refrain in their international relations from the threat or use of force against the territorial integrity or political independence of any state." This core legal principle, relevant to other legal concepts such as state sovereignty, national self-determination, and domestic jurisdiction, is related to Article 51: "Nothing in the present Charter shall impair the inherent right of individual or collective self-defense if an armed attack occurs against a Member of the United Nations." Other procedural rules are related to the prohibition of intervention and aggression on the one hand, and the right of self-defense on the other.

Thus, the Charter establishes a general prohibition against the use of force, with the only clear exception being self-defense. In an effort to indicate more explicitly the difference between impermissible aggression and permissible self-defense, the U.N. General Assembly has voted, and the U.N. International Law Commission has affirmed, that there is a general presumption against the first use of force, and that certain acts normally are impermissible. Included among these impermissible acts is "the sending by or on behalf of a State of armed bands, groups, irregulars or mercenaries, which carry out acts of armed force against another State of such gravity as to amount to [aggressive acts], or its substantial involvement therein."[4]

More generally in international law, it is widely accepted that the exercise of self-defense requires that two standards be met: necessity and proportionality.[5] Necessity implies that diplomacy and other peaceful efforts at conflict resolution are unavailable or ineffective. Proportionality requires that the defensive use of force be proportional to the preceding violation.

The United States and Nicaragua are also both members of the OAS and parties to the related Rio Treaty for hemispheric security. The OAS Charter reaffirms the basic legal principles found in the U.N. Charter, such as a general prohibition on use of force, the right of self-defense, nonintervention, national sovereignty and self-determination, and domestic jurisdiction. Article 20 mandates: "All international disputes that may arise between American States shall be submitted to the peaceful procedures set forth in this Charter, before being referred to the Security Council of the United Nations." The Rio Treaty mandates, inter alia, that conflicts between signatory states should be taken to the OAS, that the Organ of Consultation can prescribe remedies to a dispute by a two-thirds vote, and that such decisions are legally binding on the parties (military sanctions are excluded).[6]

Therefore, when the Reagan administration took office on January 20, 1981, it confronted a disliked government in Nicaragua, but it also faced long-established—if frequently violated—international legal principles for the conduct of foreign policy. The Reagan team took overt policy decisions to apply economic pressure on the Sandinistas through bilateral and multilateral channels. In a parallel development, the Executive instituted a "covert" program of military attacks in Nicaragua, carried out primarily by Nicaraguan nationals. U.S. officials were heavily involved in the organizing, training, financing, supervision, and on occasion actual military operations of the Nicaraguan opposition forces—better known as the contras. This "covert" action against the Sandinistas proved highly controversial at home and abroad. International law figured prominently in the debates.

II   EXECUTIVE POLICY

In the early years of the Reagan administration, it was not easy for those outside the inner policy circle to determine the exact nature of executive policy toward Nicaragua. As the years passed, however, it became clear that the initial rationale for U.S. covert intervention was incomplete. The original classified message to Congress concerning the start of covert operations, required by U.S. law to be delivered in a "timely" fashion, professed the goal of moderating Nicaraguan foreign policy in conformity with international law. But it became increasingly obvious that the Executive wanted the removal of the Sandinistas from power altogether. This was part of the "Reagan Doctrine" of not merely containing but rolling back communist regimes, especially weak ones in the Third World.[7]

In early 1981 President Reagan signed a secret "executive finding" authorizing the expansion of Central Intelligence Agency (CIA) activity in Nicaragua, and Central America in general, in order to prepare for increased covert action against leftists.[8] By November and December of that year, the Executive was prepared to launch a series of military attacks on Nicaragua primarily using disaffected Nicaraguans who were organized, trained, financed, and supervised by CIA and Department of Defense (DOD) personnel under the overall direction of the National Security Council (NSC). Military advisers from the highly repressive Argentine junta were also involved in 1981 and early 1982, as were nationals of other hemispheric states, referred to by the CIA as UCLAs (unilaterally controlled foreign assets).[9] Military attacks against Nicaragua, mostly against civilian and economic targets, began in early 1982. In late 1981 the congressional intelligence committees had been told that the attacks were intended to interdict the flow of arms from Nicaragua to El Salvador, or to pressure out Cubans serving in Nicaragua.[10] Neither the rest of Congress nor the American public was informed about these raids, which originated mostly from Honduras by the Nicaraguan Democratic Force, a group that had not existed as such prior to U.S. involvement.

As the press learned of these attacks and began to probe them, the covert activity became overt. In acknowledging the raids, the Executive tried to stick by the initial justification that they were designed to curtail revolutionary foreign policy moves by Managua—namely gun running and other involvement in El Salvador and elsewhere. Repeatedly, as in his address to Congress in 1983, President Reagan stated that his goal was not the overthrow of the Sandinista government, but rather the more limited objective of moderating Managua's foreign policy.[11] Initially and officially, therefore, there seemed continuity between Carter and Reagan. If the Sandinistas would behave in world affairs, the United States would maintain normal relations. Carter had recognized the Sandinista government, and Reagan did not break diplomatic relations.

This official rationale for executive conduct of foreign policy, and of course the policy of military attacks itself, led to increasing controversy. The central foreign policy issue throughout the extended controversy was the growing suspicion that executive policy was not limited and legal, but unlimited and illegal. There were many reasons for this.

First, high-level contra officials were quoted as saying that they intended to overthrow the Sandinistas.[12]

Second, top administration officials also seemed at times to be saying that the real policy was overthrow. The president himself stated in a press conference in 1985 that he would be satisfied when the Sandinistas "cried uncle."[13] That remark was widely interpreted to mean that the Sandinistas would have to give up power before the attacks would be terminated, since the president talked about changing the present structure of power in Managua. Likewise, Secretary of State George Shultz and other State Department spokespersons indicated broad U.S. objectives featuring internal changes within Nicaragua; demands for extensive domestic political reform added up to removal of the Sandinistas from power. (Elections in Nicaragua in 1984 did not satisfy the administration, although other foreign observers regarded them as reasonably fair and free.)[14] The director of the CIA, William Casey, was apparently telling members of Congress privately that the Reagan administration would do "whatever was necessary" to remove the Sandinistas.[15]

Third, the nature of concrete action taken or supported by the Executive looked like overthrow. From 1982 on, very little military activity was focused on arms interdiction. When at one point congressional elements offered to vote money for overt border control, the administration was not in favor.[16] The contras were ineffective against the Nicaraguan military, and most contra activity was directed against the social and economic infrastructure of Nicaragua. There were attacks on electric stations and power grids, agricultural cooperatives, irrigation systems, bridges important for agricultural transport, fuel storage facilities, etc.[17] In related actions, the Reagan administration overtly engaged in economic warfare against the Sandinistas, halting all foreign assistance, terminating the Nicaraguan sugar quota allowed in the U.S. domestic market, instituting a total trade embargo, and blocking private and public bank loans to Managua.[18] The overall U.S. policy looked less and less like interdiction and more and more like efforts to ruin the nation to discredit the Sandinistas.

Moreover, a former CIA official came in from the cold and out in the open to say that after early 1981 the Sandinistas had cut back on military assistance to Salvadoran rebels in an effort to pacify Washington.[19] The former U.S. ambassaor to Nicaragua was also to say eventually that Nicaraguan assistance to the Salvadoran rebels after early 1981 was "insignificant," and that in 1981 he had been in favor of a continuation of

U.S. foreign assistance as a reward for Managua's more moderate foreign policy.[20] Despite various State Department publications and speeches, hard evidence that Managua provided substantial military assistance abroad was simply not presented by the Reagan team after 1981.[21] All of this made the Reagan policy look like overthrow, whether directly through military victory or indirectly through military pressure leading to fundamental internal change.

Fourth, over time the specter of another Vietnam was raised. It was clear that the Nicaraguan people were not rallying to the contras and that there were substantial reasons for this. A number of people in the civilian and military wings of the contra movement were associated with either the CIA or the National Guard during the Somoza dictatorship; it was also eventually established that atrocities were carried out by the contras (and by the Nicaraguan army). The CIA was charged with preparing a manual for the contras that advocated assassination of civilian officials, and several lower-ranking CIA operatives were reprimanded for their part in this affair.[22] All of these factors undercut contra appeal.

Although there was an expansion of contra numbers from 1981 to about 1987, either voluntarily or by press gangs, the contras failed to take and hold a single village, much less a city or province. In contrast, from 1983 the Sandinista regime distributed weapons widely throughout the population; only a secure regime not fearful of widespread insurrection would follow such a policy. While U.S. administration policy had certainly damaged the Nicaraguan economy, the military ineffectiveness of the contras raised the question of direct involvement by Honduran or U.S. troops—or as the case might better be phrased, *more* involvement by U.S. personnel. CIA and DOD officials were already involved in training, supervision, and logistical support; some thought that CIA and DOD personnel had already taken direct part in warfare.[23] It was agreed by all that U.S. nationals had participated in the laying of mines in Nicaraguan waters and attacks on fuel storage tanks.

If Nicaragua, which had the approximate size and population of Iowa, was as clear and present a threat to U.S. national security as the administration claimed—perhaps through regional subversion or by serving as a military base for the Soviet Union—then given the military ineffectiveness of the contras and the reluctance of many Honduran officials to get fully involved, would not the United States eventually have to invade Nicaragua? This was the specter of another Vietnam.

Fifth, the administration had trouble convincing others that it had negotiated with the Sandinistas in a good faith effort to resolve differences peacefully. An early effort at bilateral negotiations under State Department official Thomas Enders may or may not have been serious.[24] Increasingly it appeared that Reagan policy was to undercut efforts at peaceful resolution, such as the Contadora negotiations led by four regional states and supported by other hemispheric states, and the Arias peace plan developed by the president of Costa Rica. A leaked State Department document seemed to indicate that its policy was to oppose such efforts because they would leave the Sandinistas in power.[25] On several occasions, when Nicaragua or some other state (for example, El Salvador or Honduras) indicated agreement with one of the peace plans, the Executive took action to sabotage the accord. The appointment of special U.S. negotiators like Richard Stone or Philip Habib seemed to many to be more window dressing to pacify critics than serious efforts; Habib resigned when undercut by the administration.[26]

A major complication arose over the Iran-contra scandal. As will be shown later, for a time Congress prohibited U.S. assistance to the contras. It eventually became known that White House officials had authorized a policy whereby foreign government, and also private, donations would be solicited and then delivered to the contras by a private network of anticommunist activists. Oliver North, an NSC staffer, was the key operative representing the executive branch, and former U.S. military officials John Singlaub and Richard Secord were the key operatives on the quasi-private side. (Some of these "private" deliveries occured from a military air base in El Salvador under the effective control of the United States.)

Thus, during the congressional ban on aid to the contras, aid was in fact delivered to them with the active involvement of U.S. government officials. Some funds were derived from covert arms sales to revolutionary Iran for the purpose of "buying" the release of U.S. citizens held hostage in Lebanon by forces linked to Iran. Considerable corruption was involved in this complicated process. All of these elements of the Iran-contra scandal were first denied, then acknowledged by Reagan and his lieutenants.[27] As a result, U.S. military assistance to the contras was once again blocked by Congress. A small amount of nonlethal assistance was authorized, but by the beginning of the Bush administration the contras had become less important in U.S. relations with Nicaragua.

A final difficulty was linked to the Iran-contra scandal, but had existed earlier as well: it was the issue of executive misrepresentation. This factor deserves emphasis not only because it indicates something about how Washington works, but also because it helps explain growing congressional assertiveness in the 1970s and 1980s.

As Congress investigated who was responsible for Iran-contra, it encountered numerous cases of conflicting testimony. Even at the time of writing (early 1990), it was still not absolutely clear what the president knew and authorized, which of his subordinates were knowledgeable and in the decision-making loop, and who was excluded or peripheral to the whole affair. A number of administration officials, as well as private individuals, were lying.

But this had long been a problem at all levels of the Reagan administration. Members of Congress in particular, not to mention foreign authorities, simply could not rely on the veracity of statements made by members of the Executive. (One did well to exercise the same skepticism when listening to Sandinistas.) When the president himself claimed that his policy toward Nicaragua was not one of overthrow, but later stated that the structure of government there would have to be changed before contra attacks would cease, his integrity was called into question.

The same problem arose at lower levels. At a time when contra attacks were being coordinated by the U.S. embassy in Honduras, under instructions from an NSC interagency group in Washington, a State Department representative told Congress: "I think that what you see along the border of Honduras and Nicaragua is first of all a rather large refugee presence. Second, the presence of very disparate groups of anti-Sandinistas, some of whom, as I indicated, are Somocistas, some of whom were apolitical, some of which are ex-Sandinistas."[28] It was no wonder that this sort of obfuscation, if not outright mendacity, led, for example, to Congress banning from its chambers Reagan's assistant secretary of state for inter-American affairs, Elliott Abrams. Needless to say, this track record created difficulties for executive policy.

In sum, it is fair to say of executive policy toward Nicaragua during the Reagan period that statements about a limited interdiction program were increasingly disbelieved by other important policymakers. Increasingly, this policy looked like coercive attempts to remove a government rather than interdict gun running. At a minimum, it seemed to be military and economic pressure disproportionate to original Sandinista conduct, and Managua's revolutionary behavior had not been proven beyond a reasonable doubt after 1981. Ultimately, these Central American issues became entangled with other questions, such as selling arms to revolutionary Iran, buying back hostages from terrorists, and violating U.S. law.

International legal claims by the Reagan team constituted a central part of the controversy.

III   EXECUTIVE LEGAL CLAIMS

Because the U.N. Charter permits the use of force for individual or collective self-defense, it is not surprising that the core Reagan legal claim in support of contra attacks appealed to that principle. The administration claimed that it was engaged in the inherent right of collective self-defense: Nicaragua had given military and other assistance to the rebels in El Salvador, so that latter state and the United States were engaged in a defensive response. (It was not until 1984 that the government of El

Salvador claimed it was under armed attack from Nicaragua and requested U.S. assistance in defense. Decisions in Washington during 1981 seemed to have been taken unilaterally; there is no known reference to any request from El Salvador.)

In retrospect one could construct a supporting legal argument, drawn from various administration statements, even if the Executive itself never put forward a coherent brief in a single document. Military attacks were necessary because, despite U.S. good-faith efforts, Nicaragua had refused to negotiate a settlement; and those attacks were proportional because Nicaragua was arming and supporting all sorts of terrorists and rebels throughout Central America and even beyond. (The Executive made no attempt, however, to seek a settlement through either the U.N. Security Council or the Organization of American States.)

A legal claim in support of other aspects of administration policy was not so clear. Even in the early 1980s and certainly more frequently thereafter, executive officials stressed not just revolutionary foreign policy by Managua but repression at home. This was true of a presentation by State Department official Thomas Enders to Congress in 1983, and by Ambassador Jeane Kirkpatrick to the United Nations in the same year. By the mid-1980s, Secretary of State George Shultz and his assistant, Elliott Abrams, argued that revolutionary foreign policy stemmed from the nature of the regime at home, so to correct the former one had to change the latter.[29] But how significant were the human rights violations at home, and what legal right did the United States have to correct them by force?

In fact, executive claims about human rights violations were exaggerated or lacking in contextual analysis. Without minimizing Sandinista violations, one should note that all governments, when faced with internal or external security problems, suspend certain human rights. This was done by President Lincoln during the U.S. Civil War under the Constitution; it is permitted by human rights treaties.[30] It was the United States that initiated significant military moves against Nicaragua at the very time Washington was claiming important human rights violations; and external attacks could only lead to more repression, not less, which raised the question of whether this was exactly what the administration desired in order to discredit the political legitimacy of Managua. A former CIA agent was to testify at the World Court that the CIA had devised a plan in the early 1980s to increase repression in Managua so as to discredit the Sandinistas.[31] Whatever the ulterior motivations of the Executive, it repeatedly misrepresented the human rights situation in Nicaragua, as when it overstated violations against the Miskito Indians and failed to reveal CIA efforts to recruit them into the armed resistance.[32]

Even if it is acknowledged that there were important human rights violations in Nicaragua (and virtually everyone agreed on this), it is not at all clear that international law permits individual states to take military action to correct those violations. While the U.N. Charter obligates states to promote human rights, it contains references to nonintervention and self-determination, not to mention a general prohibition on recourse to force (except for self-defense). And while the OAS Charter contains principles obligating states to implement democracy and social justice along with human rights, it—like the U.N. Charter—grants no explicit permission to states to compel these values on other states via force. (This will be dealt with further in the next chapter.) The administration kept repeating that the Sandinistas had promised the OAS to respect democracy and human rights, but this political statement gave no legal rights to the United States to use force.

The administration's emphasis on collective self-defense encountered early political challenge, as will be shown, when certain members of Congress viewed it as a cover argument for large-scale intervention designed to overthrow the Sandinistas. Formal legal challenge came in 1984, when Nicaragua itself petitioned the World Court to—in effect—evaluate Washington's legal claim. Most of that case is analyzed in the section below dealing with foreign responses to U.S. policy. It should be noted at this point, though, that the Reagan administration tried to keep the International Court of Justice from ruling on the merits of the case, withdrew from that phase of the case and thereby refused to argue the merits, and repeatedly attacked the court for being biased against the United States and erroneous in its legal interpretations. It bears emphasizing that while the Reagan administration put forth a legal argument in behalf of its policy toward Nicaragua, it clearly did not want the World Court—or, as we shall see, the U.N. Security Council—to pass authoritative and binding judgment on its argument. The administration wanted to be judge and jury in its own case.

IV   THE DOMESTIC RESPONSE

Three general points should be made about the domestic response to Reagan's policy and legal claims concerning Nicaragua, before proceeding to more specific matters.

First, U.S. courts were generally reluctant to treat the international and domestic legal issues. Consistent with much juridical tradition in the United States, when parties sought to involve U.S. courts to resolve highly complex legal issues touching on both international politics and conflict between the Executive and Congress, they encountered procedural rulings that avoided the merits. The Judiciary had long displayed a pronounced tendency, not ironclad, to find ways of avoiding substantive judgments when the Executive claimed that national security or other important foreign policy issues were involved. This tendency was accen-

tuated when the court also observed major disputes between the two political branches.[33]

For example, when Norwegian parties brought suit in a U.S. court
for damages to a ship struck by a mine laid in Nicaraguan waters by, or
with the support of, the United States, the court ruled that the "political
question" doctrine precluded examination of the merits.[34] Among the
reasons given by the court for this ruling was an extreme deference to
the Executive in foreign policy—a view that approached putting that
branch beyond the reach of law, either international or domestic. This
judgment went too far in this direction in the view of the normally staid
American Journal of International Law, whose commentator remarked:
"The court's assertion that the Constitution commits foreign policy decisions to the executive branch may overstate the authority of the President."[35] Be that as it may, it was clear that most domestic questions about
international law and U.S. foreign policy toward Nicaragua would be
played out in Congress, not in the courts. International law is law, but
sometimes it is not easy to get it adjudicated in national courts.

Second, as background to those congressional debates, public opinion was decidedly against U.S. military involvement in Nicaragua. Moreover, domestic public opinion was generally critical of the way in which
Reagan dealt with Nicaragua, and a substantial number of people
thought that the situation in Nicaragua could become another Vietnam.
Thus, unlike in the dispute over the ABM treaty of about the same time,
the public was at least vaguely aware of U.S. involvement in Nicaragua,
was aware of the basic controversy involved, and held opinions even if
they were not firmly grounded in detailed facts. Despite all the televised
speeches by the "Great Communicator" Reagan, and despite all the publications by the State Department, this essentially negative public opinion toward Reagan's basic policy did not shift over time—except to become more negative.

By 1985, for example, the Gallup polling organization was reporting
that only 36 percent of those sampled favored military assistance to the
contras, and only 8 percent were in favor of committing U.S. troops to
the struggle. Fifty-nine percent thought it likely or very likely that
Nicaragua could become another Vietnam. Forty-five percent disap-
proved of Reagan's overall Nicaraguan policy, and only 29 percent approved. As the Iran-contra scandal became a major event in Washington,
public opinion on Nicaraguan policy and on the president himself
shifted even more into the negative column. (Prior to the scandal, citizens distinguished between a negative view of Nicaraguan policy and a
positive view of the president himself.) In 1986, Gallup reported a disap-
proval rate of 64 percent for policy toward Nicaragua. By 1987, only 21
percent favored assistance to the contras; 69 percent were opposed. By
1986 and 1987, even a majority of Republicans opposed aid to the contras.[36]

The political significance of this public opinion was that congressional elements that opposed the president's policy felt that they could take a stand and not be punished by the voters. This had also been true of the ABM debate, but for different reasons. On that issue, the public had not been even remotely informed and did not hold opinions about the treaty. On Nicaragua, certainly from the mid-1980s on, public opinion was in the camp of the critics. Although public opinion did not necessarily determine the outcome of the debate in Washington, it was a background or indirect condition of some importance, especially as the controversy progressed.

Third, while the Congress was deeply involved in U.S. foreign policy toward Nicaragua, and while it paid considerable attention to international legal questions, the variety of legal and political issues raised, the divisions within the institution, the changing arguments and personnel by the Executive, and the changing events abroad made it difficult for Congress to take a sustained position. An overview of the pattern helps to give the big picture, before we turn to specific aspects of international law.

As early as 1982, Congress as a whole seemed to be opposed to any U.S. policy that sought the overthrow of the Sandinista government. In that year both the Democrat-controlled House and the Republican-controlled Senate approved the so-called first Boland amendment (named after the Massachusetts Democrat who chaired the House Intelligence Committee) prohibiting CIA and DOD assistance to any group trying to overthrow Nicaragua's government or promote a military exchange between Nicaragua and Honduras.[37] (This was not a tightly worded piece of legislation, and the president could simply say, as he did, that his intention was not overthrow. A more tightly worded bill prohibiting U.S. money for military or paramilitary activity in Nicaragua had been derailed by Senate Republicans.) The first Boland amendment was a clear if general congressional signal to the Executive that a policy that looked like overthrow would not find easy support. It was U.S. law (although soft law—viz., not likely to be adjudicated), based on international legal principles.

By 1984, even congressional Republicans were having major doubts about the wisdom of the Executive's continuation of military moves against Nicaragua, and in that year Congress passed legislation effectively terminating all assistance to the contras that was funneled through the CIA and DOD. This cutoff came after revelations about CIA direct involvement in the mining of harbors, attacks on fuel tanks, and provision of a manual for the contras appearing to advocate political assassination. (This was the second Boland amendment, which triggered the secret NSC program involving public and private "contributions" to the contras as coordinated by Oliver North.)

It seemed somewhat bizarre that Congress would not terminate official aid to the contras, who were violating international law by trying to overthrow the Sandinistas, until the CIA violated international law through a small set of distinct actions. But even leading Republican hawks like Senator Barry Goldwater said publicly that mining harbors was an act of war under international law and that the CIA had gone too far.[38] Part of the controversy, however, was the charge by many members of Congress that the Executive had not kept the Congress properly informed. There was widespread congressional antagonism to the substance and style of William Casey, director of the CIA.[39]

But one year later, in 1985, the Executive convinced Congress to appropriate $27 million for nonlethal aid to the contras. This occurred after Daniel Ortega had made a much-publicized trip to Moscow in search of further Soviet support, and in the context of a White House program of charging Democratic critics with being soft on, if not supporters of, communism.[40] Thus, Congress openly appropriated money for a "private" army that was obviously trying to overthrow a legally recognized government with which the United States had diplomatic relations. (In 1981–1983, U.S. money to the contras had been drawn from the CIA's unrestricted budget and was not specifically approved by Congress. Money and equipment was also funneled through U.S. programs in Honduras, without being officially designated for the contras.)

And in 1986, before the Iran-contra scandal broke but after the World Court's substantive ruling against U.S. policy, the Senate completed congressional action by voting $70 million lethal and $30 million nonlethal aid to the contras. The reasons for this congressional shift remain elusive, but Nicaragua had sent military forces into Honduras after the contras, and the administration characterized this action as blatant aggression.

(Honduras, under U.S. pressure, had allowed its territory to be used for contra attacks against Nicaragua since the winter of 1981–1982. During the Vietnam War, the United States had claimed the right to fight in Cambodia to eliminate communist bases. In the Middle East, Israel, with U.S. support, had claimed the right to fight in Jordan and Lebanon to eliminate Palestinian bases. It is reasonably clear that, under customary international law, Nicaragua was within its legal rights to try to eliminate contra bases in Honduras because the latter government was not exercising due diligence in policing its territory.[41])

Ironically, just as the Reagan team finally got Congress to okay open lethal assistance for the contras, the Iran-contra scandal caused another congressional shift, and in 1987 and 1988 Congress again terminated lethal assistance and permitted only nonlethal assistance for the purpose of food, clothing, housing, and medical care for remaining contras in Honduras.

Needless to say, the overall record of Congress on the Nicaraguan question was not one characterized by consistency. House Democrats

voted repeatedly to terminate U.S. support for the contras, except in
1986. But conservatives in the Senate, mostly Republican but including
important Democrats like Lloyd Bentsen (TX), Sam Nunn (GA), and
James Exon (NE), usually blocked a cutoff and forced compromises.
During 1982–1986, neither concern for international law nor any other
concern led to coherent, consistent policy-making by Congress as a
whole. It was only after Iran-contra, and also after the Democrats recap-
tured control of the Senate in 1987, that Congress took a firm line against
contra military actions. International legal questions repeatedly surfaced
in congressional deliberations, and it is to that specific subject that we
now turn.

*   *   *

The administration's basic international legal argument—that Nicaragua had intervened in El Salvador, that the United States was responding defensively, that military force was necessary, and that it was proportional—was repeatedly challenged by members of Congress during the
Reagan years.

Even before the World Court ruled that Nicaragua's involvement in
El Salvador did not amount to an armed attack or other aggressive action permitting the United States to respond with military force, the Executive was having difficulty persuading doubters that the Sandinistas
were substantially involved in subversion after 1981. Logically, if you
could not prove substantial subversion, the rest of the legal argument
collapsed. The skepticism and the lack of adequate response were well
captured in this exchange, which occurred between Senator John F. Kerry
(D, MA) and Secretary Shultz after five years of executive arguments:

> Senator Kerry: . . . I have had some of the private briefings which
> were supposed to give us a better sense of these things, and, candidly,
> they have not done that. I am still asking questions of the CIA about the
> reality of evidence of arms shipments into El Salvador. The evidence has
> been almost nonexistent, if not of an absolutely negligible nature.
>
> Secretary Shultz: Well, there was a car last December [that con-
> tained arms].[42]

One car (actually it was a truck) packed with weapons of dubious
origin does not establish intervention by the government of Nicaragua.
But even if one were to accept that the Sandinistas had intervened in El
Salvador (the legal question is, when does involvement constitute impermissible dictatorial intervention), a legal U.S. policy would still have to
meet the tests of necessity and proportionality. As for necessity, there
were a number of members of Congress who did not believe that the administration had tried serious negotiations with Managua or had negoti-

ated in good faith in pursuit of a peaceful resolution of this dispute.[43] Representative Gerry Studds, for example, wanted to know why the Executive had not taken the dispute to the OAS or U.N.[44] As for proportionality, another Kerry-Shultz exchange is illustrative:

> Senator Kerry: Mr. Secretary . . . it has always been my impression that what we have tried to do as a country is establish a framework within which our actions are legitimized . . . under the rule of law.
>
> It seems to me that this administration has championed a theory known as the doctrine of proportional response by which, when somebody does something, our government would respond accordingly.
>
> It appears to me that we violate both of those doctrines in our current approach, because of the way in which the Contras came into being, because of their current operation, and because of their tactics. . . .
>
> Secretary Shultz: The rule of law you are referring to certainly permits self-defense. . . .
>
> Proportionality? My gosh, we are helping people who want to fight for the freedom and independence of their country.[45]

One does not establish proportionality by reference to the cause for which one is supposedly fighting. But if one cannot prove Nicaraguan intervention abroad, then obviously the creation and direction of a fighting force of 10,000 to 20,000 contras will be disproportionate, so politically it is just as well to speak of freedom against tyranny. An old adage comes to mind: If the facts are on your side, you pound on the facts, and if the law is on your side, you pound on the law, and if neither is on your side, you pound on the table.

After the Executive had withdrawn from the Nicaraguan case at the World Court—but even before the court had struck down the administration's substantive legal claims—members of Congress had tried to persuade the administration to reevaluate its core legal argument about the Sandinistas. Speeches were made on the floor of both houses, and "Op-Ed" pieces were written in influential newspapers. The House, perennially under the control of the Democrats, held hearings on withdrawal in order to either educate or embarrass the administration. More speeches were made after the 1986 World Court judgment on the merits of the case, but all to no avail. The administration stuck to its position, however unpersuasive it might be both to the ICJ and to congressional critics.[46]

Related to core legal debates was the question of whether the Executive's real policy was overthrow of the Sandinistas. On this subject, international law was intertwined with domestic law, because the first Boland amendment had prohibited funding for the purpose of overthrow. For this and other reasons, this debate often was carried on without explicit reference to international law. Yet, concern for international law was pervasive—and sometimes even explicit. Said Representative Jim Leach (R, IA) in 1983:

Here there is a natural dilemma since, unlike domestic cases where we have courts to resolve disputes when there is disagreement between Congress and the Executive, in international policy we don't have that capacity. Therefore, I think Congress has a particular obligation to insure that the law is followed. . . .

The great challenge of our times, in a larger sense, is how we, by our actions, move to either expand or contract the rule of law in the world. . . .

. . . if we accept the view that aiding those who are attempting to overthrow the Government of Nicaragua is not attempting ourselves to overthrow that Government, we become rebels without a cause . . . . The key distinction between the United States and our allies, and those we oppose in the world is that we respect international law. . . .

Somehow we have to exercise on a unilateral basis, every degree of authority we can to demand that the administration itself conform to the rule of law. . . .

I . . . would argue quite seriously that whether we are doing the right thing or not in a practical way, from a legal perspective, we are lawbreakers.[47]

A sizable number of House Democrats were prepared to identify with these views,[48] and evasion by State Department officials did not pacify the critics. An early 1982 exchange is illustrative:

Representative Studds: Can you provide this committee and this Congress with an assurance that the United States is not and will not participate in, or encourage in any way, directly or indirectly, any effort to overthrow or to destabilize by violence the Government of Nicaragua?

Mr. [Stephen W.] Bosworth: Well, Mr. Studds, as you are aware, I believe we have been asked that question previously and I can only reiterate as a matter of longstanding policy, the U.S. Government does not address such allegations.[49]

Similar exchanges are to be found in Senate hearings, where there was comparable attention to international law and comparable concern about the United States being engaged in the overthrow of a foreign government.[50]

Related to the issue of overthrow was the issue of forceful pressure to bring about domestic reform, which can amount to the same thing. If military pressure by the contras was used to force concessions leading eventually to a new government, the government has been changed indirectly by force.

Repeatedly, congressional critics tried to clarify the role of the contras (whether the military pressure was for moderating foreign policy or compelling internal change) and under what law the administration had the right to force domestic change. Said Stephen Solarz (D, NY) in the House:

I think every member of this committee deplores the betrayal of the Nicaraguan revolution by the Sandinista leadership in that country.

I think every member of this committee would like to see genuine political pluralism . . . established in Nicaragua.

I think all of us have a good deal of admiration for the bravery and courage of those Nicaraguans who are attempting to bring about a fundamental change in the political situation in their country.

I think most of us wish them well. But many of us think it is wrong for the United States, both in terms of the principles for which we stand as well as the purposes for which we attempt to serve, to assist these people in the form of a covert operation. . . .

I doubt that there are many members of this committee who would advocate our providing paramilitary assistance to groups attempting to use violent means to overthrow established governments elsewhere in the world.

I can't imagine that my friends on the other side of the aisle would favor a covert program in Chile [under Pinochet] or Argentina [under the junta].[51]

Senator Alan Cranston (D, CA) raised a similar point in the Senate: "The American people quite rightly reject the idea that U.S. military force should be employed indiscriminately to make foreign governments in our own image." He then quoted the late American journalist Walter Lippmann: "A policy is bound to fail which deliberately violates our pledges and our principles, our treaties and our laws. In the great struggle with communism, we must find our strength by developing and applying our principles, not in abandoning them."[52]

At least some of the opposition in Congress could identify with a statement by Lee Hamilton (D, IN) who opposed military force either for overthrow or pressure:

I would make two primary arguments against covert action in Nicaragua. One is really a legal argument. And I think the gist of it is that the covert action violates the Charter of the Organization of American States. . . .

The point simply is that, when the United States is conducting a covert action in Nicaragua, we are in clear violation of the Organization of American States Treaty. I don't think a policy is going to prevail over a long period of time which violates principles like nonintervention, and violates our treaty commitments, like those to the Organization of American States. . . .

Second, I think apart from the legal argument is a very pragmatic argument . . . [that] for very little gain from the conduct of covert action, the United States is incurring a great many negatives.[53]

Other issues of international law were also treated in congressional debates, such as the role of Honduras and the tactics employed by both the contras and the CIA,[54] but space limitation precludes their discussion here.

In the final analysis, despite widespread congressional concern about executive violations of international law (and of U.S. law based frequently on international legal principles), the Reagan administration was able to continue contra military actions in Nicaragua from 1982 to about 1987 because there was enough congressional support for the administration, mainly in the Senate, to block the critics. This support took three basic forms.

One version argued essentially that in dealing with communists the United States could not afford the luxury of worrying about such niceties as international law. Senator Jesse Helms (R, NC) said in 1983 that the issue was "whether we are going to fail to do whatever we can to prevent a Marxist takeover of Central America."[55] According to Representative Gerald Solomon (R, NY): "This committee is about to sell the United States of America down the drain by aiding and abetting the spread of communism in this hemisphere and I won't stand for it."[56]

A slightly more discerning version argued that Secretary of State Shultz was right: one had to be a realist and accept that military pressure against the Sandinistas was necessary to bring about domestic change; that was the real issue. According to Senator Richard Lugar (R, IN), chair of the Foreign Relations Committee 1981–1986: "At this point, it is not enough for someone to say that he supports democracy in Nicaragua. Realism impels us to appreciate that it will take pressure, both from the Nicaraguan people and from abroad, to make the Sandinistas recall their past commitments to fellow Nicaraguans."[57]

A third view, rather than ignoring international legal considerations, accepted the administration's core legal argument that the doctrine of collective self-defense allowed support for the contras. An articulate spokesman for this view was Representative Henry Hyde (R, IL), although on occasion he seemed to fit into the first school of thought, arguing against attention to legal niceties when dealing with communists.[58]

V   FOREIGN RESPONSES

At the outset of Reagan's policy toward the Sandinistas, there was considerable foreign criticism of decisions taken in Washington. It was to be expected that the Soviet Union and its allies, as well as the Non-Aligned Movement of lesser-developed countries, would side with Nicaragua. There is no indication that criticism from such sources had any impact in Washington.

It was symptomatic of the controversy surrounding Reagan's various pressures on Managua, however, that many of Washington's friends and allies distanced themselves from the United States on this issue. France, for example, provided early military assistance to the Sandinistas and offered to clear naval mines from Nicaraguan waters. Spain, which saw itself as having a special role in the Western Hemisphere, repeatedly found fault with Washington. The Netherlands and Denmark were also clear in their criticism. Other allies, like Australia and Norway, were directly or indirectly critical of the military pressures supported by Washington.[59]

Criticism of U.S. policies from the other industrialized democracies apparently had some effect on at least a few members of Congress, because they referred to such criticism in their public comments. But friendly foreign criticism had very little evident impact on most members of the administration, except perhaps to galvanize some to make a better show of seeking a diplomatic settlement. As with other issues of this era, such as the invasion of Grenada or the attempt to block the West European deal with the U.S.S.R. to build a natural gas pipeline, the Reagan team was prepared to proceed unilaterally regardless of divisions within the Western alliance. (It seemed to be true that the other democracies regarded Central America as the U.S. backyard; while they were critical of Reagan's policies, they did not seem to press the issue, having other fish to fry.)

Various states were to criticize the Reagan team for blocking multilateral economic aid to Managua, and thus for introducing "political" issues into "economic" institutions. The General Agreement on Tariffs and Trade (GATT) ruled that U.S. manipulation of Nicaragua's sugar quota violated GATT rules. But the administration persisted in its economic warfare against the Sandinistas, even to the point of holding hostage all the operations of the Inter-American Development Bank in order to block loans to Nicaragua. This was all the more remarkable because socialist regimes in places like Yugoslavia and Tanzania had received World Bank loans without blockage by the United States.[60]

From the international legal standpoint, the most important foreign reaction to Reagan policy toward Nicaragua was the position taken by the International Court of Justice. As already observed briefly, in 1984 Nicaragua challenged U.S. legal arguments by going to the World Court. The Nicaraguan legal team relied heavily on Abram Chayes, the Harvard law professor who had been State Department legal adviser during the Kennedy administration, as well as on British and French legal counsel of world-class reputation. They had the cooperation, in addition, of David MacMichael, a former CIA official who had had access to classified information during the early 1980s. Thus, Nicaragua put together a petition of considerable legal sophistication and based on facts difficult to refute. This highly complex case can be summarized for present purposes along the following lines:

First, Nicaragua argued that, procedurally, the United States was obligated to respond to its petition in the World Court because (1) by accepting in 1946 the "Optional Clause" of Article 36(1) of the Statute of the Court, the United States had agreed to give the court jurisdiction over legal disputes, in general, provided the petitioning state had done likewise, and (2) the U.S.-Nicaraguan Treaty of Commerce, Friendship, and Navigation provided for automatic referral to the court of disputes arising under that treaty (in Managua's view, the treaty covered the mining of waters, which interrupted commerce).[61] The Reagan team, after unsuccessfully trying to block ICJ action on other grounds, argued that the court should not assume jurisdiction over this dispute because (1) Nicaragua had never given its general consent to the court to handle legal disputes, thus releasing the United States from any obligation to respond, and (2) the bilateral treaty in question was not intended to cover such subjects as the laying of mines in harbors.[62] Whether or not executive officials realized they had a weak legal case in substance, it was clear that the administration did not want the court to resolve this dispute. The ICJ, however, by overwhelming vote among its 16 judges, did assume jurisdiction in late 1984 and proceeded to examine substantive arguments about violations of international law. (A party to an ICJ case that does not find one of its nationals as a judge on the court may appoint an additional judge of its choice; Nicaragua thus appointed a judge of French nationality, making for a total of 16 rather than 15 judges.)

In early 1985, the administration withdrew from the case and refused to argue the substantive points. It said that Nicaragua was using the ICJ for political purposes and that the court had erred in assuming jurisdiction. It also argued that it could not divulge intelligence findings about Nicaraguan involvement in El Salvador without giving away its intelligence procedures and capabilities. The U.S. statement pointed out that two judges from Warsaw Pact countries sat on the court.[63]

Such action did not block court proceedings. The Republic of Iran had withdrawn from a case brought by the United States concerning the seizure of diplomats and consular officials in Tehran, and the ICJ (essentially made up of the same judges as in 1984–1986) nevertheless ruled in favor of the United States. In a similar fashion in this case, the court proceeded to the substantive phase despite the absence of U.S. officials. (At the time it began to consider jurisdiction, the court issued an interim judgment requiring the parties to cease action aggravating the case, making special reference to the mining of harbors. The Executive responded that there was nothing in the interim judgment it objected to, since the mining of harbors had already ceased.)[64]

To no one's surprise, the court ruled in 1986 in favor of Nicaragua. Usually by a vote of about 12–3 (with one judge abstaining), the ICJ held that: Nicaraguan involvement in El Salvador did not constitute an armed attack, and therefore the United States did not have the right to support the use of military force against Nicaragua; the laying of mines in Nicaraguan waters without public notice was illegal; military force linked to the United States constituted impermissible intervention into Nicaraguan affairs and a violation of Nicaraguan sovereignty; the contras had violated the laws of war on numerous occasions through such actions as attacks on civilians; the United States should cease and desist from supporting the contra organization, which the court held was effectively an agency of the U.S. government; and the United States owed monetary damages to Nicaragua, which would be set later.[65]

The Executive formally disregarded this judgment, which was binding in international law, making a series of arguments that attacked the integrity of the court. There were a number of legal scholars and others in the United States who supported at least some of the Executive's criticisms, but an equal or greater number of observers were greatly concerned by these U.S. attacks. These were carefully refuted by, inter alia, the editor of the establishment-oriented *American Journal of International Law*.[66]

In its arguments, the administration claimed that this was a political not a legal dispute; but aggression and self-defense are topics found in every source book on international law, and it is always up to a court to say what is and is not a political question. The Executive claimed that a court could not evaluate the facts of an ongoing armed conflict; but it could easily be shown how much relevant information was already in the public sector, much of it admitted by Reagan officials themselves in public. The Executive claimed that Nicaragua had used the court for political reasons; but the Carter administration had gone to the ICJ against Iran in 1979 to help isolate that revolutionary regime diplomatically and put added pressure on it to release U.S. diplomatic and consular officials. Generating political pressure through judicial action is a normal feature of both domestic and international politics.[67]

Administration officials even went so far as to say that when a state made a legal claim about self-defense, no other actor but that state was entitled to evaluate the claim. This was not a serious argument, for it would mean that when the Soviet Union invaded Afghanistan in 1979 and claimed collective self-defense because invited there by the government, the United States would have no right to evaluate that bogus claim.[68] Neither the United States itself, nor other states, had ever acted in accordance with this argument.

The administration insisted that it still was interested in international law, and it tried to show support for the ICJ by jointly submitting to it two other cases involving boundary and commercial disputes. The Executive had already (in October 1985) revoked general U.S. permission to the ICJ to treat legal disputes, but this did not affect the approximately 60 treaties that contained provision for automatic reference to the ICJ for legal disputes arising under those treaties.[69]

The most fundamental international legal problem for the administration was that it had been trying to implement the Reagan Doctrine of rolling back what it saw as communist governments. In the case of Nicaragua, this policy of dictatorial intervention by force was simply incompatible with international law as traditionally understood. But since the Reagan team, taking its lead from the president himself, manifested an ideological fixation about the Sandinistas,[70] Washington continued trying to implement its military and other pressures on Nicaragua despite the authoritative ruling by the World Court.

There were parallel events within the United Nations proper. (Technically, the ICJ is part of the extended U.N. system, but once elected its judges act independently of the rest of the United Nations.) Although the United States had not sought a role for the U.N. in the dispute with Nicaragua, Managua had gone to the Security Council in March 1983, charging the United States with aggression. Nicaragua repeatedly returned to the Security Council, and there were comparable debates in the General Assembly as well, as the Sandinistas tried to spotlight U.S. policies and marshal international opinion against them. In the debates in both organs, most opinion was against the U.S. policy of military and economic coercion of Nicaragua. The United States did, though, garner some support from formal and informal allies such as West Germany, El Salvador, and Honduras.

In April of 1984, 13 Security Council members voted for a resolution calling for a halt to military attacks on Nicaragua; the United States vetoed the resolution, while the United Kingdom abstained. In May of 1985, the United States vetoed wording in a council resolution opposed to the U.S. trade embargo and mining of harbors. And in July of 1986, the United States vetoed a council resolution calling on it to comply with the substantive judgment of the World Court; France and the U.K. abstained, along with Thailand, whose representative claimed he had received no instructions from his capital about how to vote.[71] Thus, although the great bulk of state opinion was clearly opposed to Reagan policy, it was also clear that the Reagan government would not allow the Security Council to pass authoritative judgment on U.S. policy toward Nicaragua. This made ring hollow the administration's argument that the Security Council, and not the ICJ, was the proper body to hear the Nicaraguan–U.S. dispute.

As for the Organization of American States, both the Reagan administration and most of the other member states preferred to bypass that regional body. Many hemispheric states had long feared the OAS as a front for the dominant power of the United States. And in this case, as in the invasion of Grenada, the Reagan team found it inconvenient to have recourse to an organization whose charter proclaimed repeatedly the principle of nonintervention and whose members for the most part emphasized that principle, especially when U.S. foreign policy was at issue.

There were sporadic and inconclusive debates in the OAS General Assembly concerning the Nicaraguan–U.S. dispute, but the more authoritative Organ of Consultation (similar to the U.N. Security Council) never met at all on the subject. In general, the OAS was not a significant factor, although its secretary-general played a minor role, sometimes in conjunction with the U.N. secretary-general. The Reagan team was only too happy to have the OAS mostly on the sidelines, and the hemispheric states that tried to mediate the dispute in various ways were content to operate outside the organization either in ones or twos (Mexico and Venezuela tried their hand early) or through the Contadora process (involving four principal and four support states) and the Arias process (led by the Costa Rican president and involving all of the Central American states).[72]

It was clear, nevertheless, that most hemispheric states, beyond the immediate U.S. allies in the region, took a critical view of U.S. military and economic coercion against Managua. Even those like President Arias of Costa Rica, who were clearly not enamored with the Sandinistas, felt that U.S. coercion was counterproductive to moderating Nicaraguan policy. Likewise, Mexico, Colombia, Venezuela, Alfonsin's Argentina, Cerezo's Guatemala, and others made public statements indicating dissatisfaction with the thrust of U.S. policy.[73]

This left the United States with the active support of El Salvador and Honduras (and that of the Argentine junta, before it changed its policy because of U.S. support for Britain in the Falkland-Malvinas war in 1982). Administration officials, in a process that had become rather routine in Washington, claimed that while Latin leaders felt compelled to express criticism of the United States in public, those leaders were more supportive in private. But congressional critics also claimed extensive private support. And when Daniel Ortega paid a state visit to Brazil in 1985, he was given a standing ovation in the Brazilian Congress.[74]

Consistently from the early 1980s, other foreign responses to U.S. policy toward Nicaragua were mostly negative, though there was some waxing and waning of this opinion within the overall critical thrust. For example, the Socialist International, the non-Marxist grouping of democratic socialist political parties around the world, was strongly supportive of the Sandinistas immediately after the 1979 revolution, but gradually became more critical as they observed the core Sandinistas and their policies into the 1980s.[75] France, too, became less supportive of Managua, but never fully identified with the United States. On the other hand, a group of states including Israel and most of the ultraconservative

Arab states like Saudi Arabia cooperated directly with U.S. policy. Most important for legal analysis, an overwhelming majority of ICJ judges and also members of the U.N. Security Council found U.S. coercive policies violative of international law.

VI OUTCOME FOR THE UNITED STATES

The outcome of Reagan policies toward the Sandinistas was mostly negative for the United States. As a result of the battle between Congress and the Executive, old wounds were reopened pertaining to an "imperial presidency," rogue elements within the Executive (the CIA and NSC staff), an inordinate fear of monolithic communism, pervasive lying by high executive officials, and a disregard for law whether international or domestic. The last point is perhaps the most important in the long run, and Robert Pastor has put the argument succinctly: "The Administration became so obsessed with Nicaragua that it violated the nation's core precept—respect for the rule of law internationally and at home."[76]

The Reagan presidency ended not just with Nicaraguan policy in shambles, but with fears within the administration about impeachment of the president for violating U.S. law (in particular, the second Boland amendment prohibiting official U.S. assistance to the contras via the CIA and DOD). The possibility of another national trauma—such as the one that engulfed Richard Nixon in 1974 over the Watergate Affair of illegally breaking and entering and then obstructing justice via a coverup—was in the air in 1987–1988. Violating U.S. law derived from international legal principles was not, certainly in the Nicaragua case, healthy for the nation.

The Reagan team, far from achieving a foreign policy supported by bipartisan consensus in Washington, followed its ideological convictions to the brink of national disaster. The inability of the administration to convincingly justify its policies under international law, although it made international legal arguments, contributed to the debacle. The real policy of removing the Sandinistas could not be rationalized easily in public, which drove the administration not only to "covert" action, but also eventually to the NSC "off-the-shelf" operation under Colonel North, which—when linked to arms sales to Iran and the buying of American hostages—discredited both Reagan as leader and his administration.

It should also be noted that Nicaragua was far more militarized when Reagan left office then when he entered, with more extensive ties to the Soviet Union. It is not perfectly clear that administration policy caused this military buildup and diplomatic orientation, and of course Reagan argued otherwise. But one could not reasonably expect Managua to reduce military expenditures and forgo foreign military and other support when it was being militarily attacked under U.S. guidance.

There are, of course, those who argue that the main domestic lessons to be drawn from this affair have to do with the inability of Congress and the public to appreciate the danger from communist subversion and the problems stemming from an assertive but divided Congress.[77] Just as there were three judges on the World Court—including the one from the United States, a former State Department legal adviser—who found administration arguments of fact and law persuasive across the board.[78]

VII   OUTCOME FOR WORLD ORDER

The outcome of the Reagan policy of "covert" intervention in Nicaragua was mostly negative for world order. Perhaps the most damaging aspect stemmed from the administration's attacks on the ICJ, coupled with its walkout and renunciation of the Optional Clause of the court's Statute. It is one thing to criticize a court's judgment and reasoning; it is another to claim that a court is biased and acting improperly.

The ICJ's 1986 judgment on the merits of Nicaragua's case against the United States is not beyond reasoned critique.[79] But to go beyond that, as the Reagan team did, and attack the integrity of the court, and then try to weaken it by reducing its scope of action, is to undercut one of the few operative mechanisms for peaceful resolution of conflicts in the world. Ironically, in the first year of the Reagan era a House subcommittee held hearings in an effort to generate more recourse to the ICJ (following similar Senate efforts), and the State Department went on record as favoring more use of the court, given its positive record in responding to U.S. legal concerns.[80]

It is true that the court remains on the sidelines in most of the legal disputes that arise among nations (there is an international legal dimension to every international political conflict), handling on average only about two cases per year. But, as with the U.N. Security Council, situations repeatedly arise in which the agency makes a positive contribution to the resolution of dangerous conflicts.

As Roger Fisher has pointed out, the United States, like a poker player, should not want to win all the games, because if it did, other players would quit; rather, it has an interest in keeping the peaceful game going so that it can try to win most of the time. This was the point President Dwight Eisenhower was making when he said, "It is better to lose a point now and then in an international tribunal and gain a world in which everyone lives at peace under the rule of law."[81]

The Nicaraguan affair showed that the Reagan team insisted on winning all the games, despite the minor threat posed by the Sandinistas to U.S. security. (And the 1986 judgment did not even require the United States to stop all diplomatic and economic pressure against Managua.)

By disregarding the 1986 judgment, the United States placed itself in a category with revolutionary Iran and communist Albania in ignoring final ICJ judgments on the merits.

The Reagan damage to the U.N. Security Council was slightly less, since its exercise of the veto was not coupled with charges of political bias and erroneous judgment by the council itself. But Reagan policy in the Security Council, as in the court and for that matter in Congress, showed an executive disregard for the reasoned opinions of others and an ideological determination to pursue a highly problematical (and illegal) course despite considerable cost to its reputation for wise leadership.

Relatedly, many Western Hemisphere states had their fears rekindled about U.S. interventionism in pursuit of regional domination. One of the negative side effects of the Reagan team's fixation with the Sandinistas was the buildup of Honduran military forces at a time when civilian democrats in Honduras were trying to bring the military under control. And similarly, many states within NATO worried anew about an overly belligerent alliance leader prone to see major communist threats disproportionate to reality, and prone to seek military solutions to the detriment of forward-looking diplomacy.

There was minor friction with the Soviet Union. Soviet ships were damaged at times by mines, and Soviet policies were repeatedly criticized by Washington, particularly in the early 1980s. What kept superpower conflict over Nicaragua minimal was the low level of Soviet commitment to Managua (e.g., no attack aircraft such as MIGs, and no attack missiles as in Cuba in 1962) and an improvement in other aspects of East-West relations after the rise of Mikhail Gorbachev in 1985.

In the Nicaraguan case, one sees at work on the part of the Reagan team and its supporters an extreme form of crusading moralism and hubris that is difficult for law to control. Fawn Hall, the secretary to Colonel North, when asked in a congressional hearing why she had knowingly violated U.S. law, said that sometimes one had to act beyond the law because of a higher moral cause.[82] This was the same argument made explicitly in broader form by Michael Ledeen, one of Reagan's intellectual supporters. Ledeen compared the Sandinistas to Hitler, arguing that when faced with such a threat one had to violate law, and that it was moral to do so.[83] This was, in fact, the same argument that ran through the speeches of Ronald Reagan.[84]

From the time of the 1776 Revolution, Americans have liked to draw on the Jeffersonian argument of a right to democratic revolt against tyranny. Such an argument may be morally persuasive when the democrats and the autocrats are clearly divided. In the Nicaraguan case, however, the CIA connections of the contra leaders and their civilian allies, their behavior during Somoza's rule, and their atrocities in the field all raised questions about their status as democratic freedom fighters.

On the other side of the coin, while the Sandinistas were assuredly not Jeffersonian democrats, they were equally assuredly not Hitlerian monsters. And, there was the historical fact of U.S. support for repressive regimes in the past, as in Guatemala from 1954, where the United States helped overthrow a progressive and nationalist regime in order to support a series of murderous military governments.

It was to these complexities that Senator Pell was referring indirectly when the following exhange occured about the simplistic view that lay at the heart of Reagan's attacks on Nicaragua:

> Senator Pell: What would be the difference between the situation here [Nicaragua] and the situation in Guatemala 30 years ago, when we supported the overthrow of the Arbenz government and opened up the door to a long regime of misery for the Guatemalans?
>
> Secretary Shultz: I am not familiar with that piece of history, Senator, so I cannot really make a comparison.[85]

Moral self-righteousness, based on historical ignorance, is not easily controlled by law. It is a major problem for international law, and one that reappeared in the case of the U.S. invasion of Grenada.

NOTES

The epigraphs that open Chapter 3 are quoted from Ronald Reagan, address to Congress, 1983 (*Congressional Quarterly Almanac*, 1984, E-29); from Patrick J. Leahy (D, VT), 1983 (*Congressional Quarterly Almanac*, 1984, 132); from Jesse Helms (R, NC), 1983 (Senate Hearing, April 12, 29); and from Gerry Studds (D, MA), 1987, (House Hearing, May 19, 21).

1. The literature on the United States and Nicaragua and on the United States and Central America is voluminous. Among recent publications, see especially Robert A. Pastor, *Condemned to Repetition: The United States and Nicaragua*, Princeton: Princeton University Press, 1987. Pastor was on the staff of the National Security Council during the Carter administration. For a radically different view, see Constantine C. Menges, *Inside the National Security Council*, New York: Simon and Schuster, 1988. Menges was on the NSC staff during the Reagan administration. Both Pastor and Menges dealt with hemispheric issues.

2. *Newsweek*, November 8, 1982, 44. Pastor does not mention the subject.

3. A former CIA agent, testifying for Nicaragua at the World Court in the mid-1980s, admitted under questioning that the Sandinistas had supported the "final offensive" in El Salvador in a rather significant way. See also Pastor, note 1, among others with credibility and/or access to classified information.

4. See the summary of the 40th session of the International Law Commission as reported in *American Journal of International Law*, 83, 1 (January 1989), 153–160.

5. W. Michael Reisman, et al., *International Incidents: The Law That Counts in World Politics,* Princeton: Princeton University Press, 1988, chp. 7.

6. Rio Treaty, Articles 6, 17, 20.

7. See the scholarly presentation in Barry R. Posen and Stephen W. Van Evera, "Reagan Administration Defense Policy: Departure from Containment," in Kenneth A. Oye, et al., *Eagle Resurgent? The Reagan Era in American Foreign Policy,* Boston: Little, Brown, 1987, 75–114.

8. A concise and accurate review of early decisions is found in Thomas W. Walker, "Nicaraguan-U.S. Friction: The First Four Years, 1979–83," in Kenneth M. Coleman and George C. Herring, eds., *The Central American Crisis: Sources of Conflict and the Failure of U.S. Policy,* Wilmington: Scholarly Resources, Inc., 1985, 157–192.

9. During the period April 3–5, 1983, exposés were published by the *New York Times, Washington Post,* and *Time.*

10. See especially Peter Kornbluh, "The Covert War," in Thomas W. Walker, ed., *Reagan Versus the Sandinistas: The Undeclared War on Nicaragua,* Boulder, CO: Westview, 1987, 21–38.

11. The 1983 speech is reproduced in *Congressional Quarterly Almanac,* Washington: Congressional Quarterly Press, 1984, annex E.

12. *New York Times,* December 9, 1982, 1.

13. *New York Times,* February 22, 1985, 1.

14. Walker, "Introduction," in Walker, ed., note 10, at 12 with supporting documentation.

15. Hedrick Smith, *The Power Game: How Washington Works,* New York: Ballantine Books, 1989, 47.

16. *Congressional Quarterly Almanac 1983,* Washington: Congressional Quarterly Press, 1984, 123–124.

17. Kornbluh, note 10.

18. Michael E. Conroy, "Economic Aggression as an Instrument of Low-Intensity Warfare," in Walker, note 10, at 57–79.

19. *New York Times,* September 17, 1985, 8.

20. William Goodfellow, "The Diplomatic Front," in Walker, note 10, at 144. Pastor, note 1, at 233.

21. The State Department "White Paper" entitled *Revolution Beyond Our Borders: Sandinista Intervention in Central America* of September 1985 was as general and unpersuasive to many as earlier publications had been. Even its title, taken from a speech by a Sandinista leader supposedly showing a commitment to subversion, turned out to be a distortion.

22. Walker, note 10.

23. William I. Robinson and Kent Norsworthy, *David and Goliath: The U.S. War Against Nicaragua,* New York: Monthly Review Press, 1987, 156–163. At the World Court, Nicaragua never claimed direct combat by U.S. military personnel. There appears to be consensus that Cuban military personnel participated in combat on the Nicaraguan side.

24. Goodfellow in Walker, note 10.

25. Ibid. Menges, note 1, confirms administration efforts to block "unwise" diplomatic efforts that would leave "communists" in power in Managua.

26. In addition to Goodfellow, note 10, and Menges, note 1, see *New York Times,* August 15, 1987, 1, 5.

27. "Iran-Contra Affair," *Report*, House and Senate Select Committees, 100th Congress, 1st session, November 1987, Washington: GPO, 1987.

28. Testimony of Stephen W. Bosworth, Deputy Assistant Secretary of State for Inter-American Affairs, in "Honduras and U.S. Policy," *Hearing*, House Subcommittee on Inter-American Affairs, 97th Congress, 2d session, Washington: GPO, 1982, 18.

29. According to Enders, U.S. policy sought an end to subversion, a reduction in military levels, and democracy. See "U.S. Policy Toward Nicaragua and Central America," *Hearing*, Senate Committee on Foreign Relations, 98th Congress, 1st session, Washington: GPO, 1983, 5. According to Kirkpatrick at the U.N., the United States was as much concerned with democracy within Nicaragua as with its export of revolution. See *U.N. Chronicle*, 20, 5 (May 1983), 13. Shultz and Abrams were on record many times, including "U.S. Policy Toward Nicaragua," *Hearing*, Senate Committee on Foreign Relations, 99th Congress, 2d session, Washington: GPO, 1986, 10–51.

30. The Inter-American Convention on Human Rights, the European Convention on Human Rights, and the United Nations Covenant on Civil and Political Rights permit derogation from many state obligations during public emergencies threatening the life of the nation. Certain rights such as freedom from summary execution, torture, and mistreatment remain inviolable at all times. Similar legal principles are found in the Geneva Conventions of 1949 and their Additional Protocols of 1977 regulating human rights in international and internal armed conflict. See further David P. Forsythe, *Human Rights and World Politics*, Lincoln: University of Nebraska Press, 2d ed., 1989.

31. *New York Times*, September 17, 1985, 8.

32. Walker, in Coleman and Herring, note 8, at 183–184.

33. Richard A. Falk, *The Role of Domestic Courts in the International Legal Order*, Syracuse: Syracuse University Press, 1964.

34. *New York Times*, August 14, 1985, 12.

35. *Chaser Shipping Co. v. United States* (1986) as reported in *American Journal of International Law*, 81, 2 (April 1987), 419–422. Note that the Reagan administration openly violated the U.S. neutrality laws by allowing and participating in the training of contras in U.S. territory prior to their attacking Nicaragua. No court cases definitively blocked this administration policy.

36. *The Gallup Poll: Public Opinion*, Wilmington: Scholarly Resources, Inc., annual.

37. For overviews, see *Congressional Quarterly Almanac*, annual; and William M. Leograande, "The Contras and Congress," in Walker, note 10, at 202–227.

38. Reported in both *Congressional Quarterly Almanac* and *New York Times*. Other prominent Republican senators also had strong criticism for the administration, such as Charles Percy (IL), then chair of the Senate Foreign Relations Committee, and David Durenberger (MN), member of the Senate Intelligence Committee who had seen the administration's secret testimony and evidence and who called U.S. policy "an illegal absurdity." Both House and Senate voted overwhelmingly for a nonbinding sense of the Congress resolution in opposition to CIA mining and other attacks, with large numbers of Republicans voting against the administration.

39. *New York Times*, April 11, 1984, 9.

40. Administration attacks became so vitriolic over time that Senator Nancy

Kassebaum (R, KS) finally took to the floor to denounce "distortions" by the Reagan team; *Congressional Quarterly Almanac 1986*, Washington: Congressional Quarterly Press, 1987, 398–399.

41. Gerhard von Glahn, *Law Among Nations*, New York: Macmillan, 1986, chp. 30.

42. "U.S. Policy Toward Nicaragua" (1986), note 29, at 13.

43. *Congressional Quarterly Almanac 1987*, 112.

44. "Honduras and U.S. Policy," note 28, at 17.

45. "U.S. Policy Toward Nicaragua" (1986), note 29, at 27–28.

46. See, for example, "U.S. Decision to Withdraw from the International Court of Justice," *Hearing*, House Subcommittee on Human Rights and International Organizations, 99th Congress, 1st session, Washington: GPO, 1986; and Paul Simon (D, IL), "Reagan's World Court Error," *New York Times*, October 16, 1985, 27.

47. "Concerning U.S. Military and Paramilitary Operations in Nicaragua," *Markup*, House Committee on Foreign Affairs, 98th Congress, 1st session, Washington: GPO, 1983, 34, 62, 68.

48. This was shown both by actions of the majority in the Subcommittee of Inter-American Affairs of the Foreign Affairs Committee, under Michael Barnes, and by votes on the floor of the House.

49. "Honduras and U.S. Policy," note 28, at 18.

50. "U.S. Policy Toward Nicaragua" (1986), note 29, passim.

51. "Concerning U.S. Military and Paramilitary Operations," note 47, at 52.

52. "U.S. Policy Toward Nicaragua" (1986), note 29, at 5.

53. "Concerning U.S. Military and Paramilitary Operations," note 47, at 18–19.

54. Extended attention in both hearings and floor debates was given to the U.S. role in violations of the laws of war by the contras, particularly the CIA's preparation of a manual that advised how to commit certain violations. This was not only a legal but a political issue, for the larger question was how could the administration expect the contras to gain popular support and eventually rule in a democratic method with their record of atrocities in the field. Extended attention was also given to the U.S. impact on Honduras, not just within a legal framework, but additionally within the larger political question of whether the United States was strengthening authoritarian military elements at the expense of civilian democrats.

55. "U.S. Policy Toward Nicaragua and Central America" (1983), 29.

56. "Concerning U.S. Military and Paramilitary Operations," note 47, at 14.

57. "U.S. Policy Toward Nicaragua" (1986), note 29, at 2.

58. See "Concerning U.S. Military and Paramilitary Operations," note 47, at 66, for acceptance of the self-defense argument. But see his comments at 21: "We put our white gloves on and we say no. Gentlemen don't read other gentlemen's mail. We should fight like the British Red Coats, in formation. You don't go in there and covertly interdict."

59. For one report among many, see the widespread West European criticism of U.S. policy reported in the *New York Times*, March 8, 1985, 34. West European criticism is also clear in U.N. debates as reported in the *U.N. Chronicle*. The European Economic Community maintained normal economic relations with Nicaragua, refusing to support the U.S. trade embargo.

60. Conroy in Walker, note 10; Walker in Coleman and Herring, note 8; *New York Times*, January 21, 1985, 2.

61. States must give their consent for a legal dispute to be treated by the ICJ. Under Article 36(1) of the Statute of the Court, states can give general consent. This the United States did in 1946 when it accepted this "Optional Clause" with two conditions: (a) that this permission did not extend to disputes involving domestic affairs, as determined by the United States; and (b) that this permission did not extend to disputes involving multilateral treaties unless the states involved agreed. Under Article 36(2), states could give specific consent, such as by becoming a party to a treaty that provided for automatic referral to the court of disputes under the treaty not resolved by other peaceful means.

62. The Executive first argued, upon learning of Nicaragua's intention to go to the ICJ, that the United States was altering immediately its acceptance of ICJ compulsory jurisdiction to exclude Central American disputes. The court disallowed this procedural defense because the original U.S. acceptance said it would require six months notice for termination; the ICJ held that the U.S. position was a type of termination. It was clear that the Executive was trying to find some way to head off a court test of its legal arguments. Compare a statement by Dean Acheson, later secretary of state, who said in 1946, when the United States accepted ICJ compulsory jurisdiction: "[The] record of the United States in its international dealings is such that it should not dread to have its acts reviewed by a court of law." Quoted in Thomas Franck, *Judging the World Court*, New York: Priority Press, 1986, 21.

63. The official statement of withdrawal, with supporting arguments, is reprinted in *Department of State Bulletin*, 85, 2096 (March 1985), 64–65. Judges of the ICJ sit in their individual capacity, not as representatives of their states.

64. Thus the Executive admitted at least tacitly that the placing of mines in foreign waters without notification to third-party shipping had occurred and was a violation of international law. The United States in fact ignored the rest of the interim judgment by continuing to engage in military attacks on the territorial integrity and political independence of Nicaragua.

65. The judgment is reprinted in *International Legal Materials*, 25 (1986), 1023.

66. See especially Franck, note 62, for a refutation and criticism of most executive arguments. To get a sense of the range of reactions to the ICJ judgment, see *American Journal of International Law*, 81, 1 (January 1986), 77–183. A computer search I made for law review articles on the case turned up over 100 articles, most of them critical of the United States.

67. See further, William P. Coplin, "The World Court in the International Bargaining Process," in Robert Gregg and Michael Barkun, eds., *The United Nations System and Its Functions*, Princeton: van Nostrand, 1968, 317–322.

68. See especially the clear critique by Oscar Schacter, "Self-Defense and the Rule of Law," *American Journal of International Law*, 83, 2 (April 1989), 259–277.

69. See *Department of State Bulletin*, 86, 2106 (January 1986), 67–71.

70. For an incisive argument along these lines, see the essay by Francis Fitzgerald in the *New York Times*, May 10, 1987, 36 of section VI.

71. *U.N. Chronicle*, 21, 4 (April 1984), 11–16; 21, 5 (May 1985), 16; 22, 9 (November 1986), 83.

72. Goodfellow in Walker, note 10.

73. For one example among many of reports about hemispheric dissatisfac-

tion with U.S. policy, see the *New York Times*, February 3, 1984, 6. Other than El Salvador and Honduras, Latin states refused to allow their territory to be used for contra attacks, especially after Costa Rica shut down contra camps. Latins were especially critical of the U.S. trade embargo against Nicaragua.

74. *New York Times*, March 19, 1985, 11. Brazil had long challenged administration statements that Brazilian terrorists were being trained by Nicaragua.

75. For the early situation, see *New York Times*, December 8, 1982, 3.

76. Pastor, note 1, at 257.

77. See, for example, in addition to Menges, note 1, Gordon Crovitz and Jeremy A. Rabkin, eds., *The Fettered Presidency: Legal Constraints on the Executive Branch*, Washington: American Enterprise Institute, 1989, with contributions by, among others, Kirkpatrick, Sofaer, Abrams, Perle, and Weinberger.

78. See especially the long dissent by the American judge, Stephen Schwebel, who skims over weaknesses in the U.S. position. He ends by developing the argument that because Nicaragua has lied about its policies, it does not have "clean hands" and thus is not entitled to have its central arguments prevail. He voted with the majority on only two points: that the CIA manual encouraged the violation of the laws of war (although he held that the United States was not directly responsible for violations) and that the U.S. mining of Nicaraguan harbors was legal but entailed the duty to notify neutral third parties. His dissent represents most of the U.S. legal argument on the merits that the United States chose not to make in court.

79. I agree with some critics that the ICJ assumed rather than proved the existence of customary international law on certain subjects. (The court relied on customary rather than treaty law because of the U.S. condition—the Vandenberg clause—restricting general U.S. consent for compulsory jurisdiction to disputes not involving multilateral treaties.) I also agree that the court's treatment of all facts is not beyond dispute, but find that treatment reasonable given the U.S. decision not to present factual evidence in court.

80. "Calling for the Establishment of a Special Committee on Advisory Opinions from the International Court of Justice," *Hearing*, House Subcommittee on Human Rights and International Organizations, 97th Congress, 1st session, Washington: GPO, 1981.

81. Roger Fisher, *International Conflict for Beginners*, New York: Harper and Row, 1969, chp. 7. Eisenhower is quoted by Keith Highet in "Between a Rock and a Hard Place," *American Journal of International Law*, 21, 4 (Fall 1987), 1100.

82. *New York Times*, February 22, 1987, 1.

83. *New York Times*, April 16, 1984, 23.

84. See, for example, *New York Times*, March 11, 1986, 1.

85. "U.S. Policy Toward Nicaragua" (1986), note 29, at 25.

IV

Overt Intervention
in Grenada

Let me conclude with this warning. I hope that people understand that Grenada was clearly a unique situation. Where could the President of the United States find an island where you could liberate white middle class students, capture some "bad blacks," beat up some Cubans, humiliate some Soviets, rid the island of communism, and have the majority of black people on the island say, "Thank you, Uncle Sam." Only on the island of Grenada.   —Representative Ronald Dellums

I   SOME RELEVANT FACTS

In the mid-1970s the Caribbean island of Grenada, about twice the size of the District of Columbia, was granted independence by the United Kingdom. Like many other former British colonies, Grenada retained the monarchy in London as its ultimate symbolic authority, instituted a governor-general as an intermediate and largely ceremonial head of state, and otherwise adopted the British political system that in the Caribbean is frequently called Westminster parliamentary democracy. This micro–mini-state then held elections, and Sir Eric Gairy became the nation's first prime minister. Gairy proved both bizarre and dangerous, ranting in public about how the bark of trees should be protected under human rights laws, while his "Mongoose Gang" of thugs beat up or killed political opponents.[1]

By 1979 Gairy had alienated many of his fellow citizens. While on a trip to the United Nations to promote a center for the study of unidentified flying objects (UFOs), he was overthrown in a bloodless coup led by Maurice Bishop and the Marxist New Jewel Movement (NJM). Bishop was a charismatic leader whose rhetoric tended to exceed his actions. In a speech in Havana in 1979, Bishop called for a socialist Caribbean. Grenada's economy, however, remained mixed rather than fully controlled by the government, and there was no proof of Grenadian intervention in the domestic affairs of the other Caribbean states. There was considerable social progress in education and income distribution within

Grenada. There was some genuine political participation through local councils, to which the political leadership paid some attention, but there was also considerable political repression. Promised elections were not held, and political detention drew the attention of Amnesty International and other human rights groups.

Two regional organizations, the Organization of Eastern Caribbean States (OECS), dating from 1981 and comprising seven island republics, and the larger Caribbean Economic Community (CARICOM), dating from 1973 with a membership of 13, tolerated Bishop and hoped to moderate his policies over time through interaction. The Carter administration, by contrast, responded to the 1979 coup with diplomatic pressure. The Carter team tried to isolate Bishop from the rest of the Caribbean. This policy did not mobilize much regional support, even though the Caribbean—with the notable exception of Cuba—was mostly pro-American, democratic, and socially and politically conservative. After Bishop recognized Cuba and developed close relations with other socialist countries such as Bulgaria, North Korea, the Soviet Union, and Libya, U.S. pressure increased.[2]

Early in October 1983, the NJM movement split in a power struggle between Bishop and Bernard Coard. Coard had grown impatient with Bishop's moderation at home and his search for improved relations with the United States—and no doubt also impatient with not being top dog in Grenadian politics. With the key military official, Howard Austin, tilting toward Coard, Bishop was placed under house arrest on the evening of October 13. He was freed in a spontaneous mass movement by his supporters on October 19, but that same day was killed, with a handful of his closest associates, by forces loyal to Austin and Coard. A number of Bishop's rank-and-file supporters were also killed as the military fired into a street demonstration. Austin, with Coard maneuvering behind the scenes, declared a Revolutionary Military Council (RMC) as a transitional authority and promised new elections.

Shortly after dawn on October 25, 1983, just under 2,000 U.S. troops were diverted from a naval task force on its way to Lebanon and landed in Grenada, along with token paramilitary forces from several Caribbean states. With their reinforcements, which eventually numbered some 8,000, they proceeded to occupy the island, overcoming armed resistance from some 600 Cuban construction workers who had military training. U.S. forces detained and interrogated former government officials, evacuated about 350 Americans—most of them students at the St. George's Medical College—and presided over the reconstitution of the Grenadian political system. "Combat" troops were withdrawn within several months, while "support" troops, along with police forces from neighboring Caribbean states, stayed until a new political system carried out elections in 1984.

After the invasion there followed a short but spirited debate in Washington about the relevance of the United Nations and Organization of American States Charters, and the propriety of the United States forcing a change in the Grenadian government even if under the aegis of the OECS. The central question—which was inherently a question of international law—was: is it permissible to produce democracy at the point of a bayonet in another country? This was debated at the United Nations and the Organization of American States, as well as taken up by certain states in their bilateral relations with the United States. There was also debate within Washington about the applicability of the War Powers Act (1973), asserting a role for Congress in the use of force by the Executive, short of a declaration of war.

Events in Grenada in the fall of 1983 were neither of long duration nor of cosmic importance, but they were politically and legally significant. They raised disturbing questions both about policy-making in the Reagan administration, and about the responsibility of Congress to correct deficiencies in that process. Events also demonstrated the weakness of foreign influences on Washington.

II EXECUTIVE POLICY

As with regard to U.S. policy toward Nicaragua, when one studies the policy of the Reagan administration toward Grenada, it is not easy to determine who made what decision exactly when, and with what exact motivation and objective. Even years after the invasion, executive public statements must still be probed with great care, and a wide variety of sources must be consulted to get an accurate view of executive behavior. Even then, certain events remain unclear. It is helpful to delineate three periods in Reagan's policy toward Grenada: preinvasion, invasion, and postinvasion.

Upon entering office in early 1981, the Reagan team made Bishop's Grenada one of its high-priority targets. Since Grenada was ruled by a government that was Marxist, new, and weak, it fell naturally under the Reagan Doctrine and was thus subject to "roll-back." The administration lost no time applying economic pressure to Bishop's regime because of its political coloration, managing to block new loans to Grenada in the International Monetary Fund and the World Bank. The administration offered $4 million to the Caribbean Development Bank on condition that none of the money be allocated to Grenada, but the bank refused the money with that string attached. When the administration came up with the Caribbean Basin Initiative (CBI) for the economic revitalization of Central America and the Caribbean, Grenada was explicitly excluded—along with Cuba and Nicaragua.[3]

There was also diplomatic pressure. Ambassadors were not exchanged, the United States keeping its ambassador to Grenada based in

Barbados, and refusing to accept the credentials of Bishop's nominee to Washington. President Reagan dwelt on the evils of Grenada in a speech to the OAS in early 1982. Bishop was bluntly warned to cool his rhetoric and reduce his entanglements with Cuba and the Soviet Union. Bishop's emissaries and even Bishop himself were given cool receptions by lower officials in Washington. The president increasingly focused on Grenada in televised speeches, particularly stressing the building of a long runway, which could accommodate large Cuban or Soviet aircraft, in the south of the country. (The new airport, officially for tourism, was financed by an international consortium including the Canadian government and the European Economic Community, as well as socialist states; a U.S. firm was contracted for part of the work.)

There was also military pressure. In 1981, the United States carried out war games featuring an amphibious assault on the island of "Amber," near Grenada. This was intended to be—and indeed was accepted as—a warning to Bishop. After these war games, Bishop called for and received voluntarily a sizable expansion of the Grenadian militia, as well as increased military shipments from his socialist benefactors abroad.

It was not clear what the CIA was doing vis-à-vis Grenada during this preinvasion period. It can be recalled from the previous chapter that President Reagan authorized expanded CIA action against leftists in Central America and the Caribbean in March of 1981. There were several bombings in Grenada during 1981–1983, and some observers claimed the CIA was responsible, but proof was never established. The *Miami Herald*, usually well informed on hemispheric events, reported that supporters of Eric Gairy were training in Florida, similar to the Nicaraguan contras, and the U.S. government did nothing to quell Bishop's fears about a counterrevolution launched from the United States.

I believe that the CIA was not very active in Grenada prior to October 1983, and that U.S. intelligence was poor regarding that country. At the time of the NJM split, the United States was unaware that Cuba opposed Coard. During the military invasion, U.S. troops used British tourist maps, and were unaware that the medical college had two separate campuses. The United States was also unaware of the quantity of small arms and other light weapons that the NJM had acquired. It is possible that the CIA wanted to act in Grenada but was blocked by the congressional intelligence committees, as reported in the American press. (It is also possible that the CIA was active in covert action rather than intelligence gathering, or that the CIA failed to pass along its intelligence to the military.)

There was no doubt that all this economic, diplomatic, and military pressure (with or without covert subversion) caused Bishop to seek better relations with the United States. He was in touch quietly with the U.S. ambassador to the Eastern Caribbean states, Milan Bish, and had established such a rapport with official and unofficial U.S. circles, and with similarly conservative circles among Caribbean states, that when he was placed under house arrest between October 13–19 there was discussion in these circles of his rescue by the CIA.[4] He was released, then killed before any such plans could be activated. In June of 1983 Bishop had gone to Washington on a private visit, had asked to meet with President Reagan, and after some pushing by congressional members was received for a brief talk by National Security Adviser William P. Clark and Undersecretary of State Kenneth Dam. At least at lower levels of the Reagan administration, as well as in the Caribbean, Bishop was recognized as a moderate pursuing better relations with the United States, and much preferable to either the scoundrel Gairy or the Stalinist Coard.

The invasion period of U.S. policy, covering roughly October 12–25, is more difficult to reconstruct with precision. When the NJM split, between October 12–14, some elements within the U.S. National Security Council staff immediately began to draft plans for the overthrow of whatever Marxist faction prevailed.[5] This was prior to any disruption of public order, and thus prior to any possibility of danger to U.S. students and other U.S. nationals. This was also prior to any "request" by any Caribbean state for U.S. action in Grenada.

During October 14–19, this planning for an invasion went forward within the Reagan administration, with some staff in the State Department joining those on the NSC staff in favor of an overt overthrow of any leftist Grenadian government. Some reservations were apparently expressed by the highest levels of the Department of Defense, who were in favor of a rescue mission but not clearly in favor of a broader political mission. These DOD personnel were affected both by the continuing legacy of the Vietnam War and by the then-current imbroglio in Lebanon—which was growing increasingly unpopular with Congress and public opinion. But when Secretary of State Shultz, Assistant Secretary Langhorne Motley, and other diplomats backed the plans for invasion, there emerged a broad consensus for military intervention. Friendly elements in the Caribbean, such as Tom Adams, prime minister of Barbados, were contacted, and a U.S. Marine general discussed with Adams the details of an invasion.[6]

The killing of Bishop on October 19 expedited invasion planning. In fact, the removal of this moderate and the rise of the clearly extremist Coard virtually settled the issue. Both the Reagan team and the conservative Caribbean governments believed that Coard would be a destabilizing factor in the region. No more Cubas could be tolerated, and a lesson could be sent to the Sandinistas via Grenada.[7] On October 20th Reagan permitted the diversion of the naval task force, bound for Lebanon, to facilitate an attack on Grenada. That same day the NSC staff drafted a presidential order for an attack, to have it ready for Reagan's signature. Within the Executive the consensus for a general invasion was now clear.

While these decisions were tentative, in the sense that the final order to attack had not been given, the only remaining issue, short of some unforeseen development, was how to justify the invasion. Knowing of the concern about Grenadian events particularly of Barbados and Jamaica, but also of Dominica and several other Caribbean states, the administration dispatched two envoys, Frank McNeil and General George Crist, to join Milan Bish and another U.S. official, Charles Gillespie, to produce an "invitation" from the OECS. It is not clear how hard the OECS states, plus Barbados and Jamaica, had to be pressed by the United States for a full invasion. It is reasonably clear that some states, like Barbados as led by Prime Minister Adams, were enthusiastic about invasion. It is also reasonably clear that the OECS was the only multilateral support the Reagan team could count on, since the larger CARICOM and the still larger OAS would definitely not support military intervention. Recourse to the United Nations was never considered. In any event there was a meeting of minds among half-a-dozen conservative governments, and the "invitation," drafted in Washington, was agreed to at a meeting of the OECS on October 21, then formally sent to Washington on October 22. (Barbados and Jamaica are not members of the OECS; Grenada was not notified of the meeting.) On the evening of the 22nd, President Reagan again endorsed the invasion plan drawn up by his subordinates.[8]

At some point someone decided that the involvement of the OECS was insufficient. At that point the story was released that the governor-general of Grenada, Sir Paul Scoon, had sent an oral request by unidentified, clandestine source to Barbados, asking for external assistance, and that Barbados relayed this request to the OECS and the United States.[9] This oral request, which supposedly occurred on October 23, after Reagan had already twice given approval for a general invasion, was put in writing after the invasion and then backdated to October 24.[10] The British government said it had no information about any of this, even though a British diplomat had met with Scoon on the 23rd, the day he supposedly sent his request for outside assistance.[11]

Thus, it is clear that the United States decided on an invasion during October 19–22. It took until the morning of the 25th for the military forces to be properly positioned. (In the meantime, on Sunday the 23rd, 241 U.S. Marines were killed in a terrorist attack on their barracks in Beirut, Lebanon. According to some accounts, this event increased the president's determination to move against Grenada. But the early decisions to act had already been made.)

It was, in fact, mostly irrelevant to U.S. policy that American students on Grenada were not in any imminent danger from the 19th to the 25th, as was confirmed by the chancellor of the St. George's Medical College, who was in Grenada.[12] A U.S. official who interviewed the students on

October 23 indicated that 90 percent of them wanted to stay in Grenada.[13] British and Canadian officials had no plans for any rescue operation of their nationals.[14] The Austin-Coard faction, having been warned about the invasion by friendly sources on about the 22nd, sent assurances to the Medical College and to Washington guaranteeing the safety of the students, and even provided vehicles to any students who wanted to go to the operating airport.[15] (Contrary to administration statements, the airport was open on the 24th, and at least four planes left that day. To the extent that there was difficulty in air transport, it was caused not by the Revolutionary Military Council in Grenada but by Barbados, which did not allow planes to depart *for* Grenada, in keeping with sanctions voted on the 24th by CARICOM.[16]) During the curfew declared by the RMC from the 19th, no American student, nor apparently any Grenadian, was harmed or perhaps even shot at. The island was described as tense but calm in several reports.

It was, therefore, the policy of the Reagan administration to change the government of Grenada; this it first sought by economic, diplomatic, and military pressure, and then by armed intervention when the NJM disintegrated in power and personality struggles. The question of the security of U.S. nationals in Grenada, particularly the medical students, was a convenient side-show useful to the administration in justifying the invasion to the Congress and American public. While the students might have become endangered, and while the Tehran hostage crisis of 1979–1980 might have been repeated, and while any U.S. government might have been justified in preventing such an occurrence through a genuine rescue mission, in the decision-making that actually transpired in Washington the students were mostly irrelevant. This is confirmed by the fact that the largest group of students, located on the Grande Anse campus of the Medical College, were unknown to U.S. military forces, were not reached by those forces until the third day of the invasion, and were only endangered by the fighting produced by the invasion itself.

In the postinvasion period, the United States constituted itself as an all-pervasive occupying power, detaining and questioning persons, confiscating material deemed subversive (such as Marxist literature), and supervising the subsequent elections, which were held in 1984. While police forces from several Caribbean states were visible in the streets, it was the United States—now operating through a relatively large diplomatic presence in Grenada—that actively discouraged former Premier Gairy from running again as he personally wanted to do, and actively supported acceptable politicians—such as Herbert Blaize and his New National Party, which won the general election. Just as the United States had intervened heavily with money and diplomatic influence in the elections in El Salvador in the 1980s, so the United States played a very large role in reconstituting Grenadian politics after the invasion.[17] By the mid-1980s, therefore, Grenada had returned to Westminster democracy, and sizable amounts of U.S. economic assistance underwrote the economy.

III EXECUTIVE LEGAL CLAIMS

Executive claims with regard to international law and the use of force in Grenada were shifting and ill considered, reflecting the lack of attention given to these legal factors in actual decision-making. The arguments most likely to be accepted by the international community, or in the words of one observer, "the least demonstrably false,"[18] were articulated later rather than sooner, in a defensive reaction to criticism. As the same observer remarked, the variety and inconsistency of arguments gave the impression of a rationale constructed "at the gallop."[19] Early administration statements were weak from the standpoint of international law, however much they were to succeed politically or even reflect partially the real reasons for the military intervention. On the morning of the invasion the president, accompanied by Eugenia Charles, prime minister of Dominica and president of the OECS, said the use of force was undertaken:

> First, and of overriding importance, to protect innocent lives, including up to 1,000 Americans whose personal safety is, of course, my paramount concern;
> Second, to forestall further chaos;
> And third, to assist in the restoration of conditions of law and order and of governmental institutions to the island of Grenada, where a brutal group of leftist thugs violently seized power. . . .[20]

Despite the presence of Charles, the president made no reference in his main statement to any variety of self-defense, and no one made any reference to any invitation from Governor-General Scoon. (Later it was argued that such a reference had to await the securing of his safety. His safety, however, was never in question, as he had been ignored by Austin and Coard.)

By October 27, administration statements began to mention a political version of anticipatory and preemptive self-defense, which was the crux of the argument by Charles and the other participating Caribbean states: that the RMC would constitute an aggressive or threatening state in the future, and thus the invading parties were entitled to act in anticipation of that policy.[21] The president's televised speech of the 27th gave considerable attention to this line of justification, as did Ambassador Jeane Kirkpatrick's remarks at a U.N. Security Council meeting of the same day. This was after the discovery of relatively large amounts of light, and dated, arms found by the invading forces.[22]

The president's first comments in his press conference, and Ambassador Kirkpatrick's, and the remarks in a press conference by Secretary of State Shultz, emphasized a broad right of intervention for democracy. This is a highly controversial claim since it does not exist in treaty form, does not exist clearly in customary law, is opposed by most democracies, and is roughly analogous to the Brezhnev Doctrine claimed for a time by the Soviet Union, in which it asserted a right to protect "progressive" socialist "democracies."[23]

The administration's claims shifted again by the time State Department officials testified about Grenada before Congress. Undersecretary of State Kenneth W. Dam reversed the importance of most of the legal arguments, emphasizing a more traditional argument when he stressed the invitation from the governor-general, as well as the invitation from the OECS.[24] Of course he also maintained the argument of humanitarian intervention in behalf of U.S. nationals, although he did not provide any legal support for that claim, apparently assuming such an action was clearly legal.

But Dam went out of his way to reject the president's argument of the right of military intervention to impose democracy. He stated that the United States was not making such an exceptional claim and that the U.S. legal arguments had nothing in common with the Brezhnev Doctrine. He said to the House in early November, "Those who do not see— or do not choose to see—these signal distinctions have failed to analyze the facts. We have not made, and do not seek to make, any broad new precedent for international action; we think the justification for our actions is narrow, and well within accepted concepts of international law."[25]

Likewise, when addressing the Senate, Secretary Dam sought to downplay any claim to a right of democratic intervention and to discount an intervention based on strategic considerations:

> Senator Pell: My specific question is, was the presumed threat to Americans being used as a cover or rationale for an invasion that would have occurred in any case?
> Mr. Dam: Absolutely not. There were two grounds for the action taken in response to the OECS invitation. One was the safety of Americans, the other was the response to this plea for collective security. . . .[26]

By early 1984, when a Reagan official testified before another House committee, the claim to a general right to intervene to restore democratic law and order was dropped altogether, replaced by three more traditional arguments: humanitarian intervention, invitation from the governor–general, and invitation from the OECS.[27]

If over time one looked at the various legal or quasi-legal rationales developed to justify U.S. use of force in Grenada, there seemed to be five (in no particular order beyond the first): 1) humanitarian intervention to rescue U.S. nationals; 2) collective self-defense at the invitation of the governor-general; 3) collective self-defense at the request of the OECS; 4) anticipatory self-defense linked to the OECS; 5)structural intervention in behalf of democracy. All these rationales were problematical.

1. *Humanitarian intervention* has never been codified in treaty form, since the lesser powers fear that it is a concept subject to misuse by relatively powerful states. That fear is well founded. The Johnson administration used humanitarian intervention as a primary pretext when it sent 6,000 marines into the Dominican Republic in 1965 to head off a left-of-center political movement it had misrepresented as communist.[28] India (with more justification) claimed humanitarian intervention when it used military force to stop the Pakistani army (largely Punjabi) from slaughtering Bengalis in 1971 in East Pakistan; it also seized the opportunity to dismember Pakistan by turning the eastern region into the new state of Bangladesh. Vietnam claimed humanitarian intervention when it invaded Kampuchea in 1979 to remove the murderous Pol Pot government, which had killed millions of Cambodians—but then installed a government of its choice.

Some legal theorists believe that the U.N. Charter, with its prohibition on the use of force except for self-defense, has outlawed forceful humanitarian intervention. These same theorists can cite numerous critical comments by state officials whenever the claim to such intervention is articulated.

On the other side of the coin, however, it is clear that states will use force to protect their nationals, and occasionally non-nationals, from time to time. West Germany used force, perhaps with the permission of the government in Moghidishu, to rescue passengers on a Lufthansa airliner that had been hijacked to Somalia. The Israelis did likewise at Entebbe, Uganda, after an El Al airliner with mostly Israeli nationals on board had been hijacked. The Carter administration attempted to do so in 1980 to free American hostages held with the connivance of the government of Iran, although that attempt ended in technical failure.

In these cases there was no attempt at structural political change in the state in which military force was used, and the governments utilizing force sometimes claimed self-defense rather than humanitarian intervention, leaving the status of the latter concept unclear. (Unclear also is whether the concept of self-defense can include attacks on nationals outside the state, and whether humanitarian intervention is supposed to cover the forceful protection of non-nationals.[29])

Specifically with regard to Grenada, until the actual invasion on October 25, American students and other U.S. nationals had been neither threatened nor harmed. Just the reverse had occurred: The RMC, which had the power to impose an effective curfew, and was in fact in actual control of the island, and whose spokesman at the U.N. continued to represent Grenada there, had given assurances about the safety of Americans and provided transport to the airport. It is relevant to note, however, that: in the past an American had been detained in Grenada when two Grenadians were arrested in the United States, thus constituting a type of hostage situation;[30] the students might have become hostages in the future; the Reagan team had vociferously attacked the Carter team's handling of the Iranian hostage situation and did not want to face a similar dilemma.

The concept of humanitarian intervention remains unclear in international law, depending as it does on state practice and the relation between that practice and customary international law. But even if one concludes that the Reagan administration was justified in fearing for the *future* safety of the students—given the political instability on the island, the deaths that had occurred, and the nature of the Austin-Coard faction—reconstituting the governmental structure of Grenada falls outside the bounds of humanitarian intervention. Had the administration used force to remove U.S. nationals who wanted to exit the island, there would have been little controversy at home or abroad over the operation. But from the beginning of planning within the NSC, and not withstanding early reservations by the DOD, the intention was structural change—viz., overthrow of any Marxist government or ruling authority.

2. *The request by the Grenadian governor-general* for outside assistance remains shrouded in such secrecy that we can only guess that, if such a request was really sent, it was more a fig leaf for intervention than a genuine action by a responsible government official entitled to great weight in policy-making councils. It is arguably the case that the governor-general, who normally cannot act except on the basis of a request by the prime minister, has the residual authority to take independent action in exceptional situations, and that the events of October 1983 constituted such an exceptional situation. Whether the governor-general was legally obligated to ask the British monarch for assistance before anyone else seems an unsettled point in the British Commonwealth—in any event, the Commonwealth did not condemn the intervention.[31]

A bipartisan House of Commons committee reported that it was unable to come to any firm conclusions about the oral or written request of the governor-general.[32] Given the close alliance between Britain and the United States, this conclusion has to be understood in a critical vein, for if the British had been able to verify and justify the request, surely they would have. Governor-General Scoon said after the invasion that he did not have an invasion in mind when he made his oral request, and that the first he knew of U.S. military action was when U.S. forces appeared on his front lawn.[33] His career as governor-general under Gairy, Bishop, and Austin-Coard had been as a political nonentity, a figurehead who took no action and was therefore acceptable to all. That being so, it is unlikely he would have taken decisive action except under foreign prodding.

Given such ambiguities, as well as the refusal of the United States or Barbados to clarify matters, the conclusion is justified that both the oral and written requests of the governor-general were similar to the "request" by the government of Afghanistan for "assistance" from the Soviet Union when Soviet troops moved into Afghanistan in December 1979. It is a fact that when U.S. forces landed in Grenada they made the securing of the governor-general a higher priority than the securing of the American students, and that as soon as was convenient, Scoon was taken to a U.S. ship where—at a minimum—his formal letters of request were signed.[34] The entire affair smacks of crude face-saving, and in any event the actions of the governor-general on October 23 and 24, whatever they were, had nothing to do with early U.S. decisions to invade, made between October 19–22.

3. *The claim that the OECS had the authority* to engage in military intervention in Grenada is even more transparent than the claim that the invasion was invited by the governor-general. The key article in the OECS Charter is Article 8, which reads in part:

> (4) The Defense and Security Committee shall have responsibility for coordinating the efforts of Member States for collective defense and the preservation of peace and security against external aggression and for the development of close ties among the Member States of the Organization in matters of external defense and security. . . .
> (5) The decisions and directives of the Defense and Security Committee shall be unanimous. . . .

There is no authority under the OECS Charter, in Article 8 or elsewhere, for forceful intervention into internal affairs, even in exceptional situations. Defensive action is explicitly limited to "external aggression." And all decisions must be unanimous. Not only did Grenada not vote to be invaded, since it was not invited to the meetings on October 21, 22, and 23, but also several other member states, which were invited and present, did not vote for military intervention. Moreover, the United States, Barbados, and Jamaica were not members of the OECS and could derive no authority from that body.

There was nothing in the OECS Charter that contradicted the provisions in the OAS Charter stating:

> No State or group of States has the right to intervene, directly or indirectly, for any reason whatever, in the internal or external affairs of any other State. The foregoing principle prohibits not only armed force but also any other form of interference or attempted threat against the personality of the State or against its political, economic and cultural elements (Article 16).

The OAS Charter, in turn, is consistent with the U.N. Charter, prohibiting the organization, and by implication its member-states, from intervening in a nation's internal affairs (Article 2, paragraph 7). Grenada, the United States, and most of the other states involved in this affair are members of the U.N. and the OAS.

U.S. references to the OECS Charter became so lame that Secretary Dam could only argue, in congressional hearings, that it was up to the OECS members to interpret their own charter, and the United States would defer to that interpretation.[35] The implication was clear: if they wanted to misinterpret that constitutive document, that would not affect the United States. This is a most unpersuasive argument. If states misinterpret treaties, the United States derives no justification for deferring to that violation of law.

4. *The claim of anticipatory self-defense* was raised more by the invading OECS states, plus Barbados and Jamaica, than by U.S. officials—although the latter made reference to this controversial doctrine inconsistently. There is no doubt that the socially and politically conservative Caribbean states felt threatened by the prospect of a Grenadian government controlled by Coard and backed by other socialist states. This Caribbean fear, however, does not justify the forceful intervention that transpired.

Since 1945 and the signing of the U.N. Charter, important states have not treated Article 51, the key article about self-defense, literally. The relevant part of this article, which is (as noted in the previous chapter) the only authorization for the use of force found in the Charter, reads: "Nothing in the present Charter shall impair the inherent right of individual or collective self-defense if an armed attack occurs against a Member of the United Nations. . . ." But the United States in the Cuban missile crisis of 1962, and Israel in its 1967 attack on Egypt and its 1981 attack on Iraq, argued that anticipatory self-defense was permissible. In the nuclear age, it was argued, one did not have to wait until an armed attack occurred, but could take forceful measures first.

Even for those accepting the permissibility of anticipatory self-defense—which is by no means a fully settled question in international law—a traditional rule of customary international law is generally accepted as providing guidance in these situations. This is the Caroline rule, emanating from a U.S.-Canadian (British) interaction in 1837–1841, and reads as follows:

> It will be for [a] Government to show a necessity of self-defense, instant, overwhelming, leaving no choice of means, and no moment of deliberation. It will be for it to show . . . [that it] did nothing unreasonable or excessive; since the act justified by the necessity of self-defense, must be limited by that necessity and kept clearly within it.[36]

This test was not met in the 1983 invasion of Grenada. Neither the United States nor the OECS tried any diplomacy at all after October 19. Indeed, when the CARICOM met on October 24 to vote sanctions, in an effort at a nonmilitary solution to the problems arising from Grenadian events, OECS and other informed states kept secret the fact that a decision to invade had already been taken. When the RMC and Cuba tried to avert the invasion with promises of safety for U.S. nationals, there was no response from Washington. The Executive then misrepresented the facts in testimony in Congress, saying that the RMC had "slammed the door" in the face of the United States, whereas it was the United States that had ignored CARICOM and RMC diplomatic efforts. When on the eve of attack Britain advised that the use of force was unnecessary, President Reagan went ahead anyway.[37]

It cannot be maintained that the use of force was necessary for the anticipatory self-defense of the other Caribbean states, even if one acknowledges both the absence of military forces, properly speaking, in these states, and the small size and poor training of their police forces. There was no threat that was "instant and overwhelming." There was time to try to rectify problems by diplomacy, especially since Cuba did not support Coard, and since Coard had virtually no popular support within Grenada after the killing of the relatively popular Bishop. The argument is persuasive that the Austin-Coard faction would have had to yield power, given its domestic and regional isolation.[38]

5. *The claim to a broad right to democratic intervention*, stressed by the president on the day of the invasion (which also lay at the heart of U.S. policy toward Nicaragua, as shown in the previous chapter) is the most controversial of all the shifting U.S. claims—largely abandoned by subordinates testifying in Congress. It, like the Reagan Doctrine that is its companion, is simply incompatible with provisions of the U.N. and OAS Charters stressing national self-determination and sovereignty, nonintervention, and peaceful resolution of disputes. While the U.N. and OAS Charters also mandate attention to human rights and social justice, there is nothing in these constituent documents, or any other parts of international law, that gives to an outside party the right to impose a particular version of rights or justice on national authorities. Indeed, international law mandates, and establishes procedures for, peaceful attention to human rights problems. However much these procedures may be insufficient, there remains no violent shortcut authorized by international law.[39]

It is precisely for this reason that Margaret Thatcher, a close ally of the United States and a personal friend of President Reagan, refused to support the invasion. She said later:

If you are going to pronounce a new law that wherever there is communism imposed against the will of the people then the U.S. shall enter then we are going to have really terrible wars in the world. . . . [Being opposed to communism] does not mean you are entitled to go into every country . . . which is under communist oppression.[40]

At times the administration claimed that it was restoring (democratic) law and order in a situation of anarchy in Grenada. This is a variation on the more general claim to democratic intervention; this variation is not only controversial in law, but also in fact. In Grenada from October 12 there was of course political instability, but the RMC did impose an effective curfew and was militarily in control of the island. Between October 20–24 there was little or no violence in Grenada, either between military elements or between the military and dissidents. Moreover, the United States and certain OECS states were claiming that the RMC constituted an aggressive threat. It is difficult to understand how the RMC could be both an aggressive threat and without the power to control events.

IV   THE DOMESTIC RESPONSE

When President Reagan announced the invasion of Grenada on Tuesday morning, October 25, there was considerable criticism from members of Congress. The United States was already involved in a questionable military venture in Lebanon, information was beginning to surface about policy steps regarding Nicaragua, policy toward El Salvador was subject to sharp criticism, and there was general unease throughout much of Washington about Reagan's foreign policy.

The Congressional Record for that date shows that seven members of the House of Representatives, mostly liberal Democrats, took to the floor to criticize the Grenadian venture. Only four members rose to defend it. On the following day, House critics still outnumbered backers of the administration, but only by a margin of one. By the 27th, however, only one member of the House rose to challenge the administration on the floor, while nine members, all conservative Republicans, defended the administration. The members of the Senate had been mostly quiet on the floor of their chamber, with only the ultraconservative Jesse Helms (R, NC) and Strom Thurmond (R, SC) taking the floor on the 26th and 27th to support the invasion.[41] These floor positions were indicative of the larger congressional response to the invasion: initial criticism yielded to deference.

While many numbers of Congress (especially Democrats) found the administration's actions unacceptable and its rationales unpersuasive, the return of American students on the evening of the 26th, and their obvious happiness at being back in the United States (one was televised and photographed kissing American soil), led to a surge of public opinion in support of the Executive. Public opinion polls reported anywhere from 55 percent to 90 percent support for Reagan's handling of events in Grenada.[42] Against this background, most congressional critics folded their tents. This was certainly true of the Speaker of the House, "Tip" O'Neill (D, MA), who first criticized the invasion, then, after ordering a fact-finding mission to Grenada, found the president's actions "justified."[43]

Both houses of Congress at least went through the motions of holding hearings on Grenada soon after the invasion. A number of members of Congress raised highly pertinent questions about the relevance of international law to the invasion. In the Senate on the 27th, then-chair of the Foreign Relations Committee, Charles Percy (R, IL) opened the hearing with the interesting observation that "Americans' lives were *potentially* in danger. . . ."[44] He went on to express unease about the Executive's rationales, since he was "concerned about the impact of such an operation upon world opinion and the legal justification of our intervention." Senator Pell (D, RI), the ranking Democrat then, observed pointedly: "I am concerned because the United States is committed under the charter of the OAS not to intervene in the internal affairs of any other member state, for whatever reason. It is one thing to rescue Americans; it is another to change a distasteful government at the point of a bayonet."[45] Pell also mentioned the lack of diplomatic efforts to resolve matters short of use of force.

Most of the senators who questioned the administration's point man, Secretary Dam, either went through the motions of asking—but not following-up on—questions of international law, or they switched to matters of domestic interest such as the War Powers Resolution or the restrictions imposed on American journalists during the invasion. Senator Christopher Dodd (D, CT) wanted to press the issue of Article 8 of the OECS treaty and its misinterpretation,[46] and Senator Pell wanted to emphasize the weakness of the various legal claims. Pell hit hard on Article 8. He also attacked the administration's contradictory logic on the need for intervention to restore order: "I think the very fact that there was a 24-hour curfew and a shoot-to-kill order could show that there was a government, repugnant and distasteful as it was, in place, or it could not have enforced the curfew."[47] Most senators, however, either supported the intervention or saw political problems in continuing to criticize the Reagan administration.

In the House the situation was slightly different. The Black Caucus had been interested in Grenada at least since the Reagan administration had targeted it for pressure in 1981; thus there were a few members of the House who continued to press their criticisms of executive policy despite the political hopelessness of their cause. But in the end, as in the Senate, most members exchanged criticism for deference.

The Black Caucus, led by Representatives Mervyn Dymally (D, CA) and Ronald Dellums (D, CA) had pushed Representative Michael

Barnes (D, MD) to hold hearings on Grenada in June of 1982.[48] Their criticisms intensified after the invasion. They raised questions about the real danger to American students, they challenged claims about the need for anticipatory self-defense, they noted the United States was not a member of the OECS, and they argued, not without reason, that "the greatest danger to American lives on Grenada was an American invasion."[49] They later introduced a resolution requiring that the Executive provide further information about decisions leading to the invasion.[50] All this was to no avail. It also proved pointless for Ted Weiss (D, NY) to introduce a resolution of impeachment of President Reagan for violating international and U.S. law.

During House hearings in November some comments were trenchant, but without political follow-up and support. Said Representative Sam Gejdenson (D, CT): "It seems to me that given a fair reading of that article [OECS Article 8], it would take an incredible amount of imagination to make it applicable to the invasion."[51] Mel Levine (D, CA) noted the lack of diplomatic efforts prior to the use of force.[52] George Garcia (D, NY) noted that many Americans, including many students, never left Grenada, and thus questioned the need for intervention.[53] Gerry Studds (D, MA) and Stephen Solarz (D, NY) also hit at the lack of U.S. diplomacy, as well as the Executive's misrepresentation of the RMC's assurances of safety for Americans.[54] Despite these questions and observations, as well as insightful critiques from observers from outside the government,[55] the House followed the Senate in deferring to executive action.

The administration was helped—not that it really needed further help, given American public opinion—when Carter's ambassador to the Eastern Caribbean states, Sally Shelton, endorsed the invasion despite the weakness of legal claims. In a statement remarkable for its lack of diplomatic finesse, she said: "I will leave it to the lawyers to debate the legalities of action under the OECS Treaty and how that treaty is affected by the OAS and U.N. Charters. However solid or flawed the legal base—and I deeply regret any infringements of international law which may have taken place—the fact remains that we still live in a world of realpolitik."[56]

Representative Dellums likewise cut to the heart of the matter when he said, in obvious frustration: "No one wants to hear the other side. We have taken our political views. We operate on the basis of politics by polltaking. If the American people, 85 percent, say they approve, then my colleagues will approve because it takes much less courage to go along with the polls than it does to begin to try to raise some significant and serious questions."[57]

But how could Congress debate seriously international legal restraints on the use of force when, as Dellums himself noted, President Reagan had found "an island where you could liberate white middle class students, capture some 'bad blacks,' beat up some Cubans, humiliate some Soviets, rid the island of communism, and have the majority of black people on the island say, 'Thank you, Uncle Sam'"?[58]

V   FOREIGN RESPONSES

There are indications that many Grenadians, from the rank and file as well as from educated and cosmopolitan circles, welcomed the U.S. invasion.[59] While the domestic violence had ended by October 25, the continuing presence of U.S. troops removed the threat of further violence, instability, and uncertainty. Austin and especially Coard were not popular; the presence of relatively large numbers of Cubans and others from socialist states also gave rise to considerable concern, contradicting as they did the political and economic traditions inherited from British colonialism.

At the United Nations, Nicaragua brought matters before the Security Council, and a large number of the 65 speakers clearly opposed the invasion.[60] This was not surprising since even a number of U.S. allies—including Canada, Italy, Australia, France, West Germany, and Belgium—had already issued unilateral statements of criticism. A resolution of condemnation, which sought broad support by not naming the United States explicitly as the aggressor, similar to resolutions condemning by implication the Soviet military presence in Afghanistan, was introduced by Guyana, Nicaragua, and Zimbabwe. This resolution was vetoed by the United States, with Britain abstaining along with Togo and Zaire. Voting with the 11-state majority in the Council were France, the Netherlands, Jordan, and Pakistan. The president of the Security Council remarked at one point that the United States had given the impression of following a policy of "invade first and then look for the justification later."[61]

An almost identical resolution of condemnation, declaring the U.S. military action a "flagrant violation of international law," was introduced in the General Assembly after the veto, and it passed easily, 108 to 9, with 27 abstentions. The only states to vote against, in addition to the United States and its Caribbean allies, were El Salvador and Israel. The United States did salvage some solace when a Belgian resolution calling on the United States to hold elections in Grenada also passed rather easily. This was taken as a Western victory, since by implication it distinguished the U.S. invasion from the Soviet invasion of Afghanistan, where no elections had been held or were in prospect.[62]

At the Organization of American States, debates were held with many speakers opposing the invasion of Grenada, but the United States did marshal some support from El Salvador, Guatemala, Honduras,

Costa Rica, and others. Consequently, no votes were taken and no resolutions adopted.[63]

It was clear that the organized international community, reflected in the U.N. Security Council and General Assembly, opposed the invasion as a violation of international law. It was also clear that the Reagan administration was prepared to ignore, if it could not veto, these statements of condemnation. When informed of the vote against the United States in the General Assembly, President Reagan is supposed to have said, "It didn't upset my breakfast at all."[64]

There were, however, many press reports indicating that the U.S. invasion of Grenada made its policies in Western Europe more difficult to achieve. In the fall of 1983 and shortly thereafter, the United States was engaged in a debate with many of its Western allies about strategic policy—in particular the policy of placing in Western Europe modernized intermediate-range missiles. West European criticism of U.S. policy in the Caribbean contributed to increased West European criticism of U.S. policy in Europe.[65] There was also increased Latin criticism of U.S. interventionism in the Western Hemisphere.

VI   OUTCOME FOR THE UNITED STATES

The U.S. invasion of Grenada proved a political asset at home for the Reagan administration and the president personally. The invasion, combined with an improving economy, led to high public approval ratings in various polls.[66] The invasion was mentioned repeatedly in the subsequent electoral campaign of 1984 as indicating a decisive president prepared to act abroad in the name of democracy and to protect American lives. The contrast with the Carter administration's loss of popularity through events in Iran in 1979–1980 was pronounced. The public was overwhelmingly satisfied with the outcome of the Grenada invasion, especially since there was no prospect of a long, drawn-out military engagement as in Vietnam (or Lebanon, or Nicaragua, or El Salvador).

There were also those who believed that a good signal had been sent to U.S. adversaries, especially Nicaragua and Cuba. Some believed that the Sandinistas became more interested in negotiations after the events of October 1983,[67] although in the long run there was no decisive breakthrough in the conflict between the Reagan administration and Managua. It is not known what lessons were drawn in other places, like Havana or Moscow.

The United States did have more friction with its West European allies over foreign policy questions in the short term, but in the long term the invasion of Grenada proved just a blip on the screen. The NATO allies eventually achieved a common position on the question of modernizing intermediate-range missiles; and after the rise of Gorbachev, an East-West agreement was reached on the removal of those intermediate-range weapons from Europe.

There was also some increased Latin concern about renewed U.S. gun-boat diplomacy and hegemonic interventionism in the Western Hemisphere.

Overall, from the political viewpoint of the Reagan team and its supporters, the benefits of the invasion clearly outweighed the costs—overwhelmingly so. The administration achieved its strategic, humanitarian, and political objectives quickly and without entangling involvements. It was predisposed to disregard foreign criticism, and when congressional criticism collapsed under the weight of domestic public opinion, the Reagan position easily controlled the day—thanks mainly to a politically naive student reaction to being saved from the U.S. invasion itself.[68] In this context, complicated questions about violations of international law, unlike in the case of Nicaragua, faded from public discourse quickly.

VII   OUTCOME FOR WORLD ORDER

The outcome for world order is a different matter. What proved popular in the United States and efficacious for the Reagan administration is not necessarily the same thing as a sound principle for building world order. Short-term expediency, even if accompanied by the restoration of a democratic political system, and long-term stability built on agreed standards of behavior are not the same.

U.S. traditional legal claims involving humanitarian intervention, and collective self-defense—in various forms—cannot legitimize the overall invasion of Grenada. Genuine humanitarian intervention (when separated from strategic and ideological objectives) would have arguably stood the test of close scrutiny when viewed in political context—viz., against the background of the Tehran hostage crisis of 1979–1980. U.S. structural intervention, however, clearly violated U.N. and OAS standards, not to mention the OECS treaty itself, as I have shown.

This leaves the broad claim of a right to democratic intervention, especially in situations of political instability. This claim has been put forward not only by those with a personal interest in justifying the administration they served,[69] but also by respected and more pragmatic elements in the American political elite.[70] This broad claim fails to persuade, however, not only for the reason Margaret Thatcher cited: it is a recipe for violence and international instability. The claim also fails because of an inherent double standard when applied by the Reagan administration and its ideological kin: only disliked political systems become targets of action. Marxist Grenada, Nicaragua, and Angola are

attacked in one form or another in the name of democracy. Politic
stability and violations of human rights, in comparable or greater deg
in El Salvador, Liberia, or Pakistan—or for that matter in the People's
Republic of China or the Soviet Union—are not subject to "correction"
by U.S. military force.

The international community will clearly not substitute such a dangerous double standard for the more traditional legal concepts endorsing national self-determination and national sovereignty, however problematical these concepts are to apply in the contemporary world. It is noteworthy in this regard to observe that Gorbachev has renounced the Brezhnev Doctrine asserting a special right of military intervention for the Soviet Union, and his practice to date in Soviet policy toward Eastern Europe confirms in fact that theoretical renunciation. The rest of the world, including most of the other democracies, reject special rights of intervention by the United States—or any other state, for that matter (and it can be recalled that the U.N. General Assembly repeatedly opposed both the Soviet invasion of Afghanistan and the Vietnamese invasion of Cambodia).

It is true that several U.S. presidents since 1945 (and quite a few before) engaged in forceful intervention—some of it overt and much of it covert—to try to remove distasteful governments (Eisenhower in Guatemala and Iran, Kennedy in Cuba, Johnson in the Dominican Republic). But one cannot build a just and lasting world order on a claim to unilateral military intervention that turns out to be a recipe for national dominance.[71]

At least Secretary Dam, when testifying in Congress, deemphasized claims to democratic intervention while emphasizing traditional arguments about humanitarian intervention and self-defense. An optimist might read such testimony as a wise effort by one with legal sensitivity to limit the damage done by political superiors. These traditional international legal claims, however, were ex post facto rationalizations that had little to do with the strategic and ideological objectives of the top policymakers in the Executive. U.S. policy toward Grenada in 1983 is mostly a case study in the weakness of international legal influences on those policymakers, and on the unwillingness of Congress to compensate for that weakness.

NOTES

The epigraph that opens Chapter 4 is quoted from Ronald Dellums, (D, CA), House Hearing, 1983, 10.

1. See further Gordon K. Lewis, *Grenada: The Jewel Despoiled*, Baltimore and London: The Johns Hopkins University Press, 1987; Anthony Payne, et al.,

Grenada: Revolution and Invasion, New York: St. Martin's Press, 1984; William C. Gilmore, *The Grenada Intervention: Analysis and Documentation*, London: Mansell Publishing, Ltd., 1984; Paul Seabury and Walter A. McDougall, eds., *The Grenada Papers*, San Francisco: Institute for Contemporary Studies, 1984.

2. See especially the testimony by former Ambassador Sally Shelton criticizing both the Carter and Reagan policies of trying to isolate Grenada, in "U.S. Military Actions in Grenada," *Hearings*, House Subcommittees on International Security and on Western Hemisphere Affairs, 98th Congress, 1st session, Washington: GPO, 1984, starting at 55.

3. See Kai P. Schoenhals and Richard A. Melanson, *Revolution and Intervention in Grenada: The New Jewel Movement, The United States, and the Caribbean*, Boulder, CO: Westview, 1985, 130 and passim.

4. Unimpeachable source, confirmed by remarks by Tom Adams, prime minister of Barbados, reported in the *New York Times*, October 28, 1983, 16; and by Schoenhals and Melanson, note 3, at 139.

5. Constantine C. Menges, *Inside the National Security Council: The True Story of the Making and Unmaking of Reagan's Foreign Policy*, New York: Simon and Schuster, 1989, 60–90. The U.S. ambassador to France, Evan Galbraith, a political appointee known for disregard of diplomatic tradition, said on French television that U.S. plans for an invasion had existed from October 13, which confirms Menges. See also Hugh O'Shaughnessy, *Grenada: Revolution, Invasion and Aftermath*, Bury St. Edmunds, UK: St. Edmundsbury Press, 1984, 153. The State Department later tried to contradict the ambassador's comments. See also *New York Times*, October 26, 1983, 22.

6. In addition to the sources in note 5, see also *New York Times*, October 30, 1983, 1; *New York Times*, October 28, 1983, 16.

7. *New York Times*, October 30, 1983, 1, based on interviews with government officials.

8. Menges, note 5; *New York Times*, October 30, 1983, 1; Reynold A. Burrowes, *Revolution and Rescue in Grenada*, New York: Greenwood Press, 1988, 66 and 137; Lewis, note 1, at 96; Schoenhals and Melanson, note 3, at 140–141; Franck McNeill, *War and Peace in Central America*, New York: Charles Scribner's Sons, 1988, 173–174; Paul Ramshaw and Tom Steers, eds., *Intervention on Trial: The New York War Crimes Tribunal on Central America and the Caribbean*, New York: Praeger, 1987, 115.

9. See further, among many sources, Christopher C. Joyner, "Reflections on the Lawfulness of Invasion," *American Journal of International Law*, 78, 1 (January 1984), 131–144.

10. The account is particularly trenchant in Scott Davidson, *Grenada: A Study in Politics and the Limits of International Law*, Aldershot, UK: Avebury, 1987, chps. 3, 4, and 6.

11. O'Shaughnessy, note 5, at 177.

12. *New York Times*, October 26, 1983, 20, based on interview with Charles R. Modica. Later, after he was pressured by State Department officials, he said the president's actions were justified.

13. Davidson, note 10, at 84; O'Shaughnessy, note 5, at 164–165.

14. Reported in sources too numerous to list.

15. Ibid.

16. Davidson, note 10, at 116–117.

17. See further David P. Forsythe, *Human Rights and U.S. Foreign Policy: Congress Reconsidered,* Gainesville: University Press of Florida, 1988, chp. 4. It is something of a mystery how, from the view of Washington, such heavy outside involvement can lead to "free and fair" elections, whereas the absence of that involvement in Nicaraguan elections produced a tainted procedure.

18. Davidson, note 10, at 167.

19. Ibid., at 166.

20. *New York Times,* October 16, 1983, 16.

21. The differences between U.S. and OECS claims is noted in Davidson, note 10.

22. For a political analysis sympathetic to the invasion and emphasizing the weaponry discovered in Grenada, see Nicholas Dujmovic, *The Grenada Documents: Window on Totalitarianism,* Washington: Pergamon-Brassey's, 1988. See also Richard P. Diequez, "The Grenada Intervention: Illegal in Form, Sound as Policy," *New York University Journal of International Law & Politics,* 16, 2 (Summer 1984), 1167–1204.

23. See Thomas M. Franck and Edward Weisband, *Word Politics: Verbal Strategy Among the Superpowers,* New York: Oxford University Press, 1972, comparing the Brezhnev Doctrine with U.S. claims regarding intervention in the Dominican Republic in 1965. Compare Diequez, ibid.

24. "U.S. Military Actions in Grenada," note 2, from 8; "The Situation in Grenada," *Hearing,* Senate Committee on Foreign Relations, 98th Congress, 1st session, Washington: GPO, 1983, from 3.

25. "U.S. Military Actions in Grenada," note 2, at 13.

26. "The Situation in Grenada," note 24, at 10.

27. Langhorne A. Motley, Assistant Secretary of State for Inter-American Affairs, "The Decision To Assist Grenada," *Current Policy No. 541,* Department of State, January 24, 1984, 1–4.

28. A. J. Thomas, *The Dominican Republic Crisis 1965,* Dobbs Ferry, NY: Oceana Publications, 1967.

29. See further, among many sources, Oscar Schacter, "Self-Defense and the Rule of Law," *American Journal of International Law,* 83, 2 (April 1989), 259–277; and I. I. Dore, "United States Self-Defense and the U.N. Charter," *Stanford Journal of International Law,* 24, 1 (Fall 1987), 1–19.

30. Testimony of former Ambassador Shelton, note 2. See also Schoenhals and Melanson, note 3, at 115.

31. The constitutional law of Grenada and within the British Commonwealth is reviewed in Joyner, note 9; and in Payne, note 1, at chp. 9. Many members of the British Commonwealth criticized the U.S. invasion, but no motion of censure was formally passed because some states, like New Zealand, supported the invasion and the U.K. equivocated.

32. Schoenhals and Melanson, note 3, at 146.

33. Lewis, note 1, at 96–97, based on journalists' interviews with Scoon. See also Payne, note 1, at 157; and Schoenhals and Melanson, note 3, at 146.

34. Davidson, note 10; Payne, note 1. Various reports asserted that the letters of invitation were prepared by foreign parties before the invasion and taken to Scoon for his signature. See, e.g., Payne, note 1, at 157.

35. "U.S. Military Actions in Grenada," note 2, at 26.

36. Quoted and analyzed in Davidson, note 10, at 103–107.

37. Much of Secretary Dam's testimony to both the House and Senate is a misrepresentation of the facts. For a similar defense of the administration's actions, see John Norton Moore, "Grenada and the International Double Standard," *American Journal of International Law*, 78, 1 (January 1984), 145–169. For a further distorted interpretation stressing Grenadian popular support for the invasion, which supposedly made that invasion legal under international law, see Michael J. Levitin, "The Law of Force and the Force of Law: Grenada, the Falklands, and Humanitarian Intervention," *Harvard International Law Journal*, 27, 3 (Spring 1986), 621–657.

38. Lewis, note 1, at 106.

39. See further David P. Forsythe, *Human Rights and World Politics*, Lincoln: University of Nebraska Press, 2d ed., 1989. This subject was treated by the World Court in the 1986 judgment on the merits in the Nicaraguan case. That judgment, as well as the line of reasoning developed in this book, is consistent with the analysis of the tension between peace and justice noted in Charles de Visscher, *Theory and Reality in Public International Law*, Princeton: Princeton University Press, 1968.

40. Quoted in Payne, note 1, at 171.

41. *Congressional Record*, H8580, S14610, H8643, S14753, and H8703-7, covering the period October 25–27, 1983.

42. *The Gallup Poll: Public Opinion*, Wilmington: Scholarly Resources, Inc., 1984, covering the period November 18–21, 1983. And see *New York Times*, October 29, 1983, 9; and November 6, 1983, 21. But for a careful analysis of the polls showing a public tendency to differentiate Grenada from other situations and to remain uneasy over Reagan's foreign policy, see Schoenhals and Melanson, note 3, from 153.

43. *Congressional Quarterly Almanac*, Washington: Congressional Quarterly Press, 1984; *New York Times*, November 9, 1983, 1. Interestingly, some of the members of Congress most opposed to Reagan's policies in Nicaragua finally supported the intervention in Grenada. This was true, for example, of Michael Barnes and Edward Boland.

44. "The Situation in Grenada," note 24, at 1, emphasis added.

45. Ibid., at 2.

46. Ibid., at 29–31.

47. Ibid., at 33–35.

48. "United States Policy Toward Grenada," *Hearing*, House Subcommittee on Inter-American Affairs, 97th Congress, 2d session, Washington: GPO, 1982.

49. "U.S. Military Actions in Grenada," note 2, at 7. See further Lewis, note 1, at 104–105; and O'Shaughnessy, note 5, at 219.

50. "House Resolution 383," *Hearing*, House Committee on Armed Services, 98th Congress, 2d session, Washington: GPO, 1984.

51. "U.S. Military Actions in Grenada," note 2, at 25.

52. Ibid., at 36–38.

53. Ibid., at 43.

54. Ibid., at 45–48.

55. See especially the testimony by Robert Pastor, in ibid., at 72–101.

56. Ibid., at 59–60.

57. "Visit to Grenada with Speaker's Fact-Finding Mission," *Hearing*, House Committee on Armed Services, 98th Congress, 1st session, Washington: GPO, 1984, 9–10.

58. Ibid., at 10.

59. *New York Times*, November 6, 1983, 21; Motley, note 27, at 4; testimony of Alister Hughes, a Grenadian journalist, in "U.S. Military Actions in Grenada," note 2, from 166.

60. *U.N. Chronicle*, 20, 2 (December 1983), 15–22.

61. Both Payne, note 1, and Davidson, note 10, cover the international response thoroughly.

62. Schoenhals and Melanson, note 3, at 162–163.

63. See especially Payne, note 1, and Davidson, note 10.

64. Various press reports.

65. *New York Times*, October 27, 1983, 1; Schoenhals and Melanson, note 3, at 163; Payne, note 1, at 169–171.

66. *The Gallup Poll*, note 42.

67. Menges, note 5.

68. A British officer who participated in the invasion for Barbados said eventually that the American students were not in any danger until U.S. forces invaded. According to the Associated Press, Major Mark Adkin said the invasion "was not necessary to save the lives of American medical students on the Caribbean island, as claimed by the Reagan administration, and in fact endangered them." *Lincoln Journal*, October 23, 1989, 6.

69. See the essays by Kirkpatrick, et al. in Louis Henkin, et al., *Right v. Might: International Law and the Use of Force*, New York: Council on Foreign Relations, 1989.

70. Lloyd N. Cutler, "The Right to Intervene," *Foreign Affairs*, 64, 1 (Fall 1985), 96–112. Compare V. Shiv Kumar, *U.S. Interventionism in Latin America*, New York: Advent Books, 1987.

71. See further R. J. Vincent, *Nonintervention and International Order*, Princeton: Princeton University Press, 1974.

V

Refugee Policy in the Western Hemisphere

Senator [Alan K.] Simpson [R, WY]: *I guess what I strived to set out is that this role as a country of first asylum is very unfamiliar to us.*
Attorney General [William French] Smith: *Indeed it is.*
Senator Simpson: *We kind of flunked the test on it.*

—Senate Hearings, 1981

I   SOME RELEVANT FACTS

In any given year during the 1980s there were 10 to14 million persons in the world who had fled their habitual residence because of persecution or public disorder. These persons, who fell under the good offices of the United Nations High Commissioner for Refugees (UNHCR), constituted a politically significant part of the larger phenomenon of global migration. While migrants might cross borders for social or economic reasons, refugees and those viewed as being in a refugee-like situation are defined by political realities. Refugees flee persecution (which the government in question has not prevented, even if it has not directly caused), and those in a refugee-like situation flee public disorder. Both constitute an enormous political and humanitarian problem for those states to which they flee, and for those states interested in mitigating the hardships of the situation.

Every state in the world wishes to control its own borders in order to protect national legal rights and to guarantee a certain quality of life for its nationals. No state wishes to be overwhelmed by large numbers of persons who might reduce that quality of life or change its dimensions, or upset internal political arrangements.

Table 5.1 shows the location and estimated number of people of concern to the UNHCR in 1985, according to the U.S. Committee for Refugees (a private and nonpartisan organization).[1] While these estimates may vary over time, they have remained roughly stable for several years.

International law provides a framework for dealing with refugees. The 1951 Convention on the subject, with its companion 1967 Protocol, to which a total of 102 states are parties, define a legal refugee as one

Table 5.1   Refugees and Persons in Refugee-Like Situations

Region	Estimates
Africa	3,195,600
Middle East & South Asia	5,878,500
East Asia & Pacific	560,400
Latin America & Caribbean	389,100
Europe	46,100
Total:	10,069,700

Source: World Refugee Survey, 1985 (see note 1).

who has decided to leave his or her place of habitual residence and who has crossed a national boundary because of a well-founded fear of persecution—whether political, religious, ethnic, or social.[2] Persons obtaining the legal status of refugee obtain the central right of *non-refoulement*—the right not to be returned to a situation of persecution. The generally accepted method for determing who is a refugee is through case-by-case review.

The central organization for international aid to refugees is the UNHCR. This agency was created on December 14, 1950, by a General Assembly resolution to perform the immense task of helping to protect and assist refugees and to seek "durable" solutions to their plight through resettlement, assimilation, or voluntary repatriation.[3]

The decolonization process in the late 1950s and early 1960s produced large numbers of persons fleeing political violence who, not being individualized targets of persecution, did not fall under the scope of the 1951 Convention. The 1956 Soviet invasion of Hungary and the Algerian revolt against France in 1958 both produced many migrants who resembled refugees in all but formal ways. In these and similar situations the UNHCR helped. Such UNHCR activities came to be considered part of its legitimate work, and approved by its parent, the United Nations General Assembly, as well as by state practice.[4]

The concern of the UNHCR for those fleeing "refugee-like" situations has also expanded to those persons who are internally displaced in their homelands because of political events. The first example of this expansion was the result of Secretary-General Kurt Waldheim's request to the high commissioner to coordinate assistance and provide protection for the displaced Greek inhabitants of Cyprus after the 1974 coup d'état. This kind of assistance has continued, and by the late 1980s, the UNHCR was aiding displaced persons in many African countries, as well as elsewhere.[5]

In a mass movement of persons where fear of general political unrest, individual persecution, search for economic improvement, and other incentives may be mixed on a grand scale, it has proven impossible to ascertain quickly every individual's motive. In these situations, it has become UNHCR practice to provide protection and assistance to the group. The agency makes a group determination in favor of presumptive people of concern; individual determinations of refugee status are made later, if necessary. It is important to note that only those who are granted refugee status under the Conventional definition are entitled to full international legal protection. Others aided by the UNHCR are not protected by the Convention.[6]

While the mandate of the UNHCR is to protect and assist refugees and those in a refugee-like situation, it is usually up to state authorities to make the final, legal determination of who is a genuine refugee and thus entitled to at least temporary asylum in the form of *non-refoulement*. (There are exceptions to this generalization, as some states have delegated to the UNHCR full or partial authority to make refugee determinations.) The UNHCR can persuade, lobby, involve itself in national court cases, and in other ways try to influence the national determination process. But in the last analysis it is states that are obligated under international refugee law to grant at a minimum a type of temporary asylum (non-return).[7]

More permanent grants of asylum are not regulated by international law but are given as benefits—not legal duties—by states (the wording of the Universal Declaration of Human Rights notwithstanding: Article 14, paragraph 1 of the Declaration states, "Everyone has the right to seek and to enjoy in other countries asylum from persecution." State practice confirms an individual right to seek freedom from persecution. But that same state practice confirms only a right to temporary asylum in the form of non-return).

The United States is a party to the 1967 Protocol, which incorporates the substantive terms of the 1951 Convention. The extent to which international law and UNHCR practice affect U.S. refugee policy is determined by whether the United States is the country of first asylum. The United States generally supports UNHCR determinations and practices abroad. (For instance, when the United States fashions a policy toward Vietnamese "boat people," it is likely to support refugee determinations made by the UNHCR—sometimes in contravention to determinations made by the United Kingdom [Hong Kong], Malaysia, or Singapore). The United States is a strong supporter of the work of the UNHCR globally and is the largest financial contributor to the UNHCR, providing a little over one-fifth (22 percent in 1989) of its voluntary budget.[8]

On the other hand, when the United States is the country of first asylum—i.e., the first recipient of migrants claiming refugee status—the United States is not inclined to defer to policy positions taken by the UNHCR or other states. When the United States is country of first asylum, it is legally obligated under the 1967 Protocol not to return true refugees to a situation of persecution. Since it may (and usually does) prove difficult to find another country willing to accept him or her, the United States is likely to be obligated to accept the refugee—thus the difference between U.S. support for the work of the UNHCR in dealing with Salvadorans located in Guatemala and U.S. deference to UNHCR views concerning Salvadorans located in the United States. In the latter case, the question arises of obligatory migration into the United States without numerical limit.

Many people, especially in the Western Hemisphere, wish to live in the United States. Since 1951 the United States has officially deported 20,243,143 persons who were, in the U.S. view, illegal aliens.[9] Most of these were from the Caribbean or Central America. The U.S. Immigration and Naturalization Service (INS) estimates further that for every illegal alien apprehended, two others are missed.[10] Thus the total number of those trying to enter the United States illegally was probably around 60 million over a 35-year period. Table 5.2 illustrates the number and native country of deportable aliens apprehended by the Immigration and Naturalization Service in FY 1987, 99 percent of whom were from the Western Hemisphere.

Table 5.2   Number of Deportable Aliens Apprehended
and Country of Nationality, FY 1987

All Countries	1,190,488
Europe	3,846
Poland	1,808
Other Europe	2,038
Asia	4,354
Philippines	653
Other Asia	3,701
Africa	1,455
Nigeria	661
Other Africa	794
Oceania	311
Canada, Caribbean, and Central America	1,174,464
Canada	5,256
Cuba	1,037
Dominican Republic	2,055
El Salvador	9,780
Guatemala	6,722
Haiti	536
Honduras	2,602
Jamaica	1,038
Mexico	1,139,606
Nicaragua	4,819
Other North America	1,013
South America	6,049
Colombia	3,762
Peru	681
Other South America	1,606
Other	9

Source: U.S. Department of Justice, *INS Statistical Yearbook* (see note 9).

In most cases the real locus for U.S. decisions on would-be entrants is the State Department, where political calculations often hold sway, even though its decisions are technically only recommendations. The Justice Department, through the INS, exercises formal authority for determination, but in reality usually defers to State. The would-be entrant is normally entitled to an invidual hearing before the INS.

In the United States the determination of refugee status and the determination of at least temporary asylum are rolled into one process.[11] Technically, one applies for refugee status and if that is granted, one is automatically entitled to temporary asylum. Generally, U.S. officials and reports simply speak of asylum applicants, and the successful applicant will have proven a well-founded fear of persecution. U.S. officials and reports also speak frequently of "refugees" as if these were only those persons awarded refugee status in a foreign jurisdiction, and hence only entitled to enter the United States as a country of second asylum, or a country of resettlement, at the voluntary discretion of the United States. This semantical practice does not accord technically with international law. Refugees can petition the United States as a country of either first or second asylum.

Different administrations have emphasized different means for managing the immigration of Caribbean and Central American citizens into the United States. At times the State Department has made a group determination that some nationalities are presumed to be economic migrants, whereas others are presumed to be refugees.[12] In this event individual INS hearings become meaningless formalities. Sometimes the Executive has used the parole authority to allow groups of persons to enter the United States, as if they were refugees or persons in a refugee-like situation, but without formally using the refugee label. (Congress had given the Executive parole authority—at least for individuals, if not for groups—via the Immigration and Nationality Act of 1952. The Executive used it for a group in 1956 to allow fleeing Hungarians to enter the United States. The authority was also used to permit 650,000 Cubans to enter the United States between 1959 and 1980).[13] Another U.S. substitute for formal determination of refugee status has been EVD—Extended Voluntary Departure. The Executive has sometimes used this label to provide a temporary safe haven for people of a given nationality. Such designation does not lead to permanent asylum, or a right to apply for resettlement in the United States. But EVD has been used frequently by the Executive to bypass formal determination of refugee status—and had been so used in the 1980s for Poles, Afghanistani, Ethiopians, and others.[14]

Out of this baffling array of procedures and labels employed by the United States in dealing with those seeking entry outside regular immigration (those seeking entry because of persecution or some other political reason), over the years a clear pattern of discrimination is evident: a clear pattern in which anticommunist ideology has affected refugee/asylee determinations.

U.S. refugee laws passed during the Cold War period reflected a clear emphasis on communism. The 1953 Refugee Relief Act defined a refugee as one who has been driven from his country by communist persecution, natural calamity, or military operation. This act provided over 200,000 visas for those escaping from the Soviet Union or its allies. The 1957 Refugee and Escapee Act changed the legal definition of a refugee to include those who were persecuted because of racial, political, or religious beliefs along with those fleeing communist countries and the Middle East.[15] These domestic refugee laws reflect clear emphases in U.S. foreign policy: preferences were given to anticommunists and Jews escaping Arab persecution (there was some broad concern for flight from persecution and public disorder in general). Special entry procedures such as mass parole and EVD status were used to grant exceptional entry to those fleeing communist repression—e.g., Hungarians in 1956 and Cubans after 1959.

When the United States became a party to the 1967 Protocol it was obligated to recognize a nonideological definition of a refugee, which conflicted with existing domestic law and practice. Article 3 of the 1951 Convention, which was incorporated into the Protocol, holds that the "Contracting States shall apply the provisions of this Convention to refugees without discrimination as to race, religion or country of origin." The formal change in domestic law had to wait for about a dozen years until both the Carter administration and the UNHCR lobbied Congress on the issue. The 1980 Refugee Act, initially drafted by the Carter administration and fine-tuned by the UNHCR,[16] was intended to correct discriminatory past practices and was hailed as a landmark piece of legislation, which expressed U.S. commitment to the world's refugees—and to international law.

In 1980 Congress also reasserted its legislative prerogative to set the conditions for entry by eliminating the broadened mass parole authority of the attorney general. (The attorney general retained parole authority but was restricted to individual parole for nonrefugees.) Congress distinguished between numbers of persons allowed entry as regular immigrants, and numbers of refugees resettled from foreign countries. The Executive set the ceilings on this refugee resettlement, but consultations with Congress were required, and technically Congress could raise those ceilings.

When Ronald Reagan took office in 1981, he was confronted with new U.S. legislation drawn (belatedly) from international refugee law that provided no numerical ceilings for refugees petitioning the United States as a country of first asylum. As this 1980 statute, with its openended definition of a refugee, went into effect, there was an increase in attempted immigration from the Caribbean and Central America, with many migrants claiming flight from persecution and public disorder.

II EXECUTIVE POLICY

Shortly before the new Refugee Act took legal effect on March 15, 1980, Fidel Castro opened the Port of Mariel, allowing Cubans to emigrate to the United States. The Miami Cuban community responded quickly, sending a fleet of boats to bring their friends, relatives, and other Cubans wishing to leave for the United States. This operation has been termed the "Mariel Boatlift" and it succeeded in bringing over 130,000 Cubans to Florida in a five-month period.[17] Cuban asylum applications flooded the INS, and the almost simultaneous arrival of increased numbers of Haitians further complicated what rapidly became an asylum crisis.

The Carter administration had applied a double standard to the arriving Cubans and Haitians by assuming that the Haitians were economic migrants and the Cubans were refugees; the burden of proof was placed on the Haitians to demonstrate that they were fleeing persecution, whereas no such proof was demanded of the Cubans.[18] Assistant Attorney General Charles Renfrew tried to skirt this double standard when he testified before Congress that comparing the number of Haitians excluded for admission with the number of excluded Cubans was not valid, because the Cubans were recent arrivals while the Haitian economic migration had been occurring for some time.[19] This was a non sequitur to the central issue of U.S. preferential treatment for those fleeing communism.

In addition, there was at that time a continuous influx of Central Americans as a consequence of the civil unrest in El Salvador, Nicaragua, and Guatemala; of these, Salvadoran migrants accounted for the majority. Since 1979 El Salvador had been in the midst of an internal armed conflict that had claimed some 60,000 lives and led to the internal displacement and international flight of many thousands more. Gross violations of human rights by government security forces and right-wing death squads were well documented, as were the somewhat less numerous but still important human rights abuses by left-wing guerrilla forces. The UNHCR estimated that as of 1982 some 160,000–180,000 persons had been displaced within El Salvador. Some 68,000 had fled in search of safe haven in neighboring countries and about 38,000 of these were receiving assistance from the UNHCR.[20] The State Department estimated that nearly 500,000 Salvadorans were in the United States, with many of those seeking formal asylum.

The basic refugee policy of the Reagan administration toward the Caribbean and Central America quickly became evident: to limit the number of persons allowed into the United States temporarily or perma-

nently, and to tie those admissions to Cold War preferences. (This constituted a consolidation of tendencies already evident during the Carter administration.) The Reagan administration stated formally that the number of refugees admitted to the United States would be severely limited
and that it would encourage other nations to take on a greater share of
the resettlement responsibility.[21] Further, the administration was reluctant to grant even temporary asylum, and thus afford refugee status, to
those fleeing Western Hemisphere states—with the conspicuous exception of Cubans. Haitians, Salvadorans, and Guatemalans—and even Nicaraguans through 1986—were presumed to be economic migrants.

Although the UNHCR determined that conditions in Haiti and El
Salvador in the early 1980s were such to warrant a group determination
in favor of presumptive people of concern, the administration in effect
made a group determination that the vast majority of asylum-seekers
from these two countries were economic migrants.[22]

The United States still conducted individual interviews with those
Salvadorans claiming refugee status and/or seeking asylum, but it was
INS policy to demand that these asylum applicants demonstrate a "clear
probability" of persecution, not just a well-founded fear of it.[23] Standards
of proof of probability of persecution were set exceedingly high, and in
this and other ways the INS, as advised by the State Department, found
ways to deny most Salvadoran claims. Also, the administration refused to
follow UNHCR practice and treat Salvadorans as if they were in a
refugee-like situation. Thus the United States insisted on a narrow and
rigorous test for individual persecution, while refusing to go beyond
legal requirements and institute a broader humanitarian policy.

In order to stem the movement of Haitians to the United States, the
Reagan administration began an interdiction program in 1981. The
Coast Guard, with permission from the Haitian government, was allowed
to patrol international and Haitian waters, board Haitian ships suspected
of carrying "economic migrants," and return them to Haiti. An INS official on board made determinations about refugees and economic migrants. The program was a huge success from the standpoint of limiting
numbers; the flow of Haitians to the United States practically ceased.
The administration maintained that it was only trying to curb illegal immigration.[24] The interdiction program undoubtedly served the purpose
of turning away individuals with potentially legitimate asylum claims that
the U.S. and Haitian governments would find inconvenient or embar-
rassing. If one could not physically enter U.S. legal jurisdiction, one
could not use full U.S. procedures for refugee/asylum determination,
including access to courts for a review of INS rulings.

The Reagan administration's predetermination that nearly all
Haitians attempting to enter the United States were economic migrants,
and that only communist countries produce true refugees, is evident in

administration rhetoric. Elliott Abrams, then the assistant secretary of
state for human rights and humanitarian affairs, wrote that resisting
communism is the key human rights goal because "when the government has destroyed the people's rights and freedoms and destroyed the
economy, people vote with their feet."[25] Yet, in the same text, Abrams
stated that the Haitians were not victims of persecution by the Duvalier
regime and were not "voting with their feet" (or with their boats), but
economic migrants escaping the poverty of their homeland.

The Reagan administration succeeded in tying its refugee policy to
its Cold War preferences elsewhere as well. Table 5.3 indicates the number of asylum cases, by nationality, handled during 1983–1986.[26] It is evident that the 1980 Refugee Act, derived from international law, did not
eliminate the ideological bias of U.S. refugee policy during Reagan

Table 5.3 Asylum Cases Filed with INS District Directors, Approved and Denied,
by Nationality, June 1983 to September 1986

Country	Approval Rate for Cases Decided (%)	Cases Granted	Cases Denied
Total	23.3	18,701	61,717
Iran	60.4	10,728	7,005
Romania	51.0	424	406
Czechoslovakia	45.4	99	119
Afghanistan	37.7	344	567
Poland	34.0	1,806	3,495
Hungary	31.9	137	292
Syria	30.2	114	263
Ethiopia	29.2	734	1,774
Vietnam	26.0	50	142
Uganda	25.3	75	221
China	21.4	84	307
Philippines	20.9	77	291
Somalia	15.6	74	399
Iraq	12.1	91	655
Nicaragua	14.0	2,602	15,856
Yugoslavia	11.0	31	249
Liberia	8.4	20	218
Pakistan	6.5	26	370
Cuba[a]	4.9	99	1,906
El Salvador	2.6	528	19,207
Honduras	2.5	6	234
Lebanon	2.4	34	1,338
Haiti[b]	1.8	30	1,631
Guatemala	.9	14	1,461
India	.3	1	311
Egypt	.2	3	703
Bangladesh	.0	0	403

a. There were 89,969 cases from Cuba pending at the end of FY 1986.
b. There were 2,042 cases from Haiti pending at the end of FY 1986.

Source: Immigration and Naturalization Service/U.S. Department of Justice.

years, and that discrimination on the basis of national origin continued in violation of Article 3 of 1951 Convention (applicable to the United States via the 1967 Protocol).

Other statistics show that of the 97,904 refugees and asylees from the Caribbean and Central America granted permanent resident status during 1981–1987, Cubans constituted 89,743 (or 92 percent).[27] The approval rate for Nicaraguan applicants from 1983–1986 was only 14 percent; however, it jumped to 88 percent in FY 1987.[28] When the concern for limiting the numbers of refugees clashed with traditional U.S. anticommunism, traditional Cold War preferences took precedence over limiting numbers. There was a time lag evident concerning Nicaraguans, probably for bureaucratic reasons. (Despite the fixation of top Reagan officials with the Sandinistas, the INS bureaucracy, as advised by the State Department bureaucracy, continued to deny most asylum applications from Nicaragua until the last two years of the Reagan administration. Some officials down the line of decision-making obviously failed to understand prevailing policy very easily or quickly.)

As explained above, Extended Voluntary Departure has been an important feature of U.S. immigration policy, linked to refugee policy. The Reagan administration granted continued EVD to nationals of Afghanistan and to Poles in 1981, but would not grant EVD to Salvadorans, despite the fact that use of EVD would not formally imply that the Salvadoran government, a political ally of the United States, engaged in persecution.

The 1980 Refugee Act, as already noted, eliminated the discretionary parole authority of the attorney general. Nevertheless, the parole authority was used after the act took effect to legally admit Cubans and Haitians during Mariel. The arrivals were given "special entrant" status, and could not apply for permanent resident status. In 1984, however, the Reagan Justice Department interpreted a 1966 law to mean that Cubans—but not Haitians—could apply for permanent resident status.[29]

While this chapter focuses on the Western Hemisphere, it is relevant to note that the Reagan administration was able to reduce the overall numbers of other refugees seeking entry into the United States. For those persons determined by the UNHCR or others abroad to be refugees, seeking to enter the United States as country of *second* asylum or resettlement, the Reagan administration successfully established lower ceilings, also linking those admissions to Cold War preferences. During Reagan's first year, 1981, only 159,252 refugees were admitted into the United States as a country of second asylum. The legal ceiling for the same year was 217,000. By 1986, the proposed ceiling was down to 70,000 and only 62,440 were admitted. 73.2 percent of these refugees came from Asia and the Soviet Union and involved flight from communist rule.[30]

The administration maintained throughout its tenure that it was acting in accordance with international and domestic law. Nevertheless, the success of the administration's refugee policy in accomplishing the two goals of lower numbers and preference for anticommunists undermined legal standards and humanitarian protection.

III EXECUTIVE LEGAL CLAIMS

Executive legal claims about refugee affairs have been noted in the preceding section, because one cannot analytically describe refugee policy without making reference to legal concepts and claims. The very term *refugee* is a legal term, when properly understood. To discuss different categories of persons in need of international and national protection, such as refugees, persons in a refugee-like situation, and displaced persons, as compared with economic migrants, is already to make legal distinctions.

The Reagan administration, like the Carter administration, developed legal claims with the political goal of reducing the number of lower-class, unemployed, and dark-skinned persons trying to enter the United States, and at the same time, allowing continued entry for those fleeing communism.

The Reagan administration interpreted the legal phrase "well-founded fear of persecution" to mean "a clear probability of persecution." Applicants had to produce substantial evidence to support claims of refugee status. How do people who had fled a country because of political violence to relatives prove beyond a shadow of doubt that they would be probable targets of persecution upon return? This "clear probability" standard was strictly applied to those groups the administration had predetermined to be "economic migrants."

The question of Salvadorans seeking asylum in the United States serves as a case study that illustrates Reagan legal claims pertaining to refugees. The State Department held that the majority of those who left El Salvador did so in search of better jobs or other economic opportunities, and that the migratory tradition of Salvadorans was deep-rooted and not directly related to civil strife.[31] The administration maintained that the determination of who is an "economic migrant" and who is a refugee—and therefore entitled to at least temporary asylum—rested with the United States alone. The State Department indicated no problem with the UNHCR determination that Salvadorans under the care of the UNHCR in neighboring countries were persons of legitimate concern to that agency. The United States did not try to withhold any of its voluntary contributions to the UNHCR because of its work with Salvadorans in places like Guatemala and Mexico. The United States did not, however, accept the UNHCR recommendation that the conditions prevailing in El Salvador were such that Washington should allow Salvadorans to remain in the United States as refugees or similar persons.[32] And the administra-

tion refused to use the EVD authority to grant temporary safe haven, is-
suing vague statements that did not answer the question of why the administration was so opposed to this humanitarian, if temporary, solution
to the debate over Salvadoran asylum-seekers.[33] (After all, those granted
EVD were not entitled to permanent resettlement in the United States.
When conditions changed in their home country, they could be deported.)

In the Salvadoran case, and in other cases affecting large numbers
of persons trying to enter the United States from immediately south of
U.S. borders, the Executive insisted on a narrow definition with exceedingly high standards of proof. The United States continued to support
the broad work of the UNHCR in foreign countries, but it rejected
broad conceptions of who was entitled to humanitarian protection when
that meant increased admissions into the United States.

There was also some ignoring of the law by U.S. officials during the
early 1980s. Several studies established that INS officials in particular
were ignorant of both international and national legal requirements as
they struggled to cope with ever-increasing numbers of asylum applicants. The INS was understaffed and undertrained;[34] during some periods the individual hearing for would-be entrants lasted an average six
minutes.[35] However, the main problem was not ignorance of the law by
the INS, but the political instructions about how to interpret the law
given by the State Department to the INS—and of course an underlying
problem was the willingness of the INS, and the larger Justice Department, to defer to those political instructions.

Ironically, but predictably given the Reagan administration's tunnel
vision about the East-West conflict, precisely while it was trying to use
legal conceptions and standards to exclude as many aliens as possible
from noncommunist El Salvador, the administration was preparing a
plan to handle 350,000 to 500,000 Salvadorans in the event of a Marxist
victory in El Salvador.[36]

The case study of El Salvador does not capture the entirety of the
Reagan team's legal claims about those who would enter the United
States from south of the borders. The situation in noncommunist Haiti
led to an extraordinary policy of physical interdiction—and to extraordinary legal claims, which were implausible on their face. Spokespersons
for the administration insisted it was not trying to deter genuine
refugees from Haiti, only illegal immigration. The legality of the program was defended on the grounds that when Coast Guard vessels intercepted a boat of Haitians presumed to be migrants, each individual was
correctly interviewed by an INS officer to determine asylum eligibility.[37]
During 1981–1985, however, 3,000 Haitians were intercepted and not
one was found to have a legitimate asylum claim.[38] Given the well-known
persecution in Haiti by elements loyal to the Duvalier dynasty, these
statistics belie Reagan claims to correct interpretation of the law.

The UNHCR *Handbook* was available to states to aid them in their determination proceedings. A good-faith effort to follow the *Handbook* guidelines would do much to ensure that the principle of *non-refoulement* was not breached. The UNHCR recommended that national officials (immigration officer or border police) should have clear instructions for dealing with cases that might fall under the international instruments pertaining to refugees. These national officials were to inform the asylum applicant of the procedures to be followed. The applicant should be given the services of a competent interpreter and the opportunity to contact a representative of the UNHCR. If the applicant was not recognized as a refugee, the person should also be given reasonable time to appeal.

The interdiction practice of shipboard asylum hearings deprived the asylum-seeker of counsel and appeal possibilities,[39] as well as the support of the Haitian community in the United States. None of the INS officials aboard Coast Guard ships was fluent in Creole, nor were the intercepted Haitians informed of the application procedures. In this regard the United States failed to meet the minimum procedural criteria for refugee determination as established by the international community.

It is hard to understand why it took the Reagan team until 1986 to bring its policy on Nicaraguans fleeing the Sandinistas into line with its policy on Cubans fleeing Castro. It was also strange that the Sandinistas had no death squads operating against their opponents, yet by 1987 almost 90 percent of Nicaraguan asylum applicants were proving successful. Yet in El Salvador, where death squads associated with conservative politicians had almost *carte blanche* from the government and the military, less than 3 percent of asylum applicants proved successful. But then, was it not strange that the Congress, which passed the 1980 Refugee Act, and the courts in the United States charged with correct interpretation of law, seemed to defer to executive legal claims?

IV THE DOMESTIC RESPONSE

At the start of the Reagan administration, American public opinion was skeptical of the benefits of increased immigration into the United States. A Gallup poll reported in 1981 that 57 percent of those sampled opposed entry of any more Cubans, and that 66 percent of those sampled were opposed to the United States becoming an automatic haven for those fleeing persecution. These views of the mass public remained basically constant throughout the 1980s.[40]

There were, of course, those among the American public who supported generous admission standards either in general or for particular groups. A number of American organizations, either religious or secular, harbored illegal immigrants and/or worked legally to facilitate the entry of those who appeared to be refugees or part of a refugee-like situation.[41] In the many congressional hearings on refugee policy during the period under review, there were numerous private groups lobbying the Congress to try to broaden U.S. admissions standards.[42] A number of these groups were exceedingly forthright in their criticisms of Reagan refugee policy.[43] The following is an excerpt from the American Civil Liberties Union's prepared statement to Congress in 1984, showing an attempt to use international legal standards in critiquing Reagan policies:

> It is frequently alleged that the Department of State has provided the INS with information that no individual has been returned [to his or her homeland] to subsequently suffer death or other extreme harm. This conclusion has been arrived at by way of a half-hearted investigation of an extremely small number of arbitrarily chosen cases. Clearly the likelihood of finding evidence of something depends on how carefully one is willing to look for it.
>
> While continuing to make an issue of the fate of persons returned to El Salvador, and while continuing to allege that no evidence has been found of danger to returned Salvadorans, the administration seems also to believe that a truly reliable study is infeasible. Assistant Secretary of State Elliott Abrams stated in an interview with the *Washington Monthly* (February 1984) that "Given the pressures on the embassy, all the things it has to do, it's a question of how much time they should spend on something we think is ridiculous.". . . If the administration is to continue to make an issue of the lack of proof of danger to individual Salvadorans who have been returned, it is fitting that it should reach its conclusions on the basis of sufficient investigation.[44]

Humanitarian and legal concerns aside, certain sectors of the American business community were in favor of increased access to cheap labor, and thus supportive of more immigration of all types.[45]

In larger perspective, however, throughout the Reagan administrations, American public opinion was not generally sympathetic to increased immigration into the United States. This was especially a prevalent view when directed toward dark-skinned persons without job skills, who would either be a drain on public resources or drive down blue–collar wages, even if they were Cubans and Nicaraguans.

This dominant public mood of opposition to further immigration, particularly pertaining to the immigrants from the Caribbean and Central America, found reflection in many parts of Congress. Republican Senator Alan K. Simpson of Wyoming was, for most of the Reagan era, chair of the Senate Subcommittee on Refugees, and emerged as a generally respected expert on the subject. Simpson was widely quoted when he remarked, accurately, in July 1981 that the American public was suffering from "compassion fatigue."[46] He urged the administration to promote what he termed the national interest and secure the long-term well-being of the nation's citizens and their descendents by insuring their jobs and protecting them from fear and violence.

Simpson was repeatedly troubled by the lack of a numerical ceiling on those who could be labeled as refugees when petitioning the United States as a country of first asylum. As he said openly in 1981: "I am trying to see if we could not shift numbers and not describe people as refugees if, in effect, we could describe them as some other category or as legal immigrants subject to numerical restrictions."[47]

At the same time that Simpson and others were fearful of large numbers of Haitians and Hispanics entering the United States as refugees, he and a number of his congressional colleagues had no illusions about the nature of the U.S. decision-making process in these questions. Simpson indicated, in the quote that opened this chapter, that the United States had not done well in meeting legal standards applicable to it when a country of first asylum. He also had no difficulty in pinpointing the problem: "I think sometimes that the theories and the objectives of the State Department and the diplomatic pressures make it very difficult to make decisions in that [refugee] area."[48] Others in Congress also had doubts about State Department determinations that emphasized economic motivation. Representative Romano Mazzoli (D, KY), a key player in the House on refugee affairs and one of the authors of the central Simpson-Mazzoli bill, urged the Department of Justice and the INS to stand up to State Department pressures.[49] And Representative Sam Gejdenson (D, CT) said at one point: "You know, you think about somebody who grew up in a small village in El Salvador or Guatemala, or wherever, and for that individual to make it the thousands of miles into this country shows more than just a simple desire to make more money per hour."[50]

Simpson asked the State Department formally at one point: "Hasn't the [refugee] figure for the Western Hemisphere been unrealistically low, given the large numbers of asylees coming to the U.S.?"[51]

Thus while numerous members of Congress were unhappy about the political nature of executive decisions on refugees and asylees during the Reagan period, they were also unhappy about the entry of these same persons without numerical ceilings. Even when the subject was the entry of Cubans fleeing communism, a number of members of Congress thought the United States was asking for trouble. Concerning the Mariel Boatlift, Senator Arlen Specter (R, PA) asked of a State Department official: "Are there any plans in existence, or any advance thinking, to avoid the type of situation that developed recently with the Cuban refugees? They certainly have posed an enormous problem in this country."[52]

These cross-cutting concerns—criticism of how the Executive made decisions on refugees and asylees, and fear of large numbers of persons with the legal right to enter the United States from south of the border—played themselves out in numerous congressional hearings, debates, and votes during the 1980s. Members of the Black Caucus, for example, took an interest in Haitians and tried to alter the interdiction program.[53]

The following 1984 exchange between Congressman Hamilton Fish (R, NY) and Elliott Abrams, then assistant secretary of state for inter-American affairs, reflected persistent congressional concern about the fate of Salvadorans:

> Mr. Fish: My question to you, Elliott, is do you believe there is any basis for concern that an American precedent of forcibly returning Salvadorans may be used by other countries to forcibly return persons that we consider to be refugees?
>
> Mr. Abrams: I would think not. I understand the danger. We believe we are meeting our treaty obligations and the obligations of American law by looking at every case individually to determine which individuals are in fact refugees, and allowing them to stay in the United States. We also have to acknowledge that we have perhaps a half million Salvadorans living here. No organized effort is under way, nor is anybody in Congress really suggesting one, to round up and deport those people. So if the countries of Central America were going to be following our practice, the fact is that they would be housing a very large number of Salvadorans and making no particular effort to deport them.
>
> Mr. Fish: You don't see that we could find this being used against us in our efforts in refugee work, not just today, but efforts that might occur in the future? Could I ask you if you could explain any differences that there may be in the approach of the State Department and the approach of the UNHCR to the problem of undocumented Salvadoran nationals in the United States?
>
> Mr. Abrams: The UNHCR has used the phrase, I think, of presumptive refugees [*sic.* This is incorrect.], if I remember it correctly, to describe people coming from El Salvador. There is no such term in American law nor would we be in favor of one. Our refugee and asylum laws call for the inspection of each case on its own merits . . . and it just does not stand to reason that everybody coming from El Salvador should be presumed to be a refugee. Furthermore, we have now had the chance . . . to look at thousands and thousands of Salvadoran cases and we have determined by doing so that the vast majority of those who are coming . . . are not refugees. We have looked at the cases, we have read the applications, we have interviewed the people—"we" meaning the Department of State and/or the Department of Justice Immigration Service—and they are not refugees. So I would say that to the extent that is the position of the UNH—I always get confused with the Human Rights Commission—HCR that we disagree.[54]

Senator Edward Kennedy (D, MA), who resumed the chair of the Senate Subcommittee on Refugees once the Democrats regained control of the Senate in 1987, took the opportunity to interject international law into the Salvadoran refugee debate when he submitted an internal UNHCR memo for the Congressional Record on February 11, 1982. The internal UNHCR study recommended that "the UNHCR should continue to express its concern to the United States Government that its apparent failure to grant asylum to any significant number of Salvadorans, coupled with continuing large-scale forcible and voluntary return to El Salvador, would appear to represent a negation of its responsibilities assumed upon its adherence to the Protocol."[55]

Senator Kennedy also sought to direct attention to the Executive's treatment of Salvadorans when he pursued the subject of what happened to those deported back to El Salvador. He questioned H. Eugene Douglas, U.S. coordinator for Refugee Affairs, Department of State:

> Senator Kennedy: Can you give us the kind of information you have requested of the American Embassy in San Salvador? Can you provide the Committee copies of documents, for example, that have been sent from the Department to our Ambassador asking for some follow up on this information?
>
> Ambassador Douglas: I have not always been directly involved in that. It is a State Department and Humanitarian Affairs Function, sir, the asylum area. But I will relay that request to Secretary Abrams.
>
> Senator Kennedy: Well, you must know about it. Have there been cables or have there been requests of the Embassy to follow up and, if so, when?
>
> Ambassador Douglas: Senator, I am not that directly involved in the asylum processing.
>
> Senator Kennedy: Well then, how can you come here and tell us that it is the policy of the administration to follow up—to find out what is happening to them—and come up here and indicate by your response that there does not appear to be much of a problem, unless you know from your own information or at least somebody on the panel knows what has actually been requested? If that has been done, I would like to know about it and I want to know with what degree of specificity you have followed up.
>
> Ambassador Douglas: Senator, I stand by the broad brush of what I said.
>
> Senator Kennedy: The what?
>
> Ambassador Douglas: The broad brush of the information that I have relayed.
>
> Senator Kennedy: I do not understand what broad brush of information means? Have you made specific requests that those individuals that are being sent back to El Salvador, the 500 to 1000 a month, that there is going to be some kind of an assessment about what has happened to them? Has the administration done that? Yes or no?
>
> Ambassador Douglas: I cannot answer yes or no on that.[56]

Despite such vague and defensive testimony by executive officials, the Congress as a whole was too divided to pass any forceful or meaningful refugee legislation during the period under review. At least the Democrat-controlled House of Representatives reached consensus on the fate of Salvadorans, which sent a political signal to the administration—had it wanted to listen to growing congressional concern. In 1981 the House unanimously passed Resolution 126, as a sense of Congress and therefore nonbinding resolution, recommending that the Attorney General grant EVD to Salvadorans. In 1983 Congressmen Joe Moakley (D, MA) and Edward Boland (D, MA) collected 86 signatures on a "Dear Colleague" letter to the Secretary of State again requesting that EVD be granted to Salvadorans. The House later passed two more such resolutions directed to the same end, each time attached to the State Department's Reauthorization Act and the Immigration Reform and Control Act.[57]

In 1987 Congress as a whole almost forced the administration to alter policy on both Salvadorans and Nicaraguans. On July 28, 1987, the House passed H Res 618, which required the government to grant Salvadorans and Nicaraguans in the United States EVD status. The bill passed by a vote of 237–181, with 33 Republicans voting for it and 140 voting against it. The Democratic vote was 204–41. The voting was thus generally along party lines, with Democratic and Republican defections coming from the southern and northeastern states, respectively.[58] The Senate Judiciary Committee approved a similar measure (S Res 332), but it never reached the floor for full Senate consideration and subsequently died. Hence the Reagan administration did not budge from its position that the conditions in El Salvador, or Nicaragua for that matter, did not warrant a blanket protection from deportation.[59] (By 1987, however, the Reagan administration had started approving almost 90 percent of asylum applications from Nicaragua.)

Though the Congress was too divided to effectively challenge executive refugee policy, the Judiciary was able to make a slight dent in that policy. One of the first successful legal challenges had come with the 1979 decision in *Haitian Refugee Center v. Civiletti*.[60] The plaintiffs demonstrated that the government intended to discriminate against Haitians irrespective of the credibility of the claims to flight from persecution. They showed to the satisfaction of the court that conditions in Haiti were such as to generate refugees, as defined by international law. Federal District Judge James Lawrence King enjoined the INS from holding any further deportation proceedings for those Haitians who had applied and been denied political asylum before May 1979. The Haitians were not to be deported until they were given a fair chance to present their asylum claims. Judge King went so far as to refute the government's position that all Haitians were economic migrants. In his view Haiti's poverty was a result of Duvalier's effort to maintain power; Haiti's economic condition was thus a political condition.

The decision in *Haitian Refugee Center v. Civiletti* was significant because of its substantive contribution to the debate over the distinction between economic migrants and political refugees. The kleptocracy of both François and Jean-Claude Duvalier deprived the citizens of Haiti of livelihood, education, welfare, and the protection of law, and those who spoke out against either regime were persecuted. The decision also reflected the influence of international law on the court before its domestic twin, the 1980 Refugee Act, was passed. Judge King made it clear that the discriminatory procedures of the INS would not be practiced in his district.[61] The Carter administration (and later the Reagan administration) responded by moving Haitians out of the jurisdiction of Judge King to Puerto Rico and other places away from legal counsel.[62]

The Haitian Refugee Center, Inc. is one of many public interest groups that have sought relief from administrative practices in the U.S. court system; its activities have made significant progress in securing the rights of Haitian refugees. In *Haitian Refugee Center v. Gracey*,[63] however, the effort to halt the interdiction program was unsuccessful. In this case, the plaintiffs challenged the interdiction program by alleging that it violated the obligation of *non-refoulement*. The case was dismissed on the grounds that the plaintiffs lacked standing to sue, but the district court also ruled that the United States was not bound to observe *non-refoulement* on the high seas. Although it was the intent of Congress to implement the Protocol, the court ruled that the Refugee Act does not provide any rights to aliens outside the United States.[64]

It sometimes appeared, however, that Haitians in the United States were to receive protection from the courts. *Louis v. Nelson* (which began under the case name *Marie Lucie Jean v. Nelson* and later *Louis v. Meissner)* was a class action suit to stop the deportation of Haitians who were victims of an illegal mass exclusion process. As part of the Haitian Program, 30 Haitians at a time were ordered deported while their lawyers were locked outside.[65] In this historic decision the court found that the federal government discriminated against Haitians seeking asylum in the United States. This was the first decision in American legal history where the federal government was found to discriminate in a nonemployment context.[66] The court also found that the Constitution protected excludable aliens in detention, and aliens seeking asylum had to be given notice of the right to claim asylum and allowed access to the social and legal resources.[67] This ruling had positive implications not only for aliens but for organizations such as the National Emergency Civil Liberties Committee, the National Council of Churches, the American Immigration Lawyers' Committee, the ACLU, and other groups that might wish to enter detention facilities and inform the incarcerated aliens of their rights.[68] In 1984, however, the Eleventh Circuit Court of Appeals reconsidered its decision and found that the government could discriminate on the basis of nationality, as excludable aliens did not have the protection of the Constitution.[69]

A similar decision handed down in *Nunez v. Bolden*[70] has yet to be overturned. While the decision did not have the far-reaching implications of the first *Nelson* decision, it did grant injunctive relief, requiring aliens to be informed of material procedural rights. The court reasoned that failure to give notice of the right to apply for asylum was a failure of due process to aliens in compliance with the protected interest they possess as provided in the Protocol.[71] This court decision not only had an impact on executive policy, but also showed the influence of international law in the decision-making process of the court.

In *Orantes-Hernandez v. Smith*,[72] the Central District Court of California issued an injunction against voluntary departure agreements. The court found that the INS actively sought to deport Salvadorans by misleading and coercing them into signing voluntary departure agreements. The court noted that, because of the existing condition in El Salvador, the plaintiffs would face irreparable harm if they were returned. The INS had "shown a specific pattern of conduct, akin to an explicit policy" of coercing Salvadorans to agree to depart. The court further reasoned that aliens must be given notice of their right to apply for political asylum lest the INS "effectively frustrate the intent behind the Refugee Act. . ."[73]

The above cases represent the legal process by which an alien has been afforded certain rights—especially, the right to be informed about and to apply for asylum. Grants of asylum, however, are given at the discretion of the attorney general. Sections 243(h) and 208(a) of the Immigration and Nationality Act provide two forms of relief to an otherwise deportable alien. Section 243(h), the statutory provision for mandatory withholding of deportation, requires the attorney general to halt the deportation of an alien if the alien can show that his life or freedom would be threatened upon return. In *INS v. Stevic*,[74] the Supreme Court held that the statutory provision for mandatory withholding of deportation required the alien to show that he was more likely than not to be persecuted upon his return. The "clear probability" test as practiced by the Executive was, in the court's view, totally consistent with congressional intent in the Refugee Act and its obligations under the 1967 Protocol. The court reasoned that Section 243(h) corresponded with Article 33.1 (*non-refoulement*) of the Convention Relating to the Status of Refugees. Article 33.1, however, does not extend the right of *non-refoulement* to everyone who meets the definition of a refugee. Rather it requires that an applicant demonstrate that he is indeed a refugee and to show that his life or freedom would be threatened if he were returned.[75]

In *INS v. Cardoza-Fonseca*,[76] the U.S. Supreme Court held that the "clear probability" test was *not* consistent with congressional intent in Section 208(a) or the Protocol. Section 208 provides for the broader relief of asylum. In order to be considered for asylum the refugee should have a "well-founded fear" of persecution, not a "clear probability" of persecution. It was the administration's contention, which the court rejected, that the standard applied in Section 248(h) also governed asylum applications. The court recognized that a "well-founded fear" refers to a subjective state of mind, not to an objective situation of persecution. Justice Stevens concluded:

> Our analysis of the plain language of the Act, its symmetry with the United Nations Protocol, and its legislative history, lead inexorably to the conclusion that to show a "well-founded fear of persecution," an alien need not prove that it is more likely than not that he or she will be persecuted in his or her home country. . . . In enacting the Refugee Act of 1980 Congress intended that it should give to the United States sufficient flexibility to respond to situations involving political or religious dissidents and detainees throughout the world. Our holding today increases that flexibility by rejecting the Government's contention that the Attorney General may not even consider granting asylum to one who fails to satisfy the strict Section 243(h) standard. Whether or not a "refugee" is eventually granted asylum is a matter which Congress has left for the Attorney General to decide. But it is clear that Congress did not intend to restrict eligibility for that relief to those who could prove that it is more likely than not that they will be persecuted if deported.[77]

This rather impressive list of cases indicates that since refugee policy is a blend of international and domestic law, U.S. courts will not necessarily defer to the Executive and its conduct of foreign policy but will assert themselves into the policy process. But there are limits to what each court case can achieve in broad terms, particularly if the Executive tries to continue with its initial policy orientation. The Judiciary can issue injunctions and restraining orders; it can define and clarify congressional intent. But unless the Executive chooses to act in good faith under the relevant laws, the judgments of the courts have only a slow and limited impact on policy.

V FOREIGN RESPONSES

The international response to the Reagan administration's refugee policy was muted, first of all, by the fact that many Western democracies were implementing restrictive policies of their own. On May 12, 1987, the Carriers Liability Act was passed by the British Parliament. Air carriers were to be fined £1,000 (about $2,000) for every passenger brought to the United Kingdom without the proper immigration documents. Other developed democracies adopted similar legislation to deter undocumented aliens. It was also apparent that other Western nations were dramatically dropping their acceptance rate of refugees. As the high commissioner himself stated, "All the organizations that deal with refugees, national or international, are aware that procedures to determine who is and who is not a refugee are now being used to accept as few as possible and not to determine who needs protection and who does not."[78] Thus most U.S. allies, historically the locus of safe haven for many refugees, were also implementing tighter border controls and were hence unlikely to criticize similar U.S. policies.

Second, then-adversaries of the United States, such as the Soviet Union and its allies, did not criticize the United States for its determinations about would-be immigrants because of their own sensitivity on emigration and refugee affairs. European communists, with the exception of Yugoslavia, were not parties to international refugee law during the period under review, and did not want to address the subject of international rights for those fleeing persecution. (Hungary became the second East European state to adhere to the 1967 Protocol, in 1988, but by then the overall situation in Eastern Europe and the Soviet Union had begun to change radically on refugee and other human rights matters.) During the Reagan period, most European communists, by their refusal to support the international network for refugee protection, deprived themselves of any opportunity to spotlight dubious U.S. policies. Other communist states, notably China and Vietnam, had their own expediential interests for not putting pressure on the United States.

Third, the UNHCR normally proceeded in a nonconfrontational manner vis-à-vis states, and this was certainly true of its relations with the United States. Moreover, as noted, the UNHCR receives over one-fifth of its budget from the United States and thus was confronted with the problem of being dependent on U.S. dollars—and U.S. diplomatic support in other refugee situations around the world—at the same time that it clearly differed with the United States over treatment of Salvadorans and Haitians, and probably other nationals as well.

Some observers found the UNHCR lacking in the vigor with which it might have pressed the United States about its refugee policy in the Western Hemisphere.[79] If this were true when the Dane Paoul Hartling headed the UNHCR, it might have been even more true when the Swiss J.-P. Hocke, became high commissioner. Hocke was elected with the strong backing of the United States,[80] and as he came under attack from various sources in the late 1980s for mismanagement of the organization,[81] he might have found himself even more dependent on the United States. (Hocke resigned under pressure in the fall of 1989.)

It should also be said, however, that the UNHCR clearly submitted legal briefs that were at odds with the Executive's position on deportation standards in general in the *Stevic* and *Fonseca* cases. And it is widely known that the UNHCR used its Washington office to stay in touch with private and congressional elements in favor of more generous admissions standards.

There does not appear to be any evidence that the United Nations General Assembly sought to pressure the United States to change its refugee policy on these hemispheric issues, nor does there seem to be any evidence that would suggest that the Organization of American States, through the Inter-American Commission on Human Rights, was active on these questions.

VI OUTCOME FOR THE UNITED STATES

There is no doubt that the "kindness" of the United States toward refugees has become highly "calculated," and that the "gate" of the United States has become closely "guarded."[82] This has always been true to some extent. At no time has U.S. openness to refugees been unbounded, and during several eras it has fallen far short of being generous.

What made the Reagan period remarkable was the starkness of its policies when contrasted with the 1980 Refugee Act. Given that nonideological definition of a refugee drawn directly from international law, the Reagan team could only pursue its policies of lower numbers of refugees and asylees from south of the border, and preference for those fleeing communism, by obfuscation and mendacity. These policies certainly tarnished the image of the United States as having a law-abiding (and truthful) government committed to offering at least temporary safe haven to those fleeing persecution.

Nevertheless, the Reagan administration did succeed in reducing the number of unemployed entrants from the Caribbean and Central America who were claiming flight from persecution, and this goal was broadly supported by both dominant public opinion and a majority in Congress. Furthermore, that mass public opinion and the congressional majority would have probably also deferred to further restrictions on Cubans and Nicaraguans, had not the ideology of the Reagan team permitted those two glaring loopholes in an otherwise highly restrictive hemispheric refugee policy.

In a costs–benefits analysis, probably the costs of a tarnished image were willingly paid, not only by the Reagan team but by many others in American society and the Congress, in order to achieve the benefits of fewer Haitian and Hispanic immigrants. Only the courts in the United States, stimulated by domestic and foreign legal circles, sought to uphold the full integrity of both domestic and international law. While this legal and juridical effort was not without its victories, it was not broad and fast enough to completely control widespread violations of law by the INS as advised by the State Department. Thus the Reagan team achieved its short-term objectives, but at considerable cost to the tradition of legal obedience (and truthful government). There were broader costs as well.

VII   OUTCOME FOR WORLD ORDER

While states profess their support for international (and domestic) law in general terms, there arise situations in which those same states are tempted by short-term expediential interests to violate the law. U.S. refugee policy in the Western Hemisphere is a classic study of this phenomenon—this conflict between general interest in order and humane values, and specific interest in protecting particular advantage. The Reagan administration, like Carter's, fell victim to this trap.

The Reagan administration's misinterpretation, in many individual cases, of its legal obligations to make a good-faith effort of determination of well-founded fear of persecution, and its refusal to bypass legalistic hairsplitting by using EVD for Salvadorans and others, does not bode well for attention to refugees either in the Western Hemisphere or around the world. It is likely that the U.S. posture, while lecturing other governments about their duties in responding to refugee flight, will be undercut by the memory of U.S. actions in the 1980s, when it was a highly sought-after country of first asylum by Haitians and Hispanics. If the United States finds expediential reasons to bypass its clear legal obligations, and uses those same reasons to avoid humane policies going beyond legal obligations, how can the United States, as a major actor in global refugee affairs, effectively pressure other states to provide an inconvenient and expensive safe haven? (Precisely this situation obtained in 1989 when the United Kingdom began a program of forced return of Vietnamese to their homeland from Hong Kong. The United States protested publicly and otherwise, and at least one British official remarked on American television that what the British were doing was no different from what the United States had done to Salvadorans. In his view, the British were only returning economic migrants who, since they were not refugees, had no legal right to remain in Hong Kong. It was clear that public opinion in Hong Kong supported the return program.)

There is no doubt that the plight of refugees everywhere, not to mention those persons in a refugee-like situation, has become more precarious since the United States, along with the other major and traditional safe havens, has retrenched in admissions policies. It is somewhat reassuring that the United States continues to be active in refugee affairs in places like Southeast Asia and the Horn of Africa. It is true that one continually has to draw a distinction between a country sought for first asylum and otherwise, for the legal obligations are different in the two situations. Thus the United States remains generally supportive of humanitarian protection and assistance for refugees beyond U.S. jurisdiction. Yet the refugee policies of the Reagan administration, and the inability of the Congress to bring those policies into line with legal commitments and humanitarian practices, bodes ill for the future of those fleeing persecution and public disorder.

NOTES

The dialogue between Senator Alan K. Simpson and Attorney General William French Smith that opens Chapter 5 is quoted from the Senate Hearings, 1981, 18.

1. U.S. Committee for Refugees, *World Refugee Survey*, 1985, Washington: American Council for Nationalities, 1986, 36.

2. For two excellent legal treatments, see Guy S. Goodwin-Gill, *The Refugee in International Law*, Oxford: Clarendon Press, 1983; and Atle Grahl-Madsen, *The Status of Refugees in International Law*, Leyden: Sijthoff, 1972.

3. *UNHCR: A Mandate to Protect and Assist Refugees*, New York: United Nations, 1972, 32.

4. For one overview, see David P. Forsythe, "The Political Economy of U.N. Refugee Programs," in Forsythe, ed., *The United Nations in the World Political Economy*, London: Macmillan, 1989, chp. 8.

5. For another overview, see Leon Gordenker, *Refugees in International Politics*, London: Croom Helm, Ltd., 1987.

6. See further Elizabeth G. Ferris, ed., *Refugees and World Politics*, New York: Praeger, 1985, chps. 1, 3, 5; and Mary M. Kritz, ed., *U.S. Immigration and Refugee Policy*, Lexington, MA: Lexington Books for D. C. Heath, 1983.

7. For an excellent survey of U.S. and other national decision-making processes with regard to refugees, see C. L. Avery, "Refugee Status Decision-making: The Systems of 20 Countries," *Stanford Journal of International Law*, 19, 2 (Summer 1983), 235–256.

8. See Forsythe, note 4.

9. Table 5.2 is drawn from Department of Justice, *INS Statistical Yearbook 1987*, Washington: GPO, 1988, 107.

10. Quoted in Barry Levine, *The Caribbean Exodus*, New York: Praeger, 1987, 10.

11. For an incisive treatment, see Arthur C. Helton, "The Refugee Act's Unfulfilled Asylum Promise," *World Refugee Survey, 1985*, Washington: American Council for Nationalities, 1986, 5ff.

12. The point is made in Norman and Naomi Zucker, *The Guarded Gate: The Reality of American Refugee Policy*, New York: Harcourt Brace Jovanovich, 1987.

13. Ibid., at 54–55.

14. See Goodwin-Gill, note 2.

15. Zucker, note 12, at 32.

16. David Martin, "The Refugee Act of 1980: Its Past and Future," *1982 Michigan Yearbook of International Legal Studies*, New York: Clark Boardman, Ltd., 1982, 91–123.

17. See further Gilbert Loescher and John A. Scanlan, *Calculated Kindness: Refugees and America's Half-Open Door, 1945 to the Present*, New York: Free Press, 1986, 170–187.

18. "Caribbean Refugee Crisis: Cubans and Haitians," *Hearings*, Senate Judiciary Committee, 96th Congress, 2d session, May 1980, Washington: GPO, 1980, 16.

19. Ibid., at 20.

20. See testimony of Undersecretary of State Walter Stoessel in "Annual Refugee Consultation for 1982," Senate Judiciary Committee, 97th Congress, 1st session, September 1981, Washington: GPO, 1982, 81.

21. Department of State, "International Security and Development Program," *Special Report 116*, Washington: GPO, April 1984, 9.

22. See various administration statements in "United States as a Country of Mass First Asylum," *Hearing*, Senate Judiciary Committee, Subcommittee on Immigration, 97th Congress, 1st session, July 1981, Washington: GPO, 1982, as at 27.

23. For clarification of this point, see *INS v. Stevic*, 467 U.S. 407.

24. "Annual Refugee Consultation," note 20.

25. Elliott Abrams, "Human Rights and the Refugee Crisis," *Current Policy No. 401*, Department of State, Washington: GPO, 1982, 1–3.

26. Reproduced from "Temporary Safe Haven for Salvadorans," *Hearing*, Senate Judiciary Committee, Subcommittee on Immigration, 100th Congress, 1st session, June 1987, Washington: GPO, 1988, 163.

27. *INS Statistical Yearbook*, note 9, at 63.

28. "Temporary Safe Haven," note 26, at 208.

29. Zucker, note 12, at 68.

30. Ibid., at 88.

31. "Annual Refugee Consultation," note 21, at 481.

32. Ibid., at 83.

33. See, e.g., letter from Attorney General William French Smith in "Temporary Suspension of Deportation," *Hearings*, House Subcommittee on Immigration, Refugees, and International Law, 98th Congress, 2d session, Washington: GPO, 1984, 84.

34. Avery, note 7; and Milton D. Morris, *Immigration—The Beleaguered Bureaucracy*, Washington: Brookings, 1985.

35. This was Senator Alan Simpson's estimate, in "Annual Refugee Consultation," note 20, at 19.

36. "Reauthorization of the Refugee Act," *Hearings*, Senate Subcommittee on Immigration and Refugee Policy, 98th Congress, 1st session, Washington: GPO, 1984, 53.

37. Stoessel, note 20, at 81.

38. Loescher and Scanlan, note 17, at 194.

39. Ibid.

40. *The Gallup Poll Public Opinion 1980*, Wilmington: Scholarly Resources, Inc., 120–121; *New York Times*, June 23, 1986, and July 1, 1986.

41. See, e.g., Renny Golden and Michael McConnell, *Sanctuary: The New Underground Railroad*, Maryknoll, NY: Orbis Books, 1986.

42. See, e.g., "Annual Refugee Consultation," note 20.

43. See, e.g., The Watch Committees, "—In the Face of Cruelty," *The Reagan Administration's Human Rights Record in 1984*, New York: The Watch Committees, 1985.

44. "Temporary Suspension of Deportation," note 33, at 130.

45. Vernon M. Briggs, *Immigration Policy and the Labor Force*, Baltimore: The Johns Hopkins University Press, 1984.

46. David P. Forsythe, *Human Rights and U.S. Foreign Policy: Congress Reconsidered*, Gainesville: University Press of Florida, 1988, 72.

47. "Annual Refugee Consultation," note 20, at 20–21.

48. Ibid., at 23.

49. Quoted in Forsythe, note 46, at 72.

50. "Temporary Suspension of Deportation," note 33, at 57.

51. "Annual Refugee Consultation," note 20, at 57.

52. Ibid., at 40.

53. Forsythe, note 46, at 69.

54. "Temporary Suspension of Deportation," note 33, at 57.

55. Ibid., at 140.

56. "Reauthorization," note 36, at 73.

57. See discussion of legislative history by the Refugee Policy Group in "Temporary Safe Haven," note 26, at 249.

58. *Congressional Quarterly Almanac 1987*, vol. 43, Washington: Congressional Quarterly Press, 1988, 85 (H).

59. "Temporary Suspension of Deportation," note 33, at 84.

60. *Haitian Refugee Center v. Civiletti*, 503 F. Supp. 442 (S.D. Fla. 1980).

61. *Haitian Refugee Center v. Civiletti*, Final Order Granting Relief, July 2, 1980, 162.

62. Zucker, note 12, at 98.

63. *Haitian Refugee Center v. Gracey*, 809 F.2d 794 (D.C. Cir. 1987).

64. See further Abigail King, "Interdiction: The United States Continuing Violation of International Law," *Boston University Law Review*, 68, 4 (July 1988), 773–781.

65. Zucker, note 12, at 200.

66. Ira Kurzban, "Long and Perilous Journey," *Human Rights*, 11, 2 (Summer 1983), 42.

67. Ibid.

68. Ibid.

69. Zucker, note 12, at 204.

70. *Nunez v. Bolden*, 537 F. Supp 578 (S.D. Tex. 1982).

71. King, note 64, at 777.

72. *Orantes-Hernandez v. Smith*, 541 F. Supp. 351 (C.D. Cal. 1982).

73. See further Diane Archer, "Immigration Law: Injunction Against Voluntary Departure Agreements," *Harvard International Law Journal*, 23, 2 (Winter 1983), 418.

74. *INS v. Stevic*, note 23.

75. Ibid.

76. *INS v. Cardoza-Fonseca*, 480 U.S. 421, at 440.

77. Ibid.

78. *New York Times*, March 27, 1989, 6.

79. See, e.g., Loescher and Scanlan, note 17, at 193–196.

80. Forsythe, note 4, at 139.

81. *New York Times*, October 5, 1989, 5.

82. The phrases are from Zucker, note 12, and Loescher and Scanlan, note 17.

VI

Financial Assessments to the United Nations

Mr. Fascell [D, FL] said American "frustration and anger at the U.N. is real" and comes at a time when the Congressional mood of budget stringency is strong. To argue that Congress is honor-bound to observe "treaty obligations," he predicted, would "go nowhere."—New York Times, June 27, 1986

I SOME RELEVANT FACTS

Financing the United Nations system entails a very complicated budgetary process, though the United Nations Charter lays out apparently simple and clear legal obligations for that financing. According to Article 17: "The General Assembly shall consider and approve the budget of the Organization. The expenses of the Organization shall be borne by the Members as apportioned by the General Assembly. . . ." Article 17 is buttressed by Article 19: "A Member of the United Nations which is in arrears in the payment of its financial contributions to the Organization shall have no vote in the General Assembly if the amount of its arrears equals or exceeds the amount of the contributions due from it for the preceding two full years. . . ." Thus the General Assembly approves a scale of assessments to finance its budget, and member-states are, presumably, legally obligated to meet those assessments. The penalty for noncompliance is loss of vote in the Assembly when a state falls two years behind in its payments. However, implementing these Charter provisions has not been simple. Indeed, the law and politics of financial assessments has become as complex as the budgetary process itself.

The Charter provisions on financing pertain only to assessments voted for the U.N. narrowly defined—viz., covering the operations of the principal organs. There are other assessments for certain parts of the U.N. broadly defined—viz., for the Food and Agricultural Organization (FAO), the International Labour Organisation (ILO), the United Nations Educational, Scientific, and Cultural Organization (UNESCO), and the World Health Organization (WHO). There are a few U.N. programs financed by special assessments, such as certain peacekeeping operations established by the Security Council. All other U.N. activities are financed by voluntary, not assessed, contributions. Voluntary contributions are much larger than assessed contributions.

U.N. assessments are based on the principle of the ability to pay, modified by a per capita or some other adjustment negotiated between a state and the General Assembly. The U.S. share of the assessed budget has been negotiated at different levels at different times, but always the U.S. share has been *below* its ability to pay as measured by relative gross national product. The United States started out paying almost 40 percent of the U.N. regular budget, negotiated this down to about 33 percent in 1954, then down to 25 percent in 1972—where it has remained to the time of writing. Hence when the United States thought it was paying too much, even when it should have been paying more, based on strictly economic criteria, it was able to negotiate a change that was formally approved by the Assembly. U.S. desire to reduce payments involves financial savings, but it also shrinks a basis for potential influence within the U.N. system.

This scale of assessment translates into outlays of money by the U.S. government that are definitely small relative to U.S. spending in general. Midway through the 1980s, the U.N. regular budget was about $700 million per annum, which meant the United States was presumably obligated to pay in the neighborhood of $200 million. It is interesting to compare the U.N. per annum budget of about $700–800 million in the 1980s with some facts of American spending. In 1979, Americans spent $3.2 billion for cat and dog food. The U.N. regular budget usually amounts to less than the budget of the New York City police department; in 1989 it amounted to less than half of one Stealth bomber. In 1988 the U.N. regular budget equaled .00005 percent of the U.S. GNP; this means that each American paid $0.88. (In 1987 only 29 percent of U.S. monies to the U.N. were regular assessments, 67 percent were voluntary contributions, 4 percent went for peacekeeping. Each American paid about $4.10 of the total spending of the U.N. system, which was at about $5.5 billion for 1987, excluding the World Bank and International Monetary Fund. Each Norwegian paid $39, each Swede $32, each Dane $27.10.) Furthermore, U.S. assessments were partially offset by the fact that New York City received several hundred million dollars each year from the operations of the U.N. headquarters there (estimates were in the range of $500–700 million), and more than 70 percent of all U.N. purchases worldwide went to American firms.[1]

Nevertheless, U.N. finances became an increasingly large political subject in Washington (and New York) in the 1980s. U.S. officials cited the 273 percent increase in the U.N. budget between 1972 and 1982 as one cause of alarm (inflation had increased 115 percent during the same time). They also became disgruntled that 107 members of the U.N.

were paying about 2 percent of the assessments, while the 15 major donors were paying about 85 percent. The First World of industrialized democracies was paying about 75 percent, the Second World of industrialized communist states was paying 14 percent, and the Third World of nonindustrialized states was paying 10 percent.[2] Moreover, different circles of opinion in Washington took exception to various U.N. programs, such as those benefiting Cuba, the Palestine Liberation Organization (PLO), the Southwest Africa People's Organization (SWAPO), the Law of the Sea (LOS) Preparatory Committee, Secretariat salaries, a new conference center in Ethiopia, and so on. There was a great deal of anti-American rhetoric, and some U.S. allies, such as Israel, were treated harshly. The argument was made that the U.N. budgetary process was out of control. It was said that the majority in the General Assembly, which paid very little to the U.N., voted all sorts of programs that did not make political or financial sense, then required the United States and other major donors to pay despite their objections. Congress in particular, which was used to controlling the U.S. purse strings, did not like the idea that it was obligated to authorize and appropriate monies for projects over which it had no direct say.

Events in the 1960s had complicated matters considerably. The General Assembly, using the controversial procedure known as the Uniting for Peace resolution, had taken over a peacekeeping operation in the Belgian Congo from the Security Council.[3] The Soviet Union and its allies objected, as did France, on the legal grounds that the Assembly was acting ultra vires—viz., out of bounds or beyond the rules. The Soviets may have been primarily concerned they were losing the politics of the field operation, since their client politicians were being squeezed out of power in the Congo, but they made the legal argument—joined by France—that only the Council could authorize peacekeeping. The controversy was deepened when the General Assembly, supported by an advisory opinion from the International Court of Justice, insisted that the expenses for ONUC (United Nations Operation in the Congo), as approved by the Assembly, were regular expenses of the Organization that all states were obligated to pay.

The U.S.S.R. and its allies and France withheld from their assessed payments that portion which would have gone to ONUC peacekeeping; in 1964 the General Assembly avoided all votes in order to bypass the question of whether Article 19 should be invoked (which would have deprived two members of the Council of their vote in the Assembly); and the United Nations as a whole was on the verge of financial and political chaos. At that point the United States backed away from its support of the ICJ advisory opinion and support for an authoritative Assembly, believing that it was preferable to continue with a weakened U.N. rather than a U.N. without two great powers. It is also possible, but not proven, that U.S. decision-makers began to look to the future and decided that an authoritative Assembly, even one congenial to U.S. policy on the Congo, was not in the long-term U.S. interest.

In shifting its policy, the United States issued what became known as the Goldberg Doctrine, named after Arthur Goldberg, then the U.S. ambassador to the U.N. It was a "me too" doctrine, which said in effect that if the Soviets and French were not obligated to pay for what the Assembly voted, then the United States reserved the right of nonpayment. According to Goldberg: "If any Member can insist on making an exception to the principle of collective financial responsibility with respect to certain activities of the organization, the United States reserves the same option to make exceptions if, in our view, strong and compelling reasons exist for doing so."[4] "Strong and compelling reasons" constituted a vague and broad exception to the principle of majority rule and collective financial responsibility. It was neither narrowed nor clarified when Ambassador Goldberg wrote Ambassador Jeane Kirkpatrick in the early 1980s that his 1965 language meant U.S. exemption for "national purpose."[5]

Hence by the 1980s, the precise obligation to pay what the General Assembly assessed under Articles 17 and 19 was open to debate—at least in some circles of Washington opinion. Certain rules of international law had been altered over time through the practice of states. The League of Nations had changed voting arrangements in the Council from that stated in the Covenant; the European Community had changed voting arrangements from that stated in its constituent document; even the Uniting for Peace resolution came to be widely accepted as a de facto change in the U.N. Charter. Was it therefore correct to say that Articles 17 and 19 had been altered by state practice?

The factual situation at the start of the 1990s seemed as follows: About 30 states were delinquent in meeting their assessments for various reasons. Article 19 had been automatically applied by the Secretariat to several states when they became more than two years in arrears. (The Secretariat simply turned off the electronic voting mechanism at the offending state's place in the Assembly. The only state receiving press attention for losing its right to participate in the Assembly, and hence its vote there, was the Republic of South Africa. That denial stemmed from loss of accreditation because of its policy of apartheid.[6]

In the late 1960s and early 1970s Congress began to withhold U.S. contributions to certain U.N. programs funded by voluntary contributions. For example, Congress voted to withhold certain monies from the U.N. Special Fund, later called the U.N. Development Program, for activities in Cuba. This was disliked in New York, but the American head of the UNDP made special, informal, and partially bogus bookkeeping arrangements in order to satisfy Congress. The Congress also voted withholding from the U.N. Relief and Works Agency for Palestine Refugees

(UNRWA) until certain reforms were carried out. The overall U.S.-U.N. relationship was not called into question by these withholdings, especially since they pertained to voluntary contributions.

Then in the mid-1970s Congress began to withhold from assessed contributions. It withheld part of the U.S. assessment from UNESCO until certain changes were made at the Paris headquarters; the funds were released just before the United States fell two years behind in its payments. In 1978 Senator Jesse Helms (R, NC) led a successful congressional effort to withhold from the regular U.N. budget monies under the technical assistance program. The Carter administration opposed this withholding but carried out the terms of the law after passage by Congress. Carter's legal adviser in the State Department issued an opinion that such withholding from assessed contributions was illegal,[7] and a staff report by the House Committee on Foreign Affairs concluded the same thing.[8] Congress had proceeded politically, on the basis of disliked programs or disliked actors, with scant attention to international law. In effect Congress had apparently implemented the Goldberg Doctrine: Congress, speaking for the United States, would withhold from U.N. assessed payments on grounds of challenge to particular programs, just as the Soviets and the French had done. But the Congress made no argument that the U.N. had acted beyond its proper bounds or by illegal procedures.

All of this set the stage for the Reagan administration and U.S. policy toward the U.N. in the 1980s. During the Reagan era decisions were taken in Washington that led to the United States having the largest arrearages in assessed contributions to the U.N.: over $600 million. Soviet unpaid assessments had never gone beyond $260 million, and ironically the Soviets under Mikhail Gorbachev were paying off their arrearages and renewing commitments to the U.N. just as the United States was emerging as the chief debtor to the Organization. There was a financial crisis, which was really a political crisis, in New York: a shortfall of funds so grave that daily operations had to be curtailed. The U.N. was on the edge of real bankruptcy, as it had been in the early and mid-1960s. In Washington during the 1980s there was a "crisis of multilateralism" in which the very membership of the United States in the U.N. and other international organizations was debated seriously for the first time since 1945. International law was entangled in all of this.

II EXECUTIVE POLICY

From one point of view, it was the Congress that initiated policy on U.N. financing, and the Executive that reacted: Congress initiated withholding from both voluntary and assessed contributions, forcing the Executive to take further steps that it otherwise would not have taken. This view sees the subject of U.N. financing as an aberration—a foreign policy subject on which Congress seized a leadership role within the United States. This view is not totally false. But from another point of view, the Executive was still the primary actor: Congressional withholding of U.N. funds was itself mostly a reaction to executive leadership—at least during the Reagan era. This second view also is persuasive. In both views, executive and congressional steps were intertwined, constituting an action-reaction cycle difficult to disentangle.

The Reagan administration, at its outset, was the most unilateralist, nationalistic, and ideological of any presidential team since at least 1945, if not before. The Reagan team entered office believing that the United States was a "city on a hill," a living moral lesson for the rest of the world about how to conduct public affairs.[9] Since the United States embodied political morality it had little need for international organizations that acted on the basis of compromise, not to mention majority votes, and what might be called a decent respect for world opinion. Particularly in those organizations the United States did not dominate and in which compromises were necessary, the Reagan team initially displayed considerable negativism. But even those international institutions in which U.S. influence was considerable, such as the Organization of American States, were largely ignored. The World Bank and International Monetary Fund, where U.S. influence and a commitment to capitalism were evident, were attacked by Reagan officials for promoting socialism or regulating markets excessively.[10]

It followed that the Reagan administration did not mind being the only state delegation to vote against WHO regulations recommending humanitarian restrictions on the marketing of infant formula (especially by the Nestlé corporation) in the developing countries. The Reagan team argued unfair regulation of markets (this was too much for the Congress, as both houses condemned this Reagan policy by large voting margins). It followed that the Reagan administration did not mind sabotaging the U.N. Law of the Sea Conference, refusing to negotiate on the extensive draft treaty it inherited from previous administrations, both Republican and Democratic. Particularly the provisions creating extensive regulation of the Deep Seabed Area, where mining of mineral nodules was foreseen, proved unacceptable in principle to the administration's laissez-faire ideology. It followed that the first Reagan administration should eschew U.N. peacekeeping in Lebanon, preferring a loosely coordinated Western force, the U.S. contingent of which was removed after almost 250 fatalities and the failure to secure its objectives. It followed that Reagan should withdraw U.S. membership from UNESCO in 1984, *after* proposals to restrict freedom of the press had been defeated, *after* attacks on Israel had been reduced with the help of UNESCO's director-general, *after* a start had been made on administrative and budgetary reform—as if Reagan were simply trying to find an international organization he could depart with fanfare (and against the recommendation of the United States Commission for UNESCO).

And it followed that Reagan would appoint Jeane Kirkpatrick as ambassador to the United Nations. She had written about the need for the unilateral assertion of U.S. power in the U.N. to counteract the tyranny of the communist and Third World majority, and to assert the principles of freedom the United States represented.[11] While others before her, such as Ambassador Daniel Patrick Moynihan in the Nixon administration, had made similar agruments,[12] none had done so with the evident visceral animosity toward the organization that Kirkpatrick and other Reagan officials displayed. In a much-publicized incident in the summer of 1983, one of Kirkpatrick's lieutenants in the U.S. mission to the U.N. suggested publicly that it would not be a terrible idea for the U.N. to leave New York, and the president seemed to endorse that point of view in one of his remarks to the press.[13]

The Reagan administration represented a reversal of historic roles. Since the presidency of Woodrow Wilson, the president had been associated with internationalism, cosmopolitanism, and multilateralism. U.S. presidents had fought for daily involvement in world affairs, for membership in international organizations, for a blending of American and international values. The Congress had been associated with parochialism, nationalism, nativism, and isolationism. It was the Senate that blocked membership in the League of Nations, the Congress that passed the neutrality laws to block FDR's activist foreign policy, the Congress that demanded rapid military demobilization after 1945, the Congress that led the largely irrational witch hunts for communists linked to the U.S.S.R. during the McCarthy purges of the 1950s. But particularly the first Reagan administration was associated quite accurately with ultra-nationalism rather than multilateralism.[14]

It is not surprising, then, that Reagan became the first president to engage in U.S. withholding from U.N. assessments without congressional mandate. While Congress had already initiated the practice, as noted above, Reagan took the initiative in 1982 to withhold on the basis that the cost of the Law of the Sea Preparatory Committee was not a regular expense of the U.N. Since the United States had not become a party to the LOS treaty, and did not intend to under Reagan, the United States withheld an amount equal to 25 percent of the budgeted costs for that meeting. Reagan officials argued that such costs should be borne by parties to the treaty.[15] (It can be noted in passing that some of the expenses of the U.N. Office of the High Commissioner for Refugees were covered by the U.N. regular budget through assessments, although in the 1980s some 50 states were not parties to the 1951 and 1967 treaties on refugees. While the Soviet Union, for example, protested against the

UNHCR's costs being partially covered by the regular budget, since the U.S.S.R. was not a party to the refugee treaties, it never withheld any of its assessed dues on that basis.) The Reagan administration also withheld some funds in protest against "add-ons"—viz., those U.N. costs added on by the General Assembly after the regular budget had been approved.

This executive withholding, combined with the repeated verbal attacks on the U.N. by Reagan officials, seemed to unleash a floodgate of congressional policies affecting U.S. participation in the U.N. They are mentioned in this section because they are inseparable from subsequent executive policy.

In the early 1980s Congress withheld small parts of assessments in order not to benefit the PLO or SWAPO. Then in 1983 Congress mandated (via the so-called Kassebaum amendment) that regardless of General Assembly assessments in the future, U.S. payments would be pegged to 1980 funding levels. Two years later Congress went further in legislating (via the Kassebaum-Solomon amendment) that unless the United Nations moved to a system of weighted voting in the Assembly, under which votes would be linked to payments, U.S. assessments would be limited to 20 percent, not 25 percent. Also in 1985, Congress voted (via the Sundquist amendment) a further limitation on U.S. assessed payments because of concern with Soviet financial and personnel policy toward its nationals in the Secretariat. (Congress was concerned about the practice whereby Soviets in the Secretariat were put on short-term contract only, spied for the U.S.S.R., and were required by Moscow to turn over a portion of their U.N. salary to the U.S.S.R.) As if all these limitations were not enough, in 1986 Congress voted (via the Gramm-Rudman-Hollings Act) a unilateral reduction of 4.3 percent in assessed payments, additional to the other reductions, on the basis of the U.S. deficit in federal spending.[16]

This spate of congressional action, taken in the context of executive attacks on the U.N. and indeed on the very idea of multilateral diplomacy, went beyond what the Reagan administration desired. Though the Reagan team had in effect encouraged Congress to mandate unilateral changes rather than seek negotiated changes, in its second term, the administration found itself defending the U.N. in principle, and many U.N. programs in particular, and urged Congress to meet assessments as voted by the General Assembly. From 1983 on, Reagan officials testified many times in Congress that the United States should not withdraw from the U.N., and particularly that general, across-the-board reductions (as found in the Kassebaum amendment and under Gramm-Rudman-Hollings) were not a good idea. Testifying to this effect were U.N. Ambassadors Kirkpatrick and Vernon Walters, and the various officials who held the position of assistant secretary of state for international organization affairs.[17] (While the Reagan administration was clear in its opposition to general withholdings, its position on specific withholdings, as found in the PLO/SWAPO and Sundquist amendments, was a different matter.)

In summary, the Reagan administration, starting with general and ideological attacks on the U.N. and related international organizations, moved over time to their defense. (This shift was especially marked toward the World Bank and IMF.) In his last budgetary message to Congress, Reagan sought full funding for currently assessed U.N. payments and submitted a plan for the paying of arrearages over half a decade. The second Reagan administration, having seen the problems it had unleashed in Congress through its U.N. bashing, basically sought U.N. reform through legal steps. Reform required a bonafide effort to pay the regular and valid expenses of the organization as approved by the General Assembly. (Expenses that were ultra vires might be another matter.) If good-faith payment of valid expenses were not achieved, the United States would not have the moral or financial leverage to bring about the reforms it desired.[18]

III EXECUTIVE LEGAL CLAIMS

The Reagan administration was reasonably clear in developing a legal argument on central aspects of U.N. financial assessments. Unlike some legal scholars, who argued that Article 17 had withered away through disregard, the Reagan team thought Article 17 still valid; it therefore recognized a legal obligation to pay assessments as voted by the General Assembly. Reagan officials, particularly Ambassador Kirkpatrick, argued also that selective and specific withholdings, in response to ultra vires action by the U.N., were legal. However, not all implications of these arguments were addressed.

On several occasions executive officials stated the United States was obligated to pay assessments for programs approved by the Assembly. These statements were unqualified. In 1983, when the Kassebaum amendment proposing a unilateral limitation on U.S. assessed payments linked to then-current spending levels was introduced, the acting secretary of state sent a letter to Congress saying, in part: "The administration opposes this amendment because it would place the United States in breach of its international obligations in a manner that would jeopardize United States voting rights in the affected international organization."[19] This view endorsed Articles 17 and 19 as still-binding law. On other occasions executive statements were equally categorical. In 1986 the State Department answered some congressional questions by a note that read, in part: "We do not advocate a minimum U.S. contribution to the U.N.; according to the current Scale of Assessments, the United States is assessed 25 percent of the U.N. regular budget."[20] The clear implication was that the United States should meet the 25 percent standard. In that same year Ambassador Walters said to Congress:

> The record of U.S. compliance with its treaty commitments has been excellent over the long haul of history. Our position as a leading party of the rule of law in international affairs relies in no small measure on this record.
>
> Now, with these measures [congressional statutes], the prospect is for the withholding by the United States of a very sizable amount, sizable even in the context of the large [*sic.*] U.N. budget. This inevitably would raise the question of whether the nonpayment of substantial amount could constitute a material breach of the U.S. obligation under article 17 of the U.N. Charter to pay our duly assessed share of the U.N. budget. This is an issue of which we must be aware.[21]

And in 1988, after several congressional statutes (plus the Executive's own withholding) made it impossible for the administration to meet the 25 percent standard (U.S. payments at that time equalled about 15 percent), Assistant Secretary of State Richard Williamson said, "It is of course, unfortunate that we cannot fund in full all of the organizations that we believe are serving us well, particularly considering the treaty obligations that attend our membership in each of them."[22] One of the reasons for this stand was that Washington could not demand payment of U.N. assessments by others if it did not accept the validity of assessments on itself.

The Reagan administration, by its own withholding over the issues of the LOS Preparatory Committee and budgetary add-ons, obviously believed that selective withholding in response to ultra vires action by the U.N. was legal. The State Department, through its legal office, never addressed this issue in extended fashion—which was a curious omission. But Ambassador Kirkpatrick did so in Senate and House hearings. She said in 1985:

> I believe that it is not only legally permissible but appropriate, frankly, for the United States to withhold contributions to our assessed budget in those cases, that the programs are not mandated by the charter or consistent with the Charter of the United Nations. . . .[23]
>
> I think that it is appropriate for us to withhold contributions from the United Nations when the purposes for which they are being spent are not consistent with the goals of the charter. Those assessed funds are, after all, assessed in relationship to some specific goals, and those goals are stated in the charter, and if programs are proposed that are

themselves inconsistent with the charter and with American values, I think it is appropriate for the United States under those circumstances to withhold.[24]

Kirkpatrick, in a move unusual for an executive official—most of the time, the last thing executive officials want is for Congress to take the lead on foreign policy questions—urged Congress to take the lead in reviewing U.N. programs and in exercising the claimed right of specific withholding.

One reading of Kirkpatrick's basic argument is that the Goldberg Doctrine, which speaks of "strong and compelling" national reasons for withholding assessments, should be understood to mean withholding for ultra vires action. But even if this interpretation is accepted some confusion remains: Even if one believes that Secretariat salaries are too high, it is by no means self-evident that excessively high salaries are incompatible with the Charter. Overpaid civil servants may still be working for the valid goals of international peace and security or economic development. Withholding in opposition to Secretariat salaries or the number of Secretariat positions may not be rationally justified by reference to ultra vires action. Likewise, it is by no means clear that U.N. programs that benefit the PLO and SWAPO are outside the bounds of legitimate activity as defined by the Charter. Neither the Charter nor any other part of international law provides a clear distinction between a terrorist group and a legitimate movement for self-determination using armed struggle. What is to prevent any state from erroneously charging ultra vires action when it dislikes a program on political grounds? And what if many states behaved this way; would not the U.N. be financially paralyzed, as was nearly the case in both the mid-1960s and mid-1980s?

What is clear is that all Reagan officials, including intense critics of the U.N. like Kirkpatrick, took the position that general U.S. nonpayment of assessed dues, unrelated to specific programs and agencies, was a violation of international law. The Kassebaum amendment of 1983, which put a general lid on U.S. assessments, and action under the Gramm-Rudman-Hollings Act to deal with the U.S. deficit both fell into this category. It was not clear what the administration finally thought of the Kassebaum-Solomon amendment, requiring weighted voting or a 5 percent cut in assessed payments. In politico-legal terms, administrative officials said it was unrealistic, which it was, since it would require a formal amendment to the Charter whereby most states in the General Assembly would have to give up considerable voting rights. (The Executive opposed Charter amendments because the U.S. veto in the Council would be called into question once a formal amending process got under way.) At the same time, executive officials said the amendment might prove useful in stimulating budgetary and administrative reform at the U.N.[25]

IV   THE DOMESTIC RESPONSE

It was certainly ironic that at the start of the 1980s Congress should have still on the books a statute urging the Executive to pressure members of the United Nations that had failed to pay their assessed dues within the two years mentioned in Charter Article 19. Using the foreign assistance program, as it frequently does, Congress had passed soft law—viz., law written in loose language that would never be adjudicated in court— that read as follows:

> In any decision to provide or continue to provide any program of assistance to any country under the Foreign Assistance Act of 1961, as amended, there shall be taken into account the status of the country with respect to its dues, assessments, and other obligations to the United Nations; and where such country is delinquent with respect to any such obligations for the purposes of the first sentence of Article 19 of the United Nations Charter, the President shall furnish the Committee on Foreign Relations of the Senate and the Speaker of the House of Representatives a report setting forth the assurance given by the government of the country concerned of paying all of its arrearages and of placing its payments of such obligations on a current basis, or a full explanation of the unusual or exceptional circumstances which render it economically incapable of giving such assurance.[26]

Congress, from this role of urging U.S. unilateral pressure on states to meet their legal obligations for U.N. financial assessments—a role that endorsed the binding nature of Articles 17 and 19—assumed by the mid-1980s the role of the largest debtor to the U.N. The outline of this development has already been given, and we have seen how congressional action started with withholding for specific changes within voluntary contributions, then encompassed specific withholding from assessed contributions, and also involved general limitations and reductions from those assessments.

In these actions the very large bipartisan congressional majority paid scant attention to international legal obligations. (The vote in the Senate for the first Kassebaum amendment, imposing a general and severe limitation on U.S. required payments, was 66–23.) A minority was concerned with U.S. treaty obligations, but the overwhelming majority acted on the basis of pure politics. This majority disliked a number of policies associated with the U.N., and it was tired of funding them. These policies included treatment of Israel, attempts to reduce freedom of the press in UNESCO, calls for a new international economic order, use of U.N. facilities for communist spying, Soviet violation of the political neutrality of the Secretariat, anti-American rhetoric, waste, mismanagement, bureaucratic confusion, granting of observer status to "terrorist" groups, and double standards in human rights programs.

Representative of majority sentiment was the statement by Dante Fascell (D, FL), chair of the House Foreign Affairs Committee—and by no means the most parochial member of Congress: "'Frustration and anger at the U.N. is real' and comes at a time when the Congressional mood of budget stringency is strong. To argue that Congress is honor-bound to observe 'treaty commitments' would 'go nowhere.'"[27] International legal obligations were conveniently brushed aside by Senator Nancy Kassebaum (R, KS) who pretended at one point they did not exist:

> There is nothing new about the concern expressed by my [1983] amendment nor do I believe that the amendment itself is a new or radical proposal to solve this perennial [assessment] problem. If enacted into law, this amendment would simply assert the right of the Congress to determine spending from the U.S. Treasury. This is the constitutional right of the Congress. It is also our duty.[28]

For Senator John Glenn (D, OH), agreeing with Ambassador Kirkpatrick, the issue was not whether to withhold from assessments but how to write that withholding legislation in the tightest way possible.[29] For Representative Daniel A. Mica (D, FL), the issue was not treaty obligations but whether changes were going to occur at the U.N.:

> Let me get on the record as clearly as I can that I am absolutely convinced there should be no mixed message to the United Nations. I don't care who is chairman of this committee. The Congress will balk. The Congress will say "no deal" if the United Nations reneges [on changes]. That needs to be a clear message there. I can name Member after Member who is standing out there waiting to say "If you don't follow through, we don't follow through."[30]

Or, in other words, no U.N. reform, no congressional full assessment. It was a matter of a straight political bargain. International law did not figure in at all.

A minority in Congress, throughout the debates in the 1980s, did mention the issue of treaty obligations. In 1983 Representative Don Bonker (D, WA) said:

> Senator Helms introduced an amendment several years ago to forgo our contributions if that money through U.N. agencies was to be used for technical assistance. It really put us in a state of difficulty until we could come back the following year with corrective action. It was deemed at that time imprudent and seriously jeopardized our treaty obligations payments to the United Nations. . .[31]
> . . . for a government and nation that stands on the notion that the law ought to be observed, I do not think this [the Kassebaum amendment] is a responsible action our part. . . .[32]

In the same debate, Representative Jim Leach (R, IA) said: "The question, however, remains: What are our obligations under international law? . . . [The Kassebaum amendment] isn't the way . . . our treaty obligations at this moment are written."[33] And in 1988 Representative Gus Yatron opened yet another round of hearings on contributions to the U.N. with the same point about "treaty obligations."[34] Representative Leach had already argued vigorously back in 1983:

> To this Goldberg reservation, we have appended today the Kirk-patrick corollary, which declares the desirability of national legislatures actively attempting to pick and choose among U.N. functions and to penalize those institutions and programs which have strayed from their legitimate purposes and tasks.
>
> This have-your-cake-and-eat-it-too diplomacy is analogous to tax-payers unilaterally reserving the right unto themselves to selectively decide where their tax payments should be utilized.
>
> The Kirkpatrick corollary is a prescription for global anarchy and is an irresponsibility of the highest order. . . .[35]

But the bipartisan majority in Congress did not want to hear about treaty obligations. Minority commentary was disregarded, just as the congressional majority disregarded executive testimony opposing general limitations and reductions. Congress as an institution was primarily interested in using its purse strings to save money and affect change at the U.N. Article 17 just didn't matter. This was not a matter of fine-tuning the Goldberg Doctrine; this was a matter of political pressure through the U.N. pocketbook.

Neither public opinion nor judicial opinion appeared to play a direct role in executive-congressional interactions. Public opinion, as measured in polls of the mass public, was in favor of U.S. membership in the U.N. but critical of U.N. job performance. One poll in 1985 showed that when asked, "Would the world be better off without the U.N.?" 78 percent of an American sample answered no. This compared to "no" responses from 69 percent of the British, 56 percent of the French and also the Germans, and 45 percent of the Japanese. When asked, "How is the U.N. doing in solving the problems it has had to face?" 40 percent of the Americans said poorly or very poorly. This compared to 48 percent of Japanese, but 25 percent of the French, 27 percent of the Germans, and 37 percent of the British.[36]

One way to interpret these data is that the Americans retained a commitment to the potential of the U.N.; if the United States sought to pull out of the U.N., such a decision would trigger into opposition considerable latent support for the organization. (The Reagan decision to pull out of UNESCO in 1984 did not trigger significant opposition, since important parts of the American public, chiefly journalists and Jewish voters, had been alienated by attempted restrictions on press freedoms and on Israel.) At a minimum, it was clear there was no American mass public demand for withdrawal from the U.N. in the 1980s. This was probably a background condition of indirect significance.

Public opinion in the form of interest group activity was divided. For example, the United Nations Association, represented primarily by former cabinet member Elliott Richardson, generally argued in favor of the validity of Article 17 and the obligation to meet assessments, inter alia.[37] That organization held a series of meetings in Washington, involving both citizen members and governmental decision-makers, to try to lobby for greater attention to the Charter and greater support for U.N. programs.[38] The eventual position of a committee of the American Society of International Law was similar—that is, supportive of the traditional understanding of Charter obligations and critical of any U.S. policy that refused to pay assessments on political grounds. But the Heritage Foundation, with reportedly good contacts among conservative policy-makers, argued for getting out of the U.N.[39] None of this interest group activity seemed to have a major or decisive effect on policies adopted.

U.S. courts were not involved in any decisions on U.N. financing.

V FOREIGN RESPONSES

Foreign reaction to U.S. policy on financial assessments to the U.N. was more important politically than legally.

Legally, the secretary-general and his legal office argued the expected position that Articles 17 and 19 remained valid law. The U.N. legal counsel, Carl-August Fleischhauer, circulated a lengthy statement arguing against both general failure to meet assessments as voted by the General Assembly and specific withholdings designed to coerce changes in U.N. policies. Other Secretariat officials circulated U.N. documents showing that the organization, with the knowledge of the General Assembly, had applied Charter norms against those states who had fallen two years behind in assessed payments; these officials argued this proved the continuing validity of both Articles 17 and 19. Some documents showed that in a given year the names of some states were not called out during a roll call vote in the General Assembly because they were more than two years behind in their payments. Such information, along with the fact already noted that voting was electronically blocked for states with two-year arrearages, clearly indicated a little-known application of Article 19. Other documents made clear that from the point of view of the secretary-general and Secretariat, there had been no legal change in the validity of Articles 17 and 19.[40] While these views might have been noted by officials in the State Department, there is no evidence they had any effect on congressional opinion. Apparently none of this U.N. information was ever referred to in public by executive officials.

Slightly more important was the fact that the European Community democracies sent a common communique to Washington in 1986 stating:

> The Twelve wish to express their concern that recently enacted U.S. legislation, in particular the Gramm-Rudman-Hollings act and the Kassebaum [-Solomon] amendment, is significantly affecting the administration's ability to comply with its international treaty obligations. The implementation of such legislation will result in the United States not fully meeting its financial obligation to the United Nations as contained in Article 17, paragraph 2, of the Charter. . . . Selective adherence to the principle 'pacta sunt servanda' [treaties must be obeyed] erodes the very foundation of the international order. In this respect financial obligations are no different from any other international obligations.[41]

Many of the signatories of this note were also demanding reform of the U.N., but they did not agree that specific or general withholding from assessed contributions was a legal means to the desired end. No other industrialized democracy had ever withheld from assessed payments or otherwise failed to meet those payments, except for France on the issue of peacekeeping. There is not much evidence that anyone in Washington paid much attention to this common West European position.

Politically, at the United Nations there was some movement toward reform, and this allowed the administration to argue to Congress that it should pay full assessments as the U.S. part of the bargain. (Absent that movement in the late 1980s, congressional departures from Article 17 would have been greater and more persistent than they were.)

The General Assembly, responding to leadership from Secretary-General Perez de Cueller, approved the appointment of a Group of Experts ("the Group of 18") to recommend changes in U.N. administration and finances, then approved virtually all of the report of that group in December 1986. Subsequently there was movement toward: establishing the U.N. budget through informal consensus before the formal Assembly vote (this gave the United States and every other state a veto in the process), establishing a total budgetary ceiling, establishing a ceiling for "add-on" costs after the budget was approved, establishing program priorities, reducing the number of Secretariat positions, holding budgetary expansion close to zero in real terms, and putting at least 50 percent of a state's nationals loaned to the Secretariat on long-term rather than short-term contracts (to enhance their neutrality).[42]

It was only on the basis of this movement, incomplete though it was, that the Reagan administration was able to persuade Congress, for example, to accept that the informal consensus procedure met the *intent* of the Kassebaum-Solomon amendment on weighted voting. Hence after

1987, the administration did not have to withhold part of U.S. assessed payments pending the adoption of a formal Charter amendment to that effect.[43] Also, it was on the basis of these changes in New York that the Reagan team was able to certify that there was significant reform involving the U.N. Secretariat, thus allowing the 1988 release of certain funds withheld under congressional instruction.[44]

While it cannot be said that even the second Reagan administration was enthusiastic about recommending funding for international organizations,[45] at least that administration recognized that if the United States continued to fail to pay its U.N. assessments by a wide margin, many states at the United Nations would have reduced incentive to make changes that were disagreeable from their point of view. While changes in New York were essential for changes in Washington, changes in Washington were essential for changes in New York. It is in this sense that foreign responses to U.S. policy on assessments were crucial to executive attempts to close the gap between assessments and payments in practical terms. By 1988 Reagan officials were under attack in Congress for being too quick to certify reform and release sequestered funds.[46]

The Reagan team never really stressed Article 17 and treaty obligations vis-à-vis Congress, and after 1986 it only mentioned them in passing. (This may have reflected political realism, given several congressional statutes that ignored Article 17 entirely.) But the Reagan team did, in its last years in office, try to meet as much of the assessed payment as Congress would allow. Its own specific withholdings were small, although important as a matter of legal principle. The administration's policy shift was a direct response to reform efforts by the U.N. secretary-general and states at the U.N.

VI   OUTCOME FOR THE UNITED STATES

It is undeniable that the contemporary push for reform of U.N. administration and finances came after the United States, through congressional action, started withholding, limiting, or reducing assessments that made up a vital part of the U.N. operating budget. Major impediments in U.S. assessed payments took effect in the 1984 fiscal year and continued until the time of writing. In December 1986 the General Assembly approved the start of the substantive reforms. At that time the U.N. showed a cash shortfall of over $100 million out of a budget slightly over $800 million. There were essentially no reserves. This situation created a significant incentive for the U.N. to pay serious attention to the demands of its largest donor, especially since no other state stepped forward to make up the slack created by U.S. arrears (and it can be fairly noted that U.S. policy magnified the chronic if lesser arrearages by other states). Not even Soviet payments on past and current accounts rectified the shortfall. Thus U.S. policy on financial assessments to the U.N., created out of a chaotic tug of war between the Executive and Congress, did achieve a primary objective: increased efforts at U.N. reform.

There were in addition several negative outcomes from this U.S. policy—all of which were probably regarded as minor by most decision-makers in Washington. First, there was some friction with the Common Market allies, who disagreed with the means chosen to a common end, and who thus—once again—questioned whether the U.S. was undermining the basic principles of the international legal order. Second, administration rhetoric and policy, especially in the early 1980s, encouraged the more nativistic elements in Congress and the public, who wanted either to leave the U.N. entirely or elevate domestic financial savings over reform of a sometimes useful United Nations. This inadvertent encouragement was not wise, since it subsequently made a constructive and rational policy more difficult to achieve. And third, from 1983, the administration lost control of U.S. foreign policy on this subject; there was no consistent and carefully considered rationale underlying U.S. official decisions. Rather, congressional majorities did things like pass the Kassebaum amendment while pretending that the U.N. Charter did not exist, or pass the Kassebaum-Solomon amendment without much concern about the likelihood of achieving weighted voting at the U.N., or pass the Sundquist amendment without any idea of how much money Soviet nationals in the U.N. Secretariat were required to kickback to their government under the table. Paradoxically, these and other congressional actions may have brought about desirable U.N. reform, but in themselves they were not well considered. They did not give grounds for optimism about the future rationality, effectiveness, or legality of other aspects of U.S. foreign policy.

Also, in one of those quirks for which history, or fate, is well known, U.S. policy left the U.N. in a weakened condition just as the organization showed that it could be useful to the U.S. national interest. In 1988–1989 the office of the secretary-general mediated an end to the Soviet military presence in Afghanistan; subsequently a U.N. observer force was established to monitor events. A cease-fire was negotiated in the Persian Gulf War, and a U.N. peacekeeping force was dispatched to the area. Negotiations for an independent Namibia were finally successful, and another U.N. peacekeeping force undertook the difficult job of policing withdrawal of various military forces in that region and supervising elections. The office of the secretary-general was also involved in supervising elections in Nicaragua, as well as in observing the larger Central American peace process. All of these developments were supported by the United States, and all were considered in the short-term U.S. national interest.

Yet U.S. policy in the earlier 1980s had left the U.N. in a condition that made it difficult to carry out the tasks imposed on it in the late 1980s. The organization did not have the financial resources to undertake immediately what states desired it to do, and had to secure additional funding, particularly before the peacekeeping missions could be established. (In the case of the force sent to Namibia, the United States and other major donors demanded a sizable scaling down of the proposed force before it agreed to arrangements. After deployment, there was considerable evidence that a larger, better-equipped force would have been more effective.)

This revitalization of the U.N., this renewed discovery of its usefulness especially in peace and security issues, was both an outcome relevant to the United States, defined in terms of its short-term national interests, and to world order in general.

VII OUTCOME FOR WORLD ORDER

If U.N. administrative and financial reforms continue (they are in flux at the time of writing), and if this leads to a more efficient organization with greater U.S. support, world order will be enhanced. If enhanced world order is to transpire concerning issues discussed in this chapter, Congress will have to agree with the second Reagan and first Bush administrations, and recognize its legal obligation to meet United Nations financial obligations as assessed by the General Assembly. Not only is it true that most state practice recognizes the continuing validity of Charter Articles 17 and 19 (as evidenced by state agreement on loss of Assembly vote by those two years in arrears of their U.N. payments), but also it is well to recall that even the Reagan administration, including Ambassador Kirkpatrick, reaffirmed the legal right of the General Assembly to assess for the budget under Charter Article 17, in principle, and the legal duty of the United States to pay.

Beyond this, however, the legal right of a state to engage in specific withholding of a part of its assessments, because of alleged ultra vires action by the United Nations, is very much unsettled. The Soviet Union and its allies, France, and China, all members of the Council, have withheld assessments for peacekeeping (but not for more general assessments) under the argument of improper U.N. action. The United States, through the policies of both the Executive and the Congress, has gone further, withholding for a variety of purposes and, at least on the part of the Executive, explicitly under the claim of ultra vires action. If this practice by major powers continues and expands, then an argument can be made with some reason that state practice concerning specific withholding has become the operative law, replacing the advisory opinion of the ICJ in the *Expenses Case.*

This latter view is not totally unreasonable, or, it would not be unreasonable if there emerged widespread agreement on what constituted U.N. action beyond the bounds of the Charter. As noted already, other rules found in legal instruments have been altered by the practice of states. But such a new interpretation of the implied meaning of the Charter, and the implied limits of authority to U.N. organs is not cause for optimism about world order in the current, unsettled situation. Such a new rule, if that is what specific withholding in response to alleged ultra vires action turns out to be, could confirm and formalize a serious weakness in the United Nations. There is every reason to believe that states will make this claim more on the basis of political judgment than on a considered legal judgment of the meaning of the Charter—political calculation does normally drive legal argument. During 1989 the House approved a measure restricting U.S. assessed payments to any international organization that recognized Palestine as a state; there was no accompanying legal argument suggesting that such admission was ultra vires. Likewise, in the fall of 1989, the Bush administration threatened withholding of all U.S. assessments to the U.N. if persons representing Palestine were given enhanced status in the U.N. There was no accompanying legal justification as to how this policy position could be squared with the terms of the Charter. It was straightforward political blackmail.

Thus, whatever the abstract legal reasoning behind the permissibility of specific withholding in relation to the claim of ultra vires action, actual withholdings and the threat thereof are highly likely to be political decisions devoid of serious legal consideration. At least that conclusion seems justified when looking at decisions taken in Washington. Admitting the legal possibility of such withholdings is to encourage political decisions untempered by law. One result could be a continuation of the major financial difficulties that plagued the U.N. in the mid-1960s and mid-1980s. Specific withholding is a recipe for chaos in the finances, and hence the programs, of international institutions.

A solution is available, although it is not likely to be tried. States can always seek a binding judgment from the World Court. But states have persistently shown a preference for legal ambiguity that keeps alive certain national freedoms, rather than for legal clarity that might restrict their freedom of maneuver. And while the General Assembly could request another advisory opinion from the ICJ on specific withholdings, such a judgment might meet the same indeterminate fate as the *Expenses* opinion of the 1960s.

Perhaps somewhat less pessimistically, one can note that state commitment to most international institutions reflecting majority rule or collective responsibility has been weak historically, and the financing of the U.N. only demonstrates continuing weakness. Certainly financing of U.N. peacekeeping, despite the ICJ's advisory opinion, has come to be based essentially on payment by those who are willing to pay, and while this is a messy situation, it is a messy world in which the U.N. operates.[47] If selective withholding related to the claim of ultra vires does emerge as a de facto amendment to Article 17, it may make the U.N. more cautious about the programs it adopts, more attuned to political consensus, and thus less prone to controversy in those programs. The downside or negative feature of this equation is that controversial initiatives might not be tried.

Finally, it is clear that the Congress in the 1980s, when dealing with U.N. finances, showed little inclination to temper its political hostility toward the U.N. with concern for treaty obligations. This was essentially the same Congress (Senate) that insisted on correct treaty interpretation in the matter of ABMs and SDI, and that paid considerable if inconsistent attention to international law and U.S. policy toward Nicaragua. It was also basically the same Congress that chose to ignore international law when the Reagan administration intervened with force in Grenada. This congressional inconsistency in attention to international legal issues, both between issues and within issues, is not a sound national building block of world order. In the first year of the Bush administration, the Congress agreed to full funding of current assessments, but refused to vote payments for back assessments. On the other hand, the record of the Executive on these matters of international law is not one on which one can build a strong case for excluding Congress from foreign policy influence.

NOTES

The epigraph that opens Chapter 6 is quoted from Dante Fascell (D, FL), in the *New York Times,* June 27, 1986, 8.

1. "The U.S. Role in the United Nations," *Hearings,* House Subcommittee on Human Rights and International Organizations, 98th Congress, 1st session, Washington: GPO, 1984, Appendix 8, and passim; and UNA-USA, "Financing the United Nations," New York: UNA-USA, 1989, 1–8.

2. Ibid., and Frederick K. Lister, *Fairness and Accountability in U.N. Financial Decision-Making,* New York: UNA-USA, n.d.

3. Among many studies, see David Wilkinson, "The Article 17 Crisis: The Dispute over Financing the United Nations," and Stanley Hoffmann, "A World Divided and a World Court Confused: The World Court's Opinion on U.N. Financing," both in Lawrence Scheinman and David Wilkinson, eds., *International Law and Political Crisis: A Casebook,* Boston: Little, Brown, 1968.

4. Quoted, with references, in Thomas M. Franck, *Nation Against Nation: What Happened to the U.N. Dream and What the U.S. Can Do About It,* New York: Oxford University Press, 1985, 85–86.

5. "U.S. Role in the United Nations," note 1, quoting Jeane Kirkpatrick, at 55.

6. See especially the testimony by H. K. Jacobson of Michigan University in "U.S. Policy in the United Nations," *Hearings and Markup,* House Committee on Foreign Affairs, 99th Congress, 1st session, Washington: GPO, 1986, 126–151; and John G. Stoessinger, *The United Nations and the Superpowers: United States–Soviet Interaction at the United Nations,* New York: Random House, 1977, chps. 5–6 and passim.

7. Quoted, with references, by Elisabeth Zoller, "The 'Corporate Will' of the United Nations and the Rights of the Minority," *American Journal of International Law,* 81, 3 (July 1987), 610.

8. "U.S. Participation in International Organizations and Programs," *Report,* Staff Study Mission, House Committee on Foreign Affairs, 96th Congress, 1st session, Committee Print, August 1979, Washington: GPO, 1979, 59–60.

9. Tammi R. Davis and Sean M. Lynn-Jones, "'City Upon a Hill,'" *Foreign Policy,* 66 (Spring 1987), 20–39. See also Thomas L. Hughes, "The Twilight of Internationalism," *Foreign Policy,* 61 (Winter 1985–86), 25–48.

10. Robert L. Ayres, "Breaking the Bank," *Foreign Policy,* 43 (Summer 1981), 104–120.

11. See the treatment in Leon Gordenker, "U.S. Participation in the United Nations," in David P. Forsythe, ed., *American Foreign Policy in an Uncertain World,* Lincoln: University of Nebraska Press, 1984, 243–264, which gives detailed attention to Kirkpatrick's speeches.

12. Daniel Patrick Moynihan, *A Dangerous Place,* Boston: Little, Brown, 1978.

13. The remarks by Ambassador Lichtenstein drew considerable attention in Congress. They are reprinted in "The U.S. Role in the United Nations," note 1, at Appendix 2, along with President Reagan's remarks in Appendix 4.

14. For an interpretation of U.S. policy on international human rights showing that Congress was more sensitive than the Executive to international law, see David P. Forsythe, *Human Rights and U.S. Foreign Policy,* Gainesville: University Press of Florida, 1988. The reader should compare that interpretation with the conclusions in this chapter about Congress.

15. *New York Times,* December 31, 1982, 1.

16. For overviews, see Zoller, note 7; and Richard W. Nelson, "International Law and U.S. Withholding of Payments to International Organizations," *American Journal of International Law,* 80, 4 (October 1986), 973–983.

17. In addition to "U.S. Role in the United Nations," note 1, and "U.S. Policy in the United Nations," note 6, see "International Organizations and Multilateral Diplomacy," *Hearing,* Senate Committee on Foreign Relations, 99th Congress, 1st session, Washington: GPO, 1985; "U.S. Financial and Political Involvement in the United Nations," *Hearing,* Senate Committee on Governmental Affairs, 99th Congress, 1st session, Washington: GPO, 1985; "Impact of Gramm-Rudman-Hollings on U.S. Contributions to International Organizations," *Hearing,* House Subcommittees on Human Rights and International Organizations and on International Operations, 99th Congress, 2d session, Washington: GPO, 1986; "U.S. Contributions to International Organizations," *Hearing,* House Subcommittees on Human Rights and International Operations, 100th Congress, 2d session, Washington: GPO, 1988; "Recent Developments in the United Nations System," *Hearings,* House Subcommittees on Human Rights and International Organizations and on International Operations, 100th Congress, 2d session, Washington: GPO, 1988.

18. For an example of the executive emphasis on U.S. payment of assessments as part of the push for U.N. reform, see the last entry in ibid., at 9. For a more general analysis of the Reagan "grudging acceptance of modest internationalism" (p. 150), see Robert O. Keohane and Joseph S. Nye, Jr., "Two Cheers for Multilateralism," *Foreign Policy*, 60 (Fall 1985), 148–167.

19. Quoted in "U.S. Role in the United Nations," note 1, at 63.

20. "Impact of Gramm-Rudman," note 17, at 55.

21. Ibid., at 4.

22. "U.S. Contributions," note 17, at 28.

23. "International Organizations," note 17, at 14.

24. "U.S. Financial and Political Involvement," note 17, at 25.

25. See the statement by Assistant Secretary Alan Keyes in "Impact of Gramm-Rudman," note 17, at 7.

26. *Legislation on Foreign Relations Through 1981*, U.S. Congress, Joint Committee Print, March 1982, Washington: GPO, 1982, 138, citing section 620(u).

27. *New York Times*, June 27, 1986, 8. This statement appears to reflect political realism about the mood in Congress, not Fascell's personal desire regarding attention to international law. Fascell had written the State Department about attention to Article 17, and he was generally regarded as reasonable in his voting record on U.N. issues. See his op-ed piece in the *New York Times* entitled, "Enough U.N. Bashing," September 19, 1986, 31.

28. "U.S. Role in the United Nations," note 1, at 5.

29. "U.S. Financial and Political Involvement," note 17, at 29.

30. "Status of U.S. Participation in the United Nations System, 1988," *Hearing*, House Subcommittee on Human Rights and International Organizations, 100th Congress, 2d session, Washington: GPO, 1988, 27.

31. "U.S. Role in the United Nations," note 1, at 12.

32. Ibid., at 14.

33. Ibid., at 17.

34. "U.S. Contributions," note 17, at 1–2.

35. "U.S. Role in the United Nations," note 1, at 46.

36. *New York Times*, June 26, 1985, 6. These findings were similar to those of a UNA-USA poll in the early 1980s, reprinted in ibid., at 25–36, and similar to reports from the Gallup organization.

37. See, e.g., "U.S. Role in the United Nations," note 1, at 18.

38. *New York Times*, June 27, 1986, 8.

39. See, e.g., Burton Yale Pines, ed., *A World Without a U.N.: What Would Happen If the U.N. Shut Down*, Washington: Heritage Foundation, 1984.

40. *U.N. Chronicle*, 23, 4 (August 1986), 63–65.

41. Quoted in Nelson, note 16, at 981–982.

42. *U.N. Chronicle*, 24, 1 (February 1987), 17ff.

43. See *Legislation on Foreign Relations Through 1988*, U.S. Congress, Joint Committee Print, April 1989, Washington: GPO, 1989, 44 for a congressional "finding" that the U.N. consensus decision-making procedure is a significant step toward meeting the intent of the Kassebaum-Solomon amendment.

44. "Status of U.S. Participation," note 30.

45. See Fascell, note 27.

46. "Status of U.S. Participation," note 30.

47. Alan James, "The Security Council: Paying for Peacekeeping," in David P. Forsythe, ed., *The United Nations in the World Political Economy,* London: Macmillan, 1989, 13–35.

VII

Conclusion: The Politics of International Law

Life is contradictory to law and order. . . . Only the dead are in order and obey all the laws. —Heinrich Böll

The application of international law to the controversies of public policy is not a simple and easy matter. Some policy-makers are ignorant of international law. Some find the law's strictures inconvenient, at variance with their impulses and ideology and political agenda. Some find it genuinely difficult to match the law with the factual complexities that arise. Yet international law exists, it is law, and repeatedly it intersects with the controversies of public policy. Sometimes its impact is greater, sometimes less, but never entirely absent. A brief review of our five case studies, deliberately chosen to provide a variety of important public controversies, bears out both the influences and weaknesses of international law.

*   *   *

In the five case studies reviewed in this book, the influence of international law was greatest in the controversy over Star Wars and the ABM treaty. The bizarre treaty interpretation offered by the Reagan administration, in order to remove legal restraints on development and deployment of a strategic defense system, was successfully blocked by the Senate relying on standard procedures for treaty interpretation. This situation did not transpire because some lawyers in the Senate displayed a superior knowledge of international law. Just as political calculations drove the administration's attempt to reinterpret the ABM treaty, so political factors drove the Senate majority. Many Democrats were willing to challenge a Republican administration; many Democrats opposed heavy spending on a questionable military project; and many members of both parties were concerned about loss of authority and influence for the Senate as a whole in the treaty-making process. This controversy was also one in which Senate members were not under any particular pressure from their constituents, and on which the president could not easily charge them with being soft on security matters.

141

Thus, while no doubt on the part of many senators there was genuine concern with interpreting international law correctly, a confluence of several political factors encouraged them to battle a popular president on this controversy. (And no doubt the more knowledgeable senators knew that the president himself was somewhat removed from the details of this debate, with Perle and Ikle being the primary spear-carriers for the reinterpretation effort.) It was also the case that the administration's legal arguments as presented by Sofaer were so weak and illogical that it proved extremely difficult and finally impossible to persuade the Senate majority of their correctness.

While one cannot prove scientifically which factor in the entire complex was decisive for the final outcome of this controversy, one should not overlook the fact that had the Senate agreed with the administration's reinterpretation, its own role in future treaty proceedings would have been reduced. An Executive could simply say that what the Senate had consented to ratify had been misunderstood, and that the true meaning of a treaty was up to the Executive to determine—even years after ratification. Thus a concern for institutional prerogatives strongly propelled senators to defend a correct interpretation—and correct procedure for interpretation—of the ABM treaty, whether or not they viewed a developed and deployed SDI as wise policy. Also, senators, even at a time when they were voting for much larger military budgets, were reluctant to effectively jettison an arms control treaty that had become a benchmark in relations with the Soviet Union. While other cases would show that treaty law was certainly not always viewed as sacrosanct in the U.S. political process, this treaty was viewed as having considerable importance as a confidence-building measure between the superpowers and thereby affecting the reputation of the United States for responsible behavior.

International law was less decisive but still periodically important for the outcome of Reagan's policy of "covert" intervention in Nicaragua. Some of the congressional opposition—it is impossible to say exactly how much—to the administration's policy was based on the international legal premise that forceful intervention against a sovereign state was impermissible. The first Boland amendment prohibiting U.S. action for the purpose of overthrowing the Nicaraguan government was a direct reflection of this standard international legal premise—at least in terms of its prima facie meaning. Other sources of opposition, such as fear of a Vietnam-like situation, were mixed with this concern for international law. Clearly, much congressional opposition to the laying of mines in Nicaraguan waters and to other naval operations against the Sandinistas was based on the judgment that such acts violated the normal rules of the game of international politics.

At the same time, however, one must note the inconsistency that characterized congressional efforts to check an executive policy that played fast and loose with legal arguments. If one can fairly criticize an administration that repeatedly misinterpreted international law, and at times blatantly ignored the law in the form of a binding judgment of the International Court of Justice, one should also observe that Congress was less than consistent in its attention to legal standards. Not only did the Congress as a body fail to bring the United States into compliance with international law as determined in authoritative measure by the World Court, but also it voted lethal assistance to the contras in 1986, *after* the Court's ruling on the merits. Politics may explain how members of Congress, including hawkish conservatives like Senator Goldwater, could be so incensed about mining harbors in violation of international law and so disinterested in complying with a legally binding judgment of the World Court. Certainly legal logic cannot explain so great an inconsistency.

The political factors explaining the U.S. view of international law in this Nicaraguan case are, as usual, varied and mixed. The administration displayed a fixation with potential surrogates of the Soviet Union and especially with other "Cuban model states" in the Western Hemisphere. This tunnel vision about East-West relations caused the Executive to overstate the danger to the United States from the Sandinistas, and correspondingly to downgrade the relevance of law to security policy. This caused not only willful attempts by the Executive to ignore or distort international legal standards, but also to circumvent at least the spirit of related domestic law through the covert machinations of Oliver North and the staff of the National Security Council. For its part, the Congress, despite considerable support in American public opinion for opposing Reagan's policies, found it difficult to resist the determined and dogged pressures of an Executive reverting to McCarthyite tactics. Some members of Congress appeared to be fearful of being labelled soft on communism, as charged by Reagan and his lieutenants. And a firm and sustained congressional attention to international law was made even more difficult when the Sandinista government openly sought further aid from Moscow and Havana, flagrantly repressed some of its domestic critics, and militarily pursued the contras inside Honduras (however much such pursuit might be justified in international law, questions can be raised about political wisdom and timing).

One of the important differences between the case of the ABM treaty and the case of Nicaragua was that in Nicaragua, the president of the United States was committed to the use of force over a number of years; it was extremely difficult for the Congress to counteract policies violative of international law in this context. By contrast, in the ABM case the Senate was dealing with a controversy of shorter duration not involving presidential commitment to actual force. Moreover, the shorter duration meant that the legal issues were—relatively speaking—not so varied and disparate. In the ABM case the Senate could focus on a smaller number of politico-legal questions, free from claims about *immediate* security threats—and senators from both parties had some vested interest in opposing the president on the basis of senatorial prerogatives. In the Nicaraguan case, both congressional houses were involved, the issues kept changing, the president—to put it mildly—did not easily take "no" for an answer, and significant parts of both houses were inclined to give considerable deference to the Executive in a struggle against a leftist government. These political factors explain why relying on international law was more effective in the ABM case than in the Nicaraguan case.

In the case of U.S. refugee policy, international law displayed some, but less than decisive, influence on the United States as a state of first asylum. International law, in the form of the 1951 and 1967 treaties on refugees, directly and obviously affected the 1980 U.S. statute on the subject. Both the Executive and the Congress intended to translate international legal standards into U.S. law. Beyond that point, however, international law concerning definition of a refugee, and his or her non-return to a situation of persecution, operated on the United States as a state of first asylum mainly through a small number of court cases.

The Reagan administration, once again, played fast and loose with legal interpretations, driven by a political concern to reduce to a minimum the number of migrants allowed into the United States from the Caribbean and Central America. Several considerations fed into this overriding concern: not to undermine the reputation of friendly governments, as in El Salvador; not to increase the number of unskilled blacks in the United States from Haiti; not to increase the number of unskilled Spanish-speakers in areas where the dominant Anglo cultures were resisting such an influx; not to overburden state and local authorities, which had to care for new arrivals; not to offend members of Congress from states like Florida, Texas, and California, which resisted further immigrants. These and perhaps other unarticulated considerations led to an administration policy that clearly preferred to label aliens as economic migrants rather than refugees, which was likely to result in deportation despite considerable probability of persecution upon return.

The strength of this general concern can be seen in the fact that for most of the Reagan period, aliens' claims to refugee status based on persecution by the Sandinista government were routinely dismissed by the Immigration and Naturalization Service, as advised by the State Department. It was only in the late 1980s that the administration began to grant refugee status to Nicaraguans in much higher proportion than most other nationalities from Central America and the Caribbean. There was virtually no change in the factual situation in Nicaragua that could account for this change in numbers in the United States. Only belatedly, therefore, did the administration's anticommunism make a dent in its overall policy of excluding further immigrants from the region. And thus only belatedly did the Reagan team bring its policy on Nicaraguan migrants into line with its policy on Cuban migrants, making it clear that flight from communism would still lead to preferential treatment by the U.S. government. Absent the factor of communism, claims to refugee status from Central America were routinely denied.

The Reagan team's reluctance to make a good-faith determination of refugee status under the relevant legal standards, as informed by the practice of the UNHCR, can also be seen in the extraordinary measures it took to prevent Haitians from entering U.S. jurisdiction, where their claims could be processed more equitably. The overriding desire to limit further immigration, regardless of the facts of individual cases, can also be seen in the Executive's unwillingness to grant EVD status to groups of persons fleeing political instability, as in El Salvador. Such a measure would have bypassed controversies over definition of a refugee, and would have accorded with UNHCR practice to give humanitarian protection on a group basis for a temporary period. Added to all of these factors, one could also see that INS officials were in fact poorly informed about international and U.S. law pertaining to refugees; they were thus easily manipulated by State Department political instructions.

Given this executive policy, improved implementation of refugee law was obtained only through judicial action. Spurred by public interest lawyers and amicus curiae briefs by the UNHCR, some U.S. courts did exercise some checks on the Executive concerning refugee matters. On occasion, courts were unwilling to defer to executive determinations. In part this was because Congress had acted to translate U.S. treaty commitments into reasonably clear municipal legislation. In part it was because refugee law was both international and domestic; refugee affairs constituted an "intermestic" issue on which courts felt more comfortable and competent than they did on some other, more purely international legal issues. But the judicial process worked slowly and on a case-by-case basis. The Executive was able to continue with the overall thrust of its exclusionary policy, especially after it took measures to make it more difficult for aliens to avail themselves of the courts. When Haitians were physically prevented from entering U.S. jurisdiction by action of the Coast Guard, or when aliens already within the United States were detained in facilities far from lawyers and courts, effective impediments were placed on the Judiciary. Thus the number of court cases protecting the rights of refugees remained relatively small.

Once the Congress had realigned U.S. statutory law with treaty commitments, that body was ineffective in providing oversight of the Executive's interpretation and (mis)implementation of the law. While some members of Congress displayed concern for a failure to implement law as originally intended, a large number of legislators shared the administration's exclusionary concerns. This resulted in a divided and deadlocked Congress, unable to muster the votes either to pass tightly worded legislation giving clear guidelines to the Executive, or to exercise the power of the purse in ways distasteful to the administration. In effect, a divided Congress left the policy field to the Executive, unless checked by the courts.

The congressional situation accurately reflected an American public badly fragmented on immigration and refugee matters. Some legal and religious circles worked diligently in behalf of international legal standards and international diplomatic practice designed to protect those crossing borders in flight from persecution and political unrest. But other circles of opinion in American society, particularly along the southern border but also in other areas where Anglo culture was especially dominant, were strongly supportive of an exclusionary policy whether or not it violated international (and domestic) law. Given this fragmentation, with areas of clear support for the Reagan policy, there was no concentrated and consistent public opinion pushing the Congress into improved oversight of the Executive. And the ultimate fate of international refugee law was very much affected by these political factors pertaining to public opinion and congressional (in)action.

As for U.S. financial assessments to the United Nations, it was quite clear that Congress intended to violate Article 17 of the U.N. Charter. While the Charter stipulated a U.S. legal obligation to pay assessments apportioned by the General Assembly, a bipartisan majority in Congress established financial limitations, reductions, and withholdings from those assessments, most of the time without supporting legal argument. Congress simply disliked certain programs and features of the United Nations and took action on that political motivation. That it was inadvertently encouraged in such illegal behavior by a Reagan administration that lost no opportunity in its early days to bash the U.N. and most other multilateral institutions is politically if not legally relevant.

Once Congress had taken the lead on the question of U.N. financing and reform, and once the congressional majority had repeatedly voted unilateral limitations and withholdings, the administration sought to limit the damage by endorsing, but not really emphasizing the still-binding nature of Article 17. But given the mood in Congress, such legal reaffirmations had slight policy impact. At least administration spokespersons such as Ambassador Kirkpatrick gave a legal cast to arguments about specific withholdings, arguing that such withholding should be seen as valid in response to U.N. ultra vires actions. Relatively speaking, this was preferable to withholding on straight political grounds. But the ultra vires argument did not deal with the problem of how to ensure that such a legal claim did not lead to political misuse and/or chaos in U.N. financing and programs, if practiced by any significant part of its 159 members.

The case of U.S. financial assessments to the U.N. showed not only the weakness of international law, when a powerful political body simply ignored some of its clear rules, but also showed that state power *might* lead to a change of the rules over time. One cannot conclude definitively that specific withholding for ultra vires action is now accepted as a legal exception to the general duty of states to pay assessments as voted by the General Assembly. But this *may* be emerging as a de facto amendment to Article 17, just as the Uniting for Peace resolution led to a de facto amendment to the U.N. rule that while the Security Council was treating a security issue the General Assembly was not to discuss it. Thus the case study of U.N. assessments shows well the interplay of power and law, and the way in which state exercise of power *may* change previous law over time. The case also nicely shows that while such a politico-legal process is transpiring, it can be difficult to determine with clarity the exact content of some international law.

The U.N. financing case gives rise to comparisons with the ABM case, in particular. In the latter, Congress—through the Senate—gave great emphasis to treaty law and to proper procedures for treaty interpretation. But both houses of Congress mostly ignored U.N. Charter Article 17 and proceeded on the basis of pure policy preferences. Ultimately Congress demanded a political bargain from the U.N.: payment of assessments in return for financial, administrative, and policy reform. Legal obligations figured prominently in Senate debates over the ABM, but hardly at all over U.N. assessments. From the viewpoint of the majority in Congress, Article 17 mattered about as much as did the World Court's binding judgment in the Nicaraguan case—that is to say, these manisfestations of international law mattered not at all to that majority.

Probably the only credible explanation for this great variety in congressional attention or inattention to international law is that politics varies according to issues and issue-areas. Senate prerogatives drove that body toward endorsement of the ABM treaty as traditionally understood, whereas congressional prerogatives were undermined by commitment to the U.N. Charter as traditionally understood. That is, the Senate could stay in the political game and remain an important actor by fighting the claimed right of the Executive to reinterpret treaties at will. By comparison, the Congress would have a reduced role in authorizing expenditures if it automatically had to produce the funds voted by the General Assembly. Thus institutional authority and power pushed the Senate and/or Congress into different positions about the sanctity and validity of different treaties.

Lest we become too pessimistic over congressional action and inaction relative to international law, we can at least distribute that pessimism fairly by recalling that in the case of overt intervention in Grenada it was primarily the Executive that ignored and distorted international law (al-

though Congress failed to check the Reagan administration's misrepresentations—it has long proved difficult for any Congress to oppose effectively, in the short term, a presidential decision to actually commit U.S.
military force to a foreign situation, and Grenada proved no exception
to that political rule). But it was President Reagan and his security man-
agers who made a series of decisions in favor of invasion without reference to efforts at political solutions, without reference to the U.N. and
OAS Charters, without reference to any clear and present danger to
American students, and without reference to actual order that existed in
Grenada.

Whether the shifting and belated executive legal claims were directed to humanitarian intervention, structural intervention for democracy and human rights, anticipatory self-defense, or collective self-defense in several forms, each claim failed to persuade European allies, the
Security Council, or the General Assembly. But those claims, or more accurately the politico-military action behind them, were persuasive to
Congress and American public opinion. And this proved controlling for
the situation.

That nothing succeeds like success may best explain the fate of international law pertaining to Reagan's use of force in Grenada; it could also
be applied to President Bush and his invasion of Panama. By comparison, intervention in Nicaragua raised the prospect of a Vietnam-like situation, or even—upon "victory"—a Guatemala-like situation, in which the
"freedom fighters" supported by the administration compose just another Latin tyranny. In the prolonged Nicaraguan case, many members
of Congress were willing to raise international (and domestic) legal objections to administration policy—but not in the abbreviated cases of
Grenada and Panama.

Intervention in Grenada turned out to be quick and relatively clean,
with several humanitarian and political objectives secured at low human
and political cost. No member of the administration and few members
of Congress saw any political wisdom in debating misrepresentations of
law and fact when the invasion was welcomed by most Grenadians, rid
the Caribbean of a disliked government, embarrassed leftist adversaries,
produced a return to democracy, and prevented Americans from being
held hostage. But bad cases make bad law, and Grenada was a bad case
on which to base the future of international law regulating use of force.

If the ABM case shows international law working relatively well, albeit through considerable political struggle in the Senate, the Grenada
case shows international law working very poorly, although United Nations bodies did what they could ex post facto to argue against using that
case as a valid precedent for action in the future. Condemnation by the
General Assembly and an overwhelming, if aborted, negative vote in the
Security Council makes it more difficult for any government in the fu-

ture to claim that the Grenada invasion was legally permissible. The other cases studied fall somewhere between these two poles, with some—but not decisive—international legal influences evident in the Nicaraguan and refugee cases, and considerably less impact from international law in the U.N. financing case.

*   *   *

Beyond these summaries and comparisons, one can add some further reflections on the interplay of politics and international law. Four points are stressed, in keeping with comments made in Chapter 1.

First, in all of these public controversies, there was an international legal dimension to the issue. Once the ABM treaty existed, one could not discuss development and deployment of a strategic defensive system without making reference to that treaty and its meaning. When the U.S. government organized and supported the contras against the Sandinista government, inherently the question arose as to whether such action was compatible with international legal standards concerning the use of force—indeed, this was among the first questions raised by members of Congress, and the one that was pursued throughout the Reagan administrations. After that administration intervened overtly in Grenada, the very first question for Secretary of State Shultz at a press conference was, How was such an invasion compatible with the OAS Charter and its prohibition of intervention? The very term *refugee* is derived from international law, and to understand U.S. refugee policy one must make reference to a well-founded fear of persecution and other ideas derived from international law. We cannot discuss the U.S. relationship to the U.N. in an intelligent manner without reference to the Charter and U.S. legal obligations thereunder; and we could not do so in the late 1980s without attention to Articles 17 and 19 of that Charter pertaining to financial assessments and related sanctions.

International law frames much of the debate about public policy questions, even when that law does not prove decisive in controlling politics. International law indicates many of the specific concerns that have to be addressed; thus that law affects political discourse. This is not to say that the law always adequately restrains the exercise of power, or that national policy objectives are always finally consistent with international legal standards. But international law exercises a subtle influence persistently on the political agenda, and on occasion its influence is more direct and more compelling.

Second, to understand exactly how international law interacts with the exercise of power in the policy process, we must move beyond a consideration of the United States as a unitary state. We must break down the legal fiction that the United States—or any other state—is a unitary legal actor, and look inside the "black box" that composes the decision-making process to distinguish political factors such as public opinion, legislative opinion, judicial action, and factions within the Executive. Only by doing so can we arrive at an informed understanding of the relation between U.S. policy and international law.

The traditional, formal-legal approach, consistent with the wording of the Vienna Convention on treaties,[1] emphasizes that a state (meaning the Executive that speaks for the state on the international plane) can never plead domestic legislation as a valid reason for disobeying law. But in practice, actions of the legislature, perhaps linked to public opinion, or for that matter action by domestic courts, may explain why a state is not in compliance with international law. Inaction by legislatures and courts, again sometimes linked to public opinion, may also explain why the Executive's violation of international law was not corrected. Thus an analytical approach to the functioning of law requires inquiry beyond formal-legal concepts.

Not all states permit, through their constitutions and political histories, a legislature as independent as the U.S. Congress. Not all states, and especially not the authoritarian ones, permit independent courts to restrain the Executive. Thus lessons learned about the functioning of international law relative to the United States may not be easily transferrable to other states. Even among the industrialized democracies, there are different rules and traditions pertaining to, for example, whether a treaty is to be given legal effect within the jurisdiction of the state without further action by the legislature. Despite such variations, as a general point of analysis it is advisable to look beyond the unitary state. In certain West European parliamentary democracies, for example, state adherence to or implementation of a treaty has been greatly affected by legislative pressure on the Executive—sometimes linked to public opinion and interest group activity.[2]

Third, the Reagan record relative to international law merits reflection. It is fashionable in Washington, and outside the beltway as well, to think of the United States in terms of what international law calls a "civilized nation." Pundits are prone to contrast a civilized and law-abiding United States with the likes of Qaddafi's government in Libya, or revolutionary Iran, or communist totalitarianism. The Reagan record, however, should remind us of the fragility of legal restraints when policy is driven by either ideological commitment or moral self-righteousness. Repeatedly in the cases examined in this work, the Reagan administration ignored or distorted reasonably clear international legal standards. During the Reagan era, as the most powerful state in international affairs, the United States manifested a foreign policy that left much to be desired in terms of lawful behavior under international legal standards (all apart from the question of lawful behavior under domestic legal standards).

There was adequate reason for the West European democracies, in particular, repeatedly to raise questions about U.S. global leadership and express reservations about the wisdom—and legality—of U.S. foreign policy. U.S. foreign policy during much of the 1980s was propelled by a crusading self-righteousness mixed with virulent anticommunism. In the light of the details presented in this book, we might well conclude that U.S. foreign policy would be less dangerous to ourselves and others, and better received and hence more effective in the world, if these unilateral residues of manifest destiny were replaced by greater attention to international law—especially as interpreted by multilateral institutions.

Of course it is true that some actors in world affairs do not wish the United States well, and that recourse to force and pressure remains the preferable option in certain situations—since international affairs is still characterized by a paucity of effective governing mechanisms. It is also true that other U.S. administrations have violated international law, some more blatantly than others. Senator Daniel Patrick Moynihan is correct in reminding us, for example, that Woodrow Wilson, for all his talk about international law and the League of Nations, established a Central American policy that perpetuated the traditions of gunboat diplomacy and imperial intervention.[3]

However, the United States has a relatively commendable record over two hundred years in applying the principle of constitutional government, and hence in respecting the rule of law in general—but that record is not compiled and continued without diligence on the part of citizens and political institutions. Members of both executive and legislative branches frequently boast of a commitment to international law by the United States relative to the lack of commitment by our adversaries, but in fact the United States frequently behaves just like many other nations—not like a "shining city on a hill." A particular U.S. administration may be less committed to observing legal standards than to advancing an ideological agenda or national prerogatives. Removing communists from power, re-establishing national dominance, preserving national wealth and traditional culture, simply obtaining policy objectives may override serious concern for the rule of law. Precisely that dynamic transpired all too frequently during the Reagan years.

This third point leads into the fourth. If such tendencies by executive policies violative of international law are to be checked, that restraint will have to be imposed by U.S. institutions and domestic forces. We may live in an interdependent world, but foreign influences on Washington in support of international law have been relatively weak—and are likely to continue weak in the near future. International law may be global and regional in nature, but its implementation still depends overwhelmingly on national decisions and processes. Reagan's efforts to distort the ABM treaty were checked by the Senate. Efforts to coerce the Sandinistas were impeded mostly by the Congress. Efforts to deny refugee status to most persons from south of our borders fleeing a well-founded fear of persecution were sometimes limited by U.S. courts.

In the cases examined in this book, foreign influences in support of international law were, of course, not absent. The U.N. Security Council and General Assembly, the UNHCR, European allies, and the World Court all tried to influence U.S. policy toward accommodation with international law. It is striking, however, how weak these foreign efforts turned out to be. This was due not to diplomatic and legal deficiencies on the part of these foreign parties, but rather to a collective mind-set in Washington that was mostly impervious to these influences. The American statesman George Kennan had noted the problem in the early 1950s: "If our society . . . is to retain its vitality, [we must]. . . change ourselves from an exclusive to a receptive nation in psychology and in practice. . . . There is no salvation for America in a frame of mind that tries to shut out its world environment."[4]

On occasion foreign influences were meshed with national decisions, making it difficult if not impossible to separate clearly the two complexes of influences. In some court action pertaining to refugees, the judgment by the national court appeared to be very similar to a legal brief submitted by the UNHCR. Some public statements by members of Congress in the public controversies examined in this book made explicit reference to positions taken by West European allies or spokespersons for the United Nations. In these ways American politics had become similar to a marble cake, with international and national inputs swirled together. But most of the time, what became U.S. policy could be attributed more to national than international influences. In the ABM treaty debate, the Senate was more influential than the Soviet Union, and domestic political factors driving Senate votes were more important than international legal arguments emanating from Moscow. In the Nicaraguan case, the Congress was more influential than the World Court, with the legislative-executive struggle more important than the legal reasoning of World Court judges. In the Grenada case, the collapse of congressional opposition and the endorsement of the invasion by American public opinion was far more decisive for the final outcome of policy than criticism by West European allies and condemnation by the U.N. General Assembly. Likewise, for U.S. refugee policy, the absence of congressional and public checks on executive decisions turned out to be more consistently controlling than diplomatic representations by the UNHCR. As for U.N. financial assessments, congressional demands for a political bargain proved more influential than the legal reasoning of officials in the U.N. Secretariat or a diplomatic note from West European allies.

For international law to be more effective in U.S. politics, the law itself with its supporting international influences must permeate more the national institutions that determine U.S. policy. This, in turn, suggests that those Americans who make policy in the name of the three governmental branches must become more sensitive to international law and how it can advance U.S. national interests. This is no easy goal to accomplish. It requires improved formal education for judges, and technocrats in agencies such as the INS and the Foreign Service. It requires improved informal education in international law for members of Congress, and for high executive officials who may have been businessmen (not to mention movie actors or peanut farmers). It may even require more attention to international law by at least the attentive if not the mass public, through such measures as improved public affairs programming on television and reporting in local newspapers.

While this is a difficult goal to accomplish, it is not impossible. One might note, for purposes of comparison, developments in Western Europe. There, members of parliament must become familiar with the international law of both the European Community and the Council of Europe. There, judges in national courts must become familiar with the judgments of the European Court of Human Rights and the European Court of Justice, which functions under the European Community. National administrators must be familiar with an avalanche of international rules and regulations, especially in the economic sphere. Neither high executive officials nor average citizens are free to disregard global international law or—especially—regional international law of both an economic and social (human rights) nature. In Western Europe, various international laws have deeply penetrated national decision-making processes.

The situation in the United States is very different, of course. The United States is not a party to treaties creating authoritative international organizations on a regional basis; the United States. is not so interdependent with its neighbors (although it is becoming more economically interdependent with Canada); the United States thinks of itself as being more distinct from its neighbors and more powerful relative to them. Yet the comparison remains valid for purposes of illustration. International law *can* permeate national decision-making procedures and institutions to such an extent that law becomes highly effective—viz., followed in most situations. The key to the process is through *national* political bodies and personages.

Those interested in improved international order might wish for greater authority and power on the part of international bodies. But in the world as it exists in the last decade of the twentieth century, and probably for the immediate future beyond that, national decisions will be crucial for the functioning of international law. Indeed, should international agencies eventually acquire greater authority and power, such a transformation will be based on national decisions. National decisions are required to create such agencies, imbue them with authority, and defer to their decisions—which is the ultimate source of their power or influence.

* * *

Finally, it cannot be stressed too much that there is a profound difference between what is frequently perceived in Washington as necessary for the U.S. national interest in the short term, and what turns out to be necessary for improved international order in the long term. From the cases presented in this work, this point is best demonstrated by the U.S. invasion of Grenada. This essentially unilateral use of force achieved a number of objectives approved by the Executive and public, and at least deferred to by Congress. Yet the fact remains that the invasion is not a good precedent for wise foreign policy. The Reagan administration eschewed efforts at peaceful settlement, and misrepresented both facts and law in order to exercise superior power. Similar behavior toward the more powerful Sandinistas (although the form of force was different) simply enlarged that conflict, created more suffering for both fighting parties, and undermined the rule of law both internationally and within the United States.

What is needed most fundamentally and generally in U.S. politics in order to make international law function better is a larger and longer perspective. Policy-makers at both ends of Pennsylvania Avenue need to blend concern for the pressing politics of the moment with a concern for orderly and legal international relations over the long run. When, for example, pursuing a policy that seeks reform of the United Nations, there needs to be comparable concern not to undermine the integrity of the U.N. Charter, since the Charter is a global constitution contributing to world order—which is in the U.S. national interest. This is not a naive and idealistic demand to make on Washington. The European democracies, equally concerned about U.N. reform, pursued the same goal as the United States but with precisely the respect for the Charter that particularly the Congress abjured.

When, for example, pursuing a policy designed to protect the economic and social welfare of the United States, there needs to be comparable concern not to undermine legal commitments undertaken to protect refugees. It is in the long-term U.S. national interest to uphold its legal commitments, and it aids U.S. foreign policy to do so. (The United Kingdom was not amused when the United States, having distorted refugee law in its dealings with persons from the Caribbean and Central

America, lectured the British about accepting more migrants from Vietnam in Hong Kong, not forcing their return to a situation of persecution, and treating them better in detention. No doubt U.S. influence abroad was undermined by its own policy when a country of first asylum.[5])

Had the Reagan administration been successful in its efforts to change the meaning of the ABM treaty, so as to allow development and deployment of a comprehensive Star Wars interceptor scheme, one could easily foresee great difficulty for any U.S. administration negotiating an arms control treaty with the Soviet Union. How could the U.S.S.R. be assured that some future U.S. government would not try to present it with a radically new treaty interpretation contrary to original understandings? Surely both the short-term and long-term U.S. national interests were advanced by Senate opposition to the Pentagon's efforts to secure immediate military advantage over Moscow.

Specialists in international law have long recognized that law makes an important contribution to the national interests of the United States. The contemporary case studies presented in this work indicate that U.S. policy-makers need to consider anew that truth. As Senator Moynihan wrote with regard to U.S. policy in Grenada: "A decent respect for international law . . . might have occasioned a . . . pause in which we could have considered our interests rather than merely giving in to our impulses. That, largely, is what law is about."[6]

NOTES

The epigraph that opens Chapter 7 is quoted from Heinrich Böll in the *International Herald Tribune,* July 17, 1985, 1.

1. 1969 Vienna Convention on the Law of Treaties, Article 27.

2. For an analysis of the evolution of the U.N. Convention on Torture stressing the role of the Dutch government as pressured by the Dutch Parliament—itself pressured by Amnesty International—see Peter R. Baehr, "The U.N. General Assembly: Negotiating the Convention on Torture," in David P. Forsythe, ed., *The United Nations in the World Political Economy,* London: Macmillan, 1989. Also, when the British government was pressured by the European Commission and Court of Human Rights, under the European Convention on Human Rights, the British Parliament as well as interest groups acting on that body were also involved.

3. Daniel Patrick Moynihan, *Loyalties,* New York: Harcourt Brace Jovanovich, 1984, 69.

4. From *Realities of American Foreign Policy,* as quoted in Robert Dallek, *The American Style of Foreign Policy,* New York: Oxford University Press, 1989, 154.

5. *New York Times,* December 15, 1989, 6.

6. Moynihan, note 3, at 96.

Afterword

Francis A. Boyle

Just recently, four books have been published that attempt to deal with the nature of the complex relationships between international law and politics, especially concerning the transnational threat and use of force: Reisman & Willard, *International Incidents: The Law That Counts in World Politics* (1988); Boyle, *The Future of International Law and American Foreign Policy* (1989); The Council on Foreign Relations, *Right v. Might: International Law and the Use of Force* (1989); and now David Forsythe's masterful *The Politics of International Law: U.S. Foreign Policy Reconsidered* (1990). The publication of these four volumes at this particular moment can be attributable in part to the reigning attitude of international legal nihilism that the world witnessed in Washington, D.C., during the eight-year tenure of the Reagan administration. In direct reaction thereto, from one perspective or another, all of the individuals and institutions involved in the production of these books felt some compelling need to reestablish the basic proposition that international law is relevant, if not critical, to the conduct of U.S. foreign policy, especially concerning the threat and use of force. All of these books are important because each contributes to the hitherto sparse and spotty literature in this field.[1]

Since I have already reviewed Reisman and Willard for the *American Journal of International Law*, I will not bother to repeat that analysis here.[2] In my book, *The Future of International Law and American Foreign Policy*, I attempted to critique the legal and intellectual foundations of the so-called Reagan Doctrine as well as the various manifestations of Reaganism that were produced around the world and at home: its war against international terrorism; its support for the Israeli invasion of Lebanon in 1982; its opposition to the right of the Palestinian people to self-determination and an independent state of their own; its repeatedly aggressive policies against Libya; its buildup of chemical and biological warfare capabilities; its nuclear deterrence doctrines; the Strategic Defense Initiative, etc. So, when David Forsythe kindly asked me to write a postscript to this book, I was quite pleased to discover that he had been working (completely independently of me) in the same general directions. To be sure, Professor Forsythe analyzed a different mix of problems produced by Reaganism than I had. But what seems remarkable is the consistency of the approaches taken independently by him and me with respect to criticizing various components of the Reagan administration's foreign policy—both in theory and in practice—from an international law perspective.

As Professor Forsythe noted toward the start of this book, elsewhere I have argued that the current way in which most public international law professors teach international law has become largely irrelevant to the major problems of contemporary international relations. We really have not had recently a textbook or casebook that systematically analyzes some of the major problems of contemporary international relations from a truly international law perspective and that endeavors to take into account the diversity of viewpoints on these subjects held by the different states and peoples of the world community. International law professors must take the great body of black-letter rules that has been handed down to us and attempt to make sense of them by applying them to, and testing them by, current problems of international relations. Only in this fashion will our profession continue to maintain some degree of relevance to the contemporary debate over the proper conduct of American foreign policy.

International law is thoroughly and completely grounded in fact, and it is almost impossible to reach proper conclusions about what the rules of international law are or should be without an analysis of the actual facts involved. For this reason, careful attention must be paid to the pathbreaking effort undertaken by Professor Forsythe in this book. He attempts to teach principles of international law within the context of actual real-world cases, crises, and problems. In my opinion, that is the only way we can make substantial progress toward understanding the subtleties of international relations and the role that international law and organizations do and can play in the international system. Professor Forsythe has performed a great service for the international legal studies profession by exploring these interrelationships.

Professor Forsythe's introductory chapter is quite correct to point out the complexities of the interplay among the Executive, Congress, and the Judiciary with respect to the formulation of U.S. foreign policy. The single-rational-actor model postulated by the political realists completely breaks down when it comes to explaining the manner in which U.S. foreign policy is actually made and conducted under our constitutionally mandated system of separation of powers. The United States speaks and acts with many voices on foreign affairs. Although some disagree, that diversity is all for the better.

After all, the United States is supposed to be a constitutional democracy with a commitment to the rule of law both at home and abroad. If the executive branch of the federal government decides to embark upon a course of egregiously lawless behavior abroad, then it is a testament to the strength and resilience of American democracy that Congress, the courts, and the American people at least sometimes refuse to go along with it. Forsythe's book clearly demonstrates that dynamic in a manner that has not been appreciated by most of the self-styled "realist" or "neo-realist" analysts of U.S. foreign policy. (It is a tribute to the genius of the late Hans Morgenthau that he was perhaps the only archetypal political realist who had a profound appreciation of, and deep respect for, the American democratic system of constitutional government.[3])

The only point I might add to Forsythe's excellent introduction is the power of international law in the estimation of the American people. Professor Forsythe may disagree, but based upon my extensive experience working at the grassroots level around the country for the past twelve years, I am convinced that international law arguments oftentimes exert a decisive impact upon the way the American people come to perceive events unfolding abroad in a manner that is quite different from the deceptive way their leaders have usually presented the situation to them. There is an enormous potential for proselytizing international law at the grassroots level of America that must be further exploited. Only then will more American people proceed to vigorously demand that all branches of their federal government, and especially the Executive, become respectful of the rule of law abroad as well as at home.

As far as most U.S. citizens are concerned, invoking the rule of law is as paradigmatically American as God, motherhood, apple pie, and the Eagle Scouts. Most American citizens have suckled law since they were weaned from their mother's breast. It is high time for international law teachers to tap directly into this powerful psychic reservoir of respect for law that is so uniquely and almost obsessively characteristic of the American people. Professor Forsythe's book provides us with the means whereby this task can be commenced.

Forsythe's treatment of the Reagan administration's so-called reinterpretation of the ABM treaty is far superior to the cursory examination of this subject that I presented in my book. Forsythe documents the entire disreputable affair in painstaking detail and demonstrates the strength of international law in the U.S. domestic political process, when the Senate adamantly refused to accept the Reagan administration's reinterpretation of the treaty. Forsythe also proves in this chapter the critical relevance of international law to the conduct of U.S. foreign policy on a matter of high international politics that affects the most vital national security interests of the United States. He thus convincingly refutes the confusing descriptive/prescriptive arguments made by both the political realists and the Reaganites to the effect that considerations of international law do not and should not have anything to do with such issues concerning raisons d'état. His analysis also establishes the validity of the proposition that a U.S. foreign affairs analyst cannot begin to comprehend many rudiments of U.S. foreign policy decision-making processes without possessing a sound working knowledge of international law.

For what they were worth, I have already offered my own thoughts on the illegality of the Reagan administration's war against Nicaragua in Chapter 5 of my book, *Defending Civil Resistance Under International Law* (1987). Here Forsythe does a first-rate job in demonstrating the interaction between international law and the congressional debate over U.S. funding for the contras. Forsythe stresses congressional inconsistency pertaining to international legal matters. I prefer to say that because America is a constitutional democracy with a commitment to the rule of law, it proved to be exceedingly difficult for the Reagan administration to sustain its illegal war against the people of Nicaragua over the strenuous efforts of an organized domestic opposition that invoked the rule of international law and domestic law to their cause.

The Reagan administration's covert war against Nicaragua was generally said to have been the exemplar of the self-styled Reagan Doctrine of supporting anticommunist guerrilla movements around the world. Perhaps the best explanation and defense of the Reagan Doctrine was made by Reagan's first ambassador to the United Nations, Jeane Kirkpatrick, and her legal adviser, Allan Gerson, entitled "The Reagan Doctrine, Human Rights and International Law," which can be found in *Right v. Might: International Law and the Use of Force.* Here Kirkpatrick and Gerson quite correctly (though perhaps unwittingly) pointed out that on May 5, 1985, Reagan took the opportunity to publicly announce his so-called doctrine at Bitburg, West Germany (p. 22). There Reagan laid a memorial wreath at the cemetery that he knew contained the remains of dead Nazi Waffen SS stormtroopers despite the vigorous protestations of the justifiably outraged American Jewish community and U.S. veteran organizations, among others. As I argued in a general debate with Gerson and others before the annual convention of the American Society of International Law on April 26 of that year:

> It is the Reagan administration's Machiavellian approach to foreign affairs that sponsored the Israeli invasion of Lebanon. It is the Reagan administration that brought you the United States invasion of Grenada. It was the Reagan administration that brought you the U.S. invasion of Nicaragua, which still goes on today. It is the Reagan administration's policy of constructive engagement that has encouraged the South African invasion of Angola. It is the Reagan administration which has launched an all-out vicious assault on the integrity of the International Court of Justice. And it is now the Reagan administration that is going to be paying tribute to 39 SS soldiers at a cemetery in West Germany. I think nothing could be a more eloquent and symbolic statement of what motivates the foreign policy of this administration than that act.[4]

Due to the gravity of the moral, legal, and political issues at stake, it becomes critical for the reader to study seriously David Forsythe's definitive repudiation of the supposed legal basis for the Reagan Doctrine. Both in this chapter and in the next, on the Reagan administration's invasion of Grenada, Forsythe's analysis vigorously reaffirms the integrity and the utility of the traditional interpretation to international law concerning the threat and use of force that has been historically espoused—albeit with some lapses—by the U.S. government since the foundation of the United Nations in 1945. By contrast, the Reagan administration advocated nothing more sophisticated than an across-the-board anticommunist crusade to form the overall basis for the conduct of American foreign policy, and the illegal invasion of Grenada was yet another case in point.

As Professor Forsythe demonstrates, Grenada was the paradigmatic example of how much naked power the U.S. president sometimes has, and how little influence Congress, the courts, and the American people ultimately wield if the president decides to use military force. Reagan's illegal bombings of Tripoli and Benghazi in 1986 are other examples. So much for the argument put forth by many political scientists and international lawyers that the president has been unduly burdened by legal restrictions imposed upon him by Congress in the area of foreign affairs and defense policies.

Those who have argued that the president has been somehow "fettered" by the rule of law with respect to the conduct of foreign affairs are either generally ignorant of or else purposely dissembling over the fact that under the Constitution, treaties, statutes, and relevant Supreme Court and Courts of Appeal decisions, the president of the United States of America is the most powerful person in the world. The president has the political initiative to do whatever he wants in foreign affairs and defense policies, and there is little that Congress, let alone the courts, can do to stop him in the short term.[5] Witness Nicaragua and Vietnam, where it took many long years and much hard work by the American people and Congress to finally terminate these clearly illegal wars.

By comparison, in Grenada the president was able to act expeditiously and unilaterally to accomplish his objectives before Congress could respond and despite the fact that such action clearly violated international law and U.S. statutory restrictions (e.g., the War Powers Resolution). Professor Forsythe's analysis of the Reagan administration's invasion of Grenada shows that our much-vaunted constitutional system of separation of powers under the rule of law can be easily circumvented or overthrown by a headstrong and belligerent president in the heat of an immediate crisis (even when that crisis has been manufactured by the president himself). Professor Forsythe also demonstrates the inherent dangers of the American rally-round-the-flag phenomenon that is so prevalent during times of real or self-induced international crises.

The American people must somehow come to grips with this phenomenon before it overwhelms us in yet another Tonkin-Gulf-Resolution/Vietnam-War scenario. The War Powers Resolution was originally intended to solve this problem. But a long line of abusive and usurpatory presidents—both Democrats and Republicans—have negated this supreme law of the land on the bogus grounds that the act is said to be unconstitutional.

Article 1, Section 8, Clause 11 of the U.S. Constitution emphatically states: "*The Congress* shall have Power . . . to declare War . . ." (emphasis added.) Nevertheless, an entire series of imperial presidents have reinterpreted out of existence this critical protection for the American Republic against an unjust, unwise, or precipitous war. The framers of our Constitution decided for good cause to lodge the awesome power to resort to warfare only in the hands of the representatives of the entire populace by requiring both houses of Congress to act together. Two hundred years later, however, today's monarchical presidents—like George III before them—contemptuously assert that they are above the law as well as above the American social contract founded by the U.S. Constitution. Unfortunately a number of our court decisions have deferred to this line of argument, as Forsythe shows. It is high time for the American people to declare their independence from the tyranny of an imperial presidency.

As Professor Forsythe demonstrates with respect to the Reagan administration's belligerent policies toward—especially—Grenada (and I would add toward Nicaragua, El Salvador, and Haiti), perhaps it is sometimes true that in today's world, the strong do what they will and the weak suffer what they must.[6] The sophistic teaching that "might makes right" is a great self-legitimizing philosophy for the strong—but what about the weak? Their hopes and expectations are dependent upon the strength and the integrity of the international legal order.

As Thucydides dramatically portrayed in his book, the Athenian democracy's adherence to the philosophy of realpolitik was ultimately responsible for the outbreak of the Peloponnesian War and eventually the defeat of Athens at the hands of authoritarian Sparta. Today, like Athens before it, blinded by hubris, the U.S. Executive might very well lead the civilized world into another cataclysm. Only this time, there will be no Philip of Macedon around to pick up the radioactive pieces.

My cursory viewpoints on the Reagan administration's callous policies toward Central American refugees can be found on pages 189 to 197 of *Defending Civil Resistance Under International Law*. The Reagan administration illegally intervened into the civil war in El Salvador by providing enormous amounts of military and economic assistance to a brutal mili-

tary dictatorship that used that assistance to perpetrate a gross and consistent pattern of violations of basic human rights of the people of that
country, thus creating an enormous number of refugees fleeing in fear
for their lives. Nevertheless, the Reagan administration took the position
that these individuals were generally not entitled to qualify as refugees,
and thus for political asylum, because they were alleged to be in the
United States primarily for economic reasons. On its face this claim was
at odds with the obvious facts of a prolonged civil war in El Salvador, as
well as the brutal genocide practiced against the indigenous people of
Guatemala by their government. The Reagan administration's disingen-
uous position on these matters constituted a clear-cut violation of its obligations under both the U.S. Refugee Act of 1980 and the 1967 U.N. Protocol to the Refugee Convention.

As Professor Forsythe shows, the reason the Reagan administration
denied reality in these cases was that to have acted otherwise, by deter-
mining that such refugees were entitled to asylum, would have constituted tacit recognition of the violations of fundamental human rights
being perpetrated every day by the military dictatorships that were and
still are ruling El Salvador and Guatemala. This in turn would have undercut the pseudo-legitimacy of the democratic facades of the Duarte
and Cristiani governments in El Salvador and the Cerezo government in
Guatemala in the perceptions of both American public opinion and the
international community. Furthermore, in the event foreign governments, such as those in El Salvador and Guatemala, are found to be en-
gaging in a gross and consistent pattern of violations of the fundamental
human rights of their own citizens, a number of U.S. statutes should be
triggered that would mandate the cut-off of various forms of U.S. military and economic assistance.

The Reagan administration sought to forestall that day by denying
these legitimate refugees their recognized right to asylum under both
U.S. domestic law and international law, and indeed continued to deport
refugees back to Central America even in the face of mounting evidence
that many suffered persecution, torture, and death upon their return.
The Reagan administration sacrificed the lives of these human beings in
the name of its own determination of U.S. national security interests despite the rules of international and U.S. domestic law.

Professor Forsythe patiently takes the reader through all the legalistic lies, distortions, and half-truths put forth by various members of the
Reagan administration in order to justify their inhumane policies. He
concludes the chapter by correctly observing the highly deleterious impact these policies might exert upon the future peace and stability of the
Western Hemisphere in particular, and the cause of world order in general. This latter topic is then taken up and pursued at greater length in

the chapter dealing with the financial crisis at the United Nations, which was produced by the Reagan administration's decision to withhold the United States' legally obligated assessments.

In my opinion, the entire crisis over the nonpayment of U.S. assessments to the United Nations resulted from the Reagan administration's willingness to paralyze that organization. The Reaganites seemed to see the U.N. as some sort of international conspiracy of Third World and communist states that vaguely directed against the national security interests of the United States. The Reagan administration's comprehensive attack upon the integrity of the United Nations organization as well as its affiliated organs and institutions represented a serious setback to the long-term cause of world order, and to the immediate demands of maintaining international peace and security. Here Professor Forsythe performs an excellent service by reporting the arguments and actions of the administration and also the Congress to justify U.S. withholding of its legally obligated assessments from the United Nations and its affiliated organizations.

Quite obviously, it would take an entire book to refute their collective criticisms of the United Nations organization. Until that book is produced, however, I would recommend *The United Nations and the Maintenance of International Peace and Security* (1987), which was published under the auspices of the United Nations Institute for Training and Research (UNITAR). In response to the anti-U.N. onslaught launched by the Reaganites, UNITAR and the School of International and Public Affairs at Columbia University organized a joint conference on "The United Nations and the Maintenance of International Peace and Security: A Retrospective and Prospective View," held in September 1986. This UNITAR book contains the background papers prepared for that conference. Topics included the peaceful settlement of disputes, peacekeeping, outlawing the use of force, the International Court of Justice, the office of the secretary-general, disarmament, arms control, nuclear proliferation, and international terrorism.

For readers of Forsythe's book, the most important contribution to the UNITAR volume was the introductory chapter by Ernst Haas—a virtuoso survey of the actual record of the United Nations organization's successful management of international conflict during the first forty years of its existence. Haas's research was a powerful antidote to the polemical attacks against the U.N. mounted by the Reagan administration and its supporters located throughout the academic world and in the mainstream news media. Because of the general prevalence of these latter criticisms in public discourse, I believe it is important to reproduce Haas's summary of conclusions here:

> 1. The most intense disputes are the most likely to be successfully managed. Insignificant and very low intensity disputes can be margin-

ally influenced. Disputes in the intermediate range are the most resistant to management.

2. Success comes most readily when the fighting is very limited. The most contagious disputes are the ones most frequently influenced, very often with great success. Disputes that the neighbours of the contending parties are about to enter actively are the most difficult to manage, whereas it seems relatively simple to score minimal impacts on purely bilateral disputes.

3. Disputes free of decolonization and Cold War complications are the most successfully managed, *provided* that no civil war is involved. On the other hand, such disputes arising out of an internal conflict are the most intractable. Decolonization issues are the next most amenable to United Nations management. Cold War disputes score lowest, though 37 per cent of them were influenced by United Nations action.

4. Success is easier to achieve if the contending parties are members of the same Cold War bloc or if both are non-aligned. Cold War alliances complicate conflict management.

5. Conflicts involving middle powers (such as Argentina, Mexico, Egypt, Pakistan, The Netherlands) are most easily managed, particularly when the opposing party is smaller. Conflicts involving the superpowers as a party are the most intractable.

6. Strong United Nations decisions bring results. However, the failure to make a strong decision does not necessarily imply inability to influence the outcome of a dispute.

7. United Nations operations of a military nature are almost always successful. Field operations involving only the Secretariat are also successful over half of the time. The failure to launch any operations results in failure of management two-thirds of the time.

8. Successful action is associated most strongly with the joint leadership of the superpowers and the active intervention of the Secretary-General. But even the leadership of a single superpower brought success in 53 per cent of the cases in which it occurred. When leadership is exercised by large and middle powers the rate of success declines sharply. Small powers make the poorest leaders. Successful United Nations intervention requires a wide or very wide consensus of the membership. (pages 17–18)

Perhaps the most important lesson to be learned from analyzing Haas's meticulous study is that the United Nations will become even more effective at the task of maintaining international peace and security to the extent that it has the active support of the U.S. government.

Now that the Bush administration has come into power and somewhat returned—at least in relative terms—to the traditional American support for international law and organizations, we are experiencing for the first time in forty-five years, support from both superpowers—at least in principle—of the United Nations and its international regime. It is incontestable that Mikhail Gorbachev has launched a foreign policy with a central component being to strengthen the international regime concerning the threat and use of force that is found in the United Nations Charter. In significant part, Gorbachev was spurred into action by the curious spectacle of the Reagan administration striving to undermine this very regime—which the United States had created after the end of World War II in order to serve its own interests—the declining hegemon seeking to devour its own children. Once it became clear that the overall objective of the Reagan administration was to bypass or undercut the United Nations regime, the Soviet Union was compelled to recognize its stake in the effectiveness of the United Nations, and thus immediately acted to shore it up, using all its influence and power as well as those of its allies and supporters.

Indeed, under Gorbachev and Bush it now seems that the Soviet Union and the United States are attempting to reach a formal understanding to reinforce and expand the currently existing U.N. regime regulating the threat and use of force. The successful completion of that task will only serve the respective national interests of both superpowers, no matter what disagreements they might have *inter se*, and produce an international political climate that is even more conducive to a real international security regime (as that term has been traditionally defined by international political scientists) between them.[7] In my opinion, this latter objective is what Gorbachev is striving to accomplish now. In any event, his initiative is certainly worth U.S. reciprocation. Even from a realpolitik perspective, that is the only reasonable alternative the United States has in today's world of "existential deterrence."

Therefore, I would say that the United Nations regime regulating the threat and use of force is alive and well, and will remain so for the immediate future. Witness the efflorescence of United Nations peacekeeping operations or proposals for their deployment around the world today: in the Middle East, the Persian Gulf, Namibia, Angola, Central America, Cambodia, Afghanistan. Extending this list in the future is the only way most of these serious international conflicts possessing systemically destabilizing tendencies can be effectively dealt with. But as Professor Forsythe's analysis suggests, none of these worthwhile goals can be achieved unless and until the Bush administration repays the money owed to the United Nations by the U.S. government, and then stops making clearly illegal threats to withhold America's lawfully obligated U.N. assessments in the future.

In his conclusion, Professor Forsythe does a superb job summing up the political dynamics between international law and the formulation of U.S. foreign policy. I would add that the future of international law and U.S. foreign policy is whatever the American people want to make of it. Right now, international law is alive and well in the United States of America. For it resides in the hearts, hands, and minds of the American people, and, as David Forsythe proves, even those of some judges, legislators, bureaucrats, lobbyists, think-tankers, professors, and self-styled experts who inhabit Washington, D.C., and New York City.

We must all be grateful to Professor Forsythe for elucidating the complicated dynamics of the interaction between international law and U.S. foreign policy in this incisive, well-written, and accessible study. Both the strengths and weaknesses of international law in American foreign policy decision-making processes have been laid bare for all Americans to see. We must ponder and wrestle with the conclusions. But above all, we should give thanks for his insights, and for his deep personal and professional commitment to reestablishing the rule of law in the conduct of U.S. foreign policy.

NOTES

1. See, e.g., M. Kaplan and N. Katzenbach, *The Political Foundations of International Law* (1961); W. Coplin, *Functions of International Law* (1966); C. de Visscher, *Theory and Reality in Public International Law* (rev. ed. 1968); L. Scheinman and D. Wilkinson, eds., *International Law and Political Crisis* (1968); R. Fisher, *International Conflict for Beginners* (1969); W. Gould and M. Barkun, eds., *International Law and the Social Sciences* (1970); K. Deutsch and S. Hoffmann, eds., *The Relevance of International Law* (1971); R. Fisher, *Improving Compliance With International Law* (1981); F. Boyle, *World Politics and International Law* (1985); "Enhancing Order (and Law) in Future International Crises," 70 *Am. Soc. Int'l L. Proc.* 123 (1976) (panel discussion by R. Bowie, T. Farer, R. Fisher, and C. Parry); Rubin, "Order and Chaos: The Role of International Law in Foreign Policy," 77 *Mich. L. Rev.* 336 (1979). See also R. Bowie, *Suez 1956* (1974); A. Chayes, *The Cuban Missile Crisis* (1974); T. Ehrlich, *Cyprus 1958–1967* (1974); G. Abi-Saab, *The United Nations Operation in the Congo 1960–1964* (1978); R. Fisher, *Points of Choice* (1978). The latter five books compose the International Crises and the Role of Law Series published under the auspices of the American Society of International Law.

2. See 83 *Am. J. Int'l L.* 403 (1989).

3. See H. Morgenthau, *The Purpose of American Politics* (1960).

4. See the verbatim taperecording of these proceedings produced by Audio-Stats, Inglewood, California, in Tape ASIL 681-85, No.14A (at end of Boyle speech).

5. See generally L. Henkin, *Foreign Affairs and the Constitution* (1972).

6. See *The Complete Writings of Thucydides: The Peloponnesian War* 331 (Modern Library College ed. 1951) (emphasis added):

> Athenians.—For ourselves, we shall not trouble you with specious pretences—either of how we have a right to our empire because we overthrew the Mede, or are now attacking you because of a wrong that you have done us—and make a long speech which would not be believed; and in return we hope that you, instead of thinking to influence us by saying that you did not join the Lacedaemonians, although their colonists, or that you have done us no wrong, will aim at what is feasible, holding in view the real sentiments of us both *since you know as well as we do that right, as the world goes is only in question between equals in power, while the strong do what they can and the weak suffer what they must.*

See also F. Boyle, "The Law of Power Politics," 1980 *Univ. Ill. L. Rev.* 901, 907–915.

7. See R. Keohane and J. Nye, *Power and Interdependence* (1977); R. Keohane, *After Hegemony* (1984); S. Krasner, ed., *International Regimes* (1982); Haggard and Simmons, "Theories of International Regimes," 41 *Int'l Org.* 491 (1987). But compare Ashley, "The Poverty of Neorealism," 38 *Int'l Org.* 225 (1984).

Selected Bibliography

Abi-Saab, G., *The United Nations in the Congo 1960–1964.* New York: Oxford University Press, 1979.

Bowie, Robert R., *Suez 1956.* New York: Oxford University Press, 1974.

Boyle, Francis A., *The Future of International Law and American Foreign Policy.* Ardsley-on-Hudson, NY: Transnational Publishers, 1989.

———, *World Politics and International Law.* Durham, NC: Duke University Press, 1985.

Bull, Hedley, *Intervention in World Politics.* New York: Oxford University Press, 1984.

Cassesse, Antonio, *International Law in a Divided World.* New York: Oxford University Press, 1986.

Chayes, Abram, *The Cuban Missile Crisis: International Crises and the Role of Law.* New York: Oxford University Press, 1974.

Chen, Lung-Chu, *An Introduction to Contemporary International Law: A Policy-Oriented Perspective.* New Haven: Yale University Press, 1989.

Coplin, William D., *The Functions of International Law: An Introduction to the Role of International Law in the Contemporary World.* Chicago: Rand McNally, 1966.

Davidson, Scott, *Grenada: A Study In Politics and the Limits of International Law.* Aldershot, UK: Avebury, 1987.

Deutsch, Karl W., and Stanley Hoffmann, eds., *The Relevance of International Law: Essays in Honor of Leo Gross.* Cambridge: Schenman Publishing Co., 1971.

Falk, Richard A., *The Status of Law in International Society.* Princeton: Princeton University Press, 1970.

———, *The Vietnam War and International Law,* 3 vols. Princeton: Princeton University Press, 1968.

Falk, Richard A., and Wolfram F. Hanrieder, *International Law and Organization: An Introductory Reader.* Philadelphia: Lippencott, 1968.

Falk, Richard A., Friedrich Kratochwil, and Saul H. Mendlovitz, eds., *International Law: A Contemporary Perspective.* Boulder, CO: Westview, 1985.

Fisher, Roger, *Improving Compliance with International Law.* Charlottesville: University of Virginia Press, 1981.

———, *International Conflict for Beginners.* New York: Harper and Row, 1969.

Forsythe, David P., *Human Rights and U.S. Foreign Policy.* Gainesville: University Press of Florida, 1988.

———, *Human Rights and World Politics.* Lincoln: University of Nebraska Press, 2d ed., 1989.

————, *Humanitarian Politics: The International Committee of the Red Cross*. Baltimore: The Johns Hopkins University Press, 1977.

Franck, Thomas M., *Nation Against Nation: What Happened to the U.N. Dream and What the U.S. Can Do About It*. New York: Oxford University Press, 1985.

Franck, Thomas M., and Edward Wiesband, *Word Politics: Verbal Strategy Among the Superpowers*. New York: Oxford University Press, 1972.

Garthoff, Raymond L., *Policy Versus the Law: The Reinterpretation of the ABM Treaty*. Washington: Brookings Institution, 1987.

Goldstein, Joseph, Burke Marshall, and Jack Shwartz, *The My Lai Massacre and Its Cover-up: Beyond the Reach of Law?* New York: Free Press, 1976.

Gordenker, Leon, *Refugees in International Politics*. London: Croom Helm, Ltd., 1987.

Gould, Wesley L., and Michael Markun, eds., *International Law and the Social Sciences*. Princeton: Princeton University Press, 1970.

Henkin, Louis, *How Nations Behave: Law and Foreign Policy*. New York: Columbia University Press, 1979.

Henkin, Louis, et al., *Right v. Might: International Law and the Use of Force*. New York and London: Council on Foreign Relations Press, 1989.

Hoyt, Edwin C., *Law and Force in American Foreign Policy*. Lanham, MD: University Press of America, 1985.

Kaplan, Morton A., and Nicholas Katzenbach, *The Political Foundations of International Law*. New York: Wiley, 1961.

Levi, Werner, *Contemporary International Law: A Concise Introduction*. Boulder, CO: Westview, 1979.

————, *Law and Politics in the International Society*. Beverly Hills, CA: Sage, 1976.

Loescher, Gilbert, and John A. Scanlan, *Calculated Kindness: Refugees and America's Half-Open Door, 1945 to the Present*. New York: Free Press, 1986.

McDougal, Myres S., and Florentino Feliciano, *Law and Minimum World Public Order*. New Haven: Yale University Press, 1961.

Moore, John N., *Law and Civil War*. Baltimore: The Johns Hopkins University Press, 1974.

Moynihan, Daniel P., *Loyalties*. New York: Harcourt Brace Jovanovich, 1984.

Peterson, M. J., *The General Assembly in World Politics*. Boston: Allen & Unwin, 1986.

Rasmussen, Hjalte, *On Law and Policy in the European Court of Justice: A Comparative Study in Judicial Policymaking*. Dordrecht, The Netherlands: Martinus Nijhoff Publishers, 1986.

Reisman, W. Michael, and Andrew R. Willard, eds., *International Incidents: The Law That Counts in World Politics*. Princeton: Princeton University Press, 1988.

Scheinman, Lawrence, and David Wilkinson, eds., *International Law and Political Crisis: An Analytic Casebook*. Boston: Little, Brown, 1968.

Stoessinger, John G., *The United Nations and the Superpowers: China, Russia, and America*. New York: Random House, 4th ed., 1977.

Stone, Julius, *Visions of World Order: Between State Power and Human Justice*. Baltimore: The Johns Hopkins University Press, 1984.

Vincent, R. J., *Nonintervention and International Order*. Princeton: Princeton University Press, 1974.

de Visscher, Charles, *Theory and Reality in Public International Law.* Princeton: Princeton University Press, 1968.

Zucker, Naomi and Norman, *The Guarded Gate: The Reality of American Refugee Policy.* New York: Harcourt Brace Jovanovich, 1987.

Index

About the Book

Intended for students in international relations, international law, and U.S. foreign policy courses, this book demonstrates how international law really functions in foreign policymaking in Washington. David Forsythe views politics as the driving force behind legal interpretation. Examining a series of controversies in public policy during the Reagan administration—the clash of "Star Wars" with the ABM treaty, use of the contras against the Sandinistas in Nicaragua, the invasion of Grenada, refugee policy in the Western Hemisphere, and the payment of dues to the United Nations—he inquires into the interplay of international law and U.S. foreign policy, stressing the political factors that make for adherence to, or violation of, international law.

Each of the controversies is analyzed according to a framework raising seven questions: What are the basic facts of the case? What was the Executive's main policy objective? What legal claims were argued in support of that objective? What was the domestic response from the public, the Congress, and the courts? What was the response of other states and of international organizations? What was the outcome for the short-term interests of the United States? And what was the outcome for world order?

Forsythe also breaks new ground in showing the crucial relationship between public opinion, Congress, and the Judiciary, on the one hand, and executive primacy in the conduct of foreign policy on the other. One of the main themes emerging from this new analysis is that domestic political factors often decide the fate of international law, frequently being more influential than such legal factors as judgments by the World Court or positions taken by U.N. agencies.

Francis A. Boyle is professor of international law and a member of the Program in Arms Control, Disarmament, and International Security at the University of Illinois–Champaign. His books include *Defending Civil Resistance Under International Law* (1987), *The Future of International Law and American Foreign Policy* (1989), and the forthcoming *The Foundations of World Order* (1991).

Richard A. Falk is Milbank Professor of International Law and Practice at Princeton University. He is the author of numerous publications, including *Revitalizing International Law* (1989) and *The Promise of World Order* (1988). Currently he is completing an exploration of time, social movements, social justice, and world order. He is also working on an analysis of the 1986 World Court case brought by Nicaragua against the United States.

David P. Forsythe is professor of political science at the University of Nebraska–Lincoln. He has been especially interested in human rights and humanitarian diplomacy, within the context of international law and organization and U.S. foreign policy. Among his recent books are a second edition of *Human Rights and World Politics* (1989), and *Human Rights and U.S. Foreign Policy: Congress Reconsidered* (1988), which won the Manning J. Dover prize. His *International Human Rights: Patterns and Prospects* will be published in 1991. Among his current research projects are those concerning the relationship between human rights and international peace, and a further study of politics and international law.